The Anthem Angelic, and Other Sermons

THE ANTHEM
ANGELIC

AND

Other Sermons

BY

Rev. William Henry Bancroft
Author of "SHINING PATHWAYS"

✠

Printed by
GEORGE W. JACOBS & CO.
PHILADELPHIA

Foreword

A SHOWER of sparks; a rush of wind; a burst of flame; and a beloved church building was totally destroyed, that building having stood for many years.

This book is sent forth to aid my flock in putting up a new sheepfold. It has been prepared as a labor of love.

The book takes its title from the first sermon within it. The opening notes are from the song of the angels at the birth of Christ; its closing notes are from the song of Redemption in praise of the glorified Christ.

The sermons herein have been left just as they were delivered to the congregation of Buckingham Presbyterian Church, of Berlin, Md., the edifice of that congregation now a heap of ashes. It was thought best to print the sermons in their original form. May they do good among many to whom the author is a stranger!

With that prayer in the heart of him who spoke these sermons, they are launched from the press upon the sea of publicity. Take passage, my friend, upon any one of these sermonic ships and let it carry you to God.

WILLIAM HENRY BANCROFT.

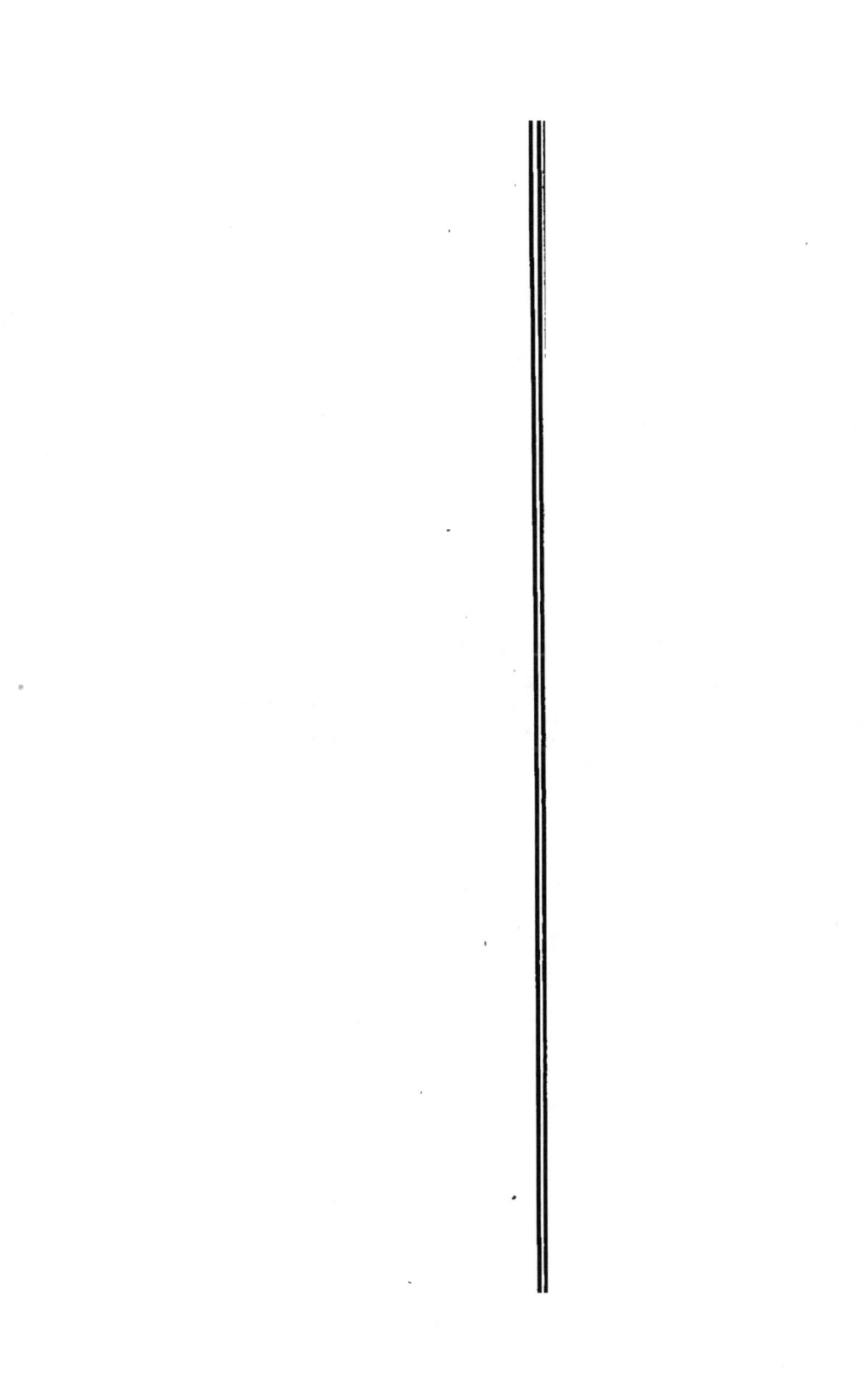

To My Wife,

Margaret,

Whose encouragement made this book possible,

and

To the dear friends of Buckingham Church,

This volume is affectionately dedicated.

CONTENTS

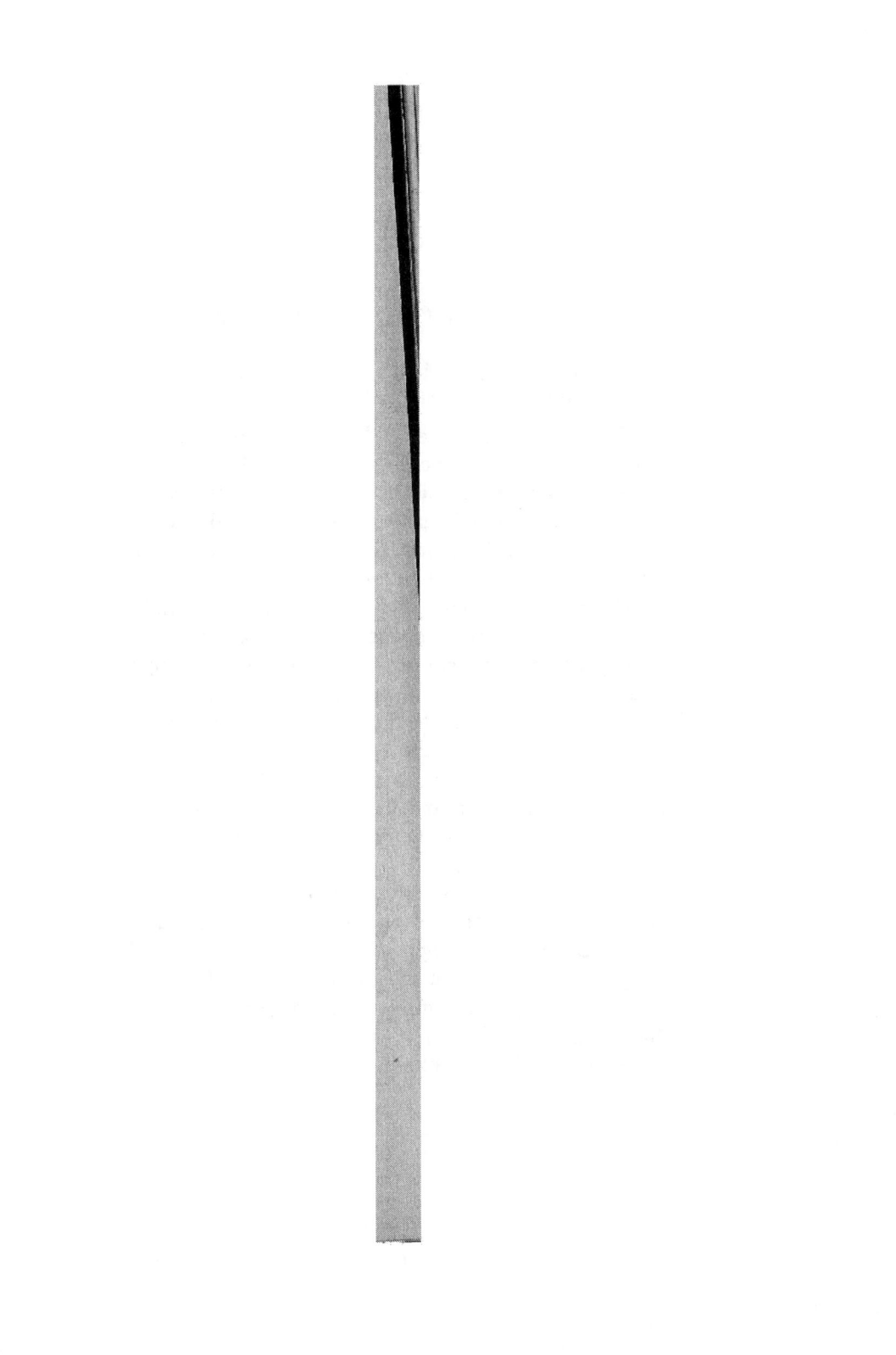

The Anthem Angelic

And suddenly there was with the angel a multitude of the heavenly host praising God. Luke 2: 13.

WITHIN the vestibule of this Christmas sermon of mine, I wish you to note that the angels of heaven have had two great holidays. The first holiday was at the laying of the foundations of the world, the omnipotence of God setting the rocks in order, when those angels winged their way to the scene of that wondrous achievement and let fall upon the rising temple of humanity a chorus of song. Their second holiday was at the birth of Christ, when they dropped a sublime anthem from their lips beneath the stars of Bethlehem. They are to have a third holiday, when they shall accompany the Lord in the clouds in the majesty of His second coming to earth, a seraphic courier announcing that mighty event with a trumpet-blast that shall startle the living and wake the dead.

But we are concerned this Christmas morn with the second angelic holiday. Over the world-cradle in which the infant God was rocked the inhabitants of heaven wove a canopy of song, threading it with the grandest notes that ever passed along the air of earth. I ask you to study with me to-day that anthem angelic, and with no thought of weariness, if the study should be prolonged.

I. I remark, that anthem angelic was a joyous anthem. It was rendered by a numerous company of celestial inhabitants. The text calls that augmented choir of angelic choristers "a multitude of the heavenly host." The idea in the Greek is that they were representative of the immense army of the Lord. I suppose that nearly all heaven came forth that night to sing the earth's first Christmas carol. What wings cleft the shadowed air! Wings in groups! Wings in crowds! Wings in battalions! Wings in regiments! Legions of wings! Those wings so brilliant that they outshone the stars; the splendor of those wings blinding the stars with a darkness that did not lift, until those wings had flashed back through the gates of pearl and were folded reverently before heaven's highest throne.

For what did that multiple choir come to earth? Was it to sound a dirge? Oh, no! Nothing funereal in the music that parted the lips of those celestial hosts. The leader of those choristers had just announced to the wondering shepherds of the Bethlehem hills the thrilling message, "Behold, I bring you good tidings of great joy." Whether that seraphic messenger voiced his proclamation melodiously or not, I do not know. But I do know that the proclamation was unanimously sustained by a burst of music that flowed from shining tongues and lips. "And suddenly there was with the angel a multitude of the heavenly host praising God."

You have seen the picture, "St. Cecelia at the Organ." Down upon the keys of the instrument, those keys pressed by the fairest of fingers, bright-winged cherubs are dropping roses. With the harmony that ripples from beneath those gentle fingers is mingled the sweetness of heavenly gardens, those roses gathered from some clustered sunrise. But the chant that broke from those lips angelic that first Christmas night was fragrance itself. Upon the senses of the Bethlehem shepherds came pouring down the perfume of joy. There were roses of joy, and heliotropes of joy, and mignonettes of joy. Those choristers had gathered their flowers of song from the conservatory of the King's palace. Joy! Music abloom with joy!

Away with the idea that religion is a groan! It is a song of joy. Those who present religion, either by words or conduct, as a form clad in midnight robes, and showing a face upon which shadows rest, give you a caricature, not a real picture. A true child of God does not go through the world with a frown upon the brow, and with features that have been distorted by acid fingers. A sour disposition is not born of piety, but of the devil. My study of the Bible has brought to me the knowledge that the religion of Jesus Christ is the gladdest, the brightest and the sweetest thing that ever came to this world. Ask Peter; and he will answer you with fallen prison fetters and an opened prison door. Ask Paul and Silas; and they will answer you with a duet at twelve o'clock at night under the roof of a noisome

Philippian jail. Ask Paul again; and he will answer
you with good cheer upon the deck of a storm-driven
ship in the Mediterranean. Ask Paul again; and he
will answer you with a smile within Neronic dungeon
walls. There are thousands of witnesses. Interro-
gate them every one. They will all answer you with
words of gold set with rubies and amethysts and
pearls and diamonds. Religion is a host of angels
shaking joy from their wings, and scattering
joy from their lips over a world of pain and
sin. Let religion have full sway within the soul, and
it will hush all discord with heavenly harmonies.

The trouble with many Christians is that they have
never taken a full course in the university of God's
grace. They have only partially studied the melodies of the Christian life. They have learned only a
few chords, preferring the "rag-time" music of
earth. Once come to the realization of the fact of
pardoned sin and help divine in trouble and the sure
prospect of heaven through the righteousness of
Jesus Christ, and the heart will then be an organ
from which will roll melodies accordant with the anthem angelic of Bethlehem's heights, that anthem
breaking when Christ was born. Joy will press the
keys of that organ; joy will tramp the pedals. It
was to give joy that Christ stripped Himself of celestial glory for the robes of earth. No wonder that
the hosts of the army of God followed Him through
the gates of pearl, strewing His path below earthly
skies with the flowers of joy!

II. Again, I remark, that anthem angelic was a hopeful anthem. Those Judean shepherds saw that night what no other human eyes ever saw. Astrology was the mother of astronomy. For hundreds of years had learned minds studied the heavens, and out of that study of signs and omens issued the glorious science of the stars known in this present age. But no Egyptian sight, no sight Persian, no sight Chaldean, no sight of a Copernicus, or a Galileo, or a Herschel, or a Kepler, or a Proctor, or a Mitchell ever witnessed the splendor that blazed before the vision of those sheep-watchers on the hill-top of Bethlehem. In our day, taking a telescope as a mountain-stock, learned men climb from their rotating observatories among the Alps and the Andes and the Himalayas of stellar magnificence piled in the heavens of the night. But in all their astronomical journeys they have never yet found any inhabitants beyond this world, lofty as have been their numerous ascents, traveling upward through more miles than arithmetic can count. It was reserved for the vision of a few rustics to witness the fact that somewhere in God's universe there are beings other than men. First came a flashing presence, filling them with fear, and a tuneful voice; then "suddenly there was with the angel a multitude of the heavenly host praising God."

Let this Christmas narration, inspired of God, forever settle the fact that there is a place called heaven. Where it is I do not know; neither do I

anxiously care. Enough for me to know that it is.
Wherever it is, it overflowed that night and flooded
earth with its glistening grandeurs. No wonder!
The jeweled walls of God's metropolis could not hold
back the tide of glory that swept against them when
Christ robed Himself in the swaddling clothes of the
Bethlehem manger. Those angels came rushing to
earth with the news of that royal advent. They
voiced the tidings in song. He who had come was
the Hope of the world.

All through the past ages had men been looking
forward to the advent of this Christ. Jacob told of
His coming in dying prophecy. David sang of His
coming in marvelous lyrics, those lyrics accompanied
by the strains that David brushed from the strings
of his sanctified harp. Isaiah climbed the highest
peaks of divine vision and beheld His coming like
that of the dawn breaking through the shadows of
the night. Without His coming the world was without hope. The angelic choral of that first Christmas
hour told that He had come. The birth of Christ
brought to the world the most cheering news ever
published. It was good news when it was learned
that Wellington had defeated Napoleon Bonaparte at
Waterloo. It was good news when it was known
that the guns of Dewey, and Schley, and Shafter
had silenced the tyranny of Spain. But these tidings
announced Him who is yet to replace a lost Eden
with a better Eden than the one with which the world
started. No wonder that the angels expressed the

fact with song! Their anthem was charged with the melody of hope.

III. Again, I remark, that anthem angelic was an anthem which musically proclaimed a glorious truth. What was that truth? It was that a Saviour was born. What a theme that was for the songful lips of those choristers celestial! It is a Saviour that the world still needs, after the lapse of over nineteen hundred years since the occupancy of the Bethlehem manger by the Christ. This is a lost world. It is a ship loosed from its moorings of safety and astray upon a wide ocean of tempest and storm. It needs to be piloted back to God. It needs a mighty hand at the wheel. Hear it, O wandering earth! One has come who is strong to save. Let the anthem angelic of long ago echo in every set of ringing chimes within churchly towers, in every bell of every village steeple, in every trumpet-blast at Christmastide, in every pealing organ and tinkling piano and trembling harp, in every song and carol of the advent season within every home and sanctuary. Carry the notes of that anthem angelic to every corner of heathenism on the globe, whether that benighted place be close to our own doorstep or far over the seas. Let it be everywhere known that a Saviour has come.

I often think that too much thought is given at Christmas to a mythical Santa Claus, and not enough to the real Christ. Do not misunderstand me. I would not sour a single joy of childhood. I have no sympathy with those whose mission it is to banish

all the sweets from the banqueting table of young
life, replacing those sweets with vinegar, and mus-
tard, and horse-radish, and cayenne pepper. I look
back to-day and call up most pleasant memories of
tender years, when, as a small boy, I went to sleep
Christmas eve firmly believing that Santa Claus
would visit my home in the night, making entrance
and exit by way of the chimney, though wondering
how so stout a form could possibly accommodate
itself to the narrowness of so small an opening. But
childhood is the paradise of the imagination. It is
through the imagination of childhood that we prepare ourselves for the richer faith of after years.
That I am now one strongly anchored to the reality
of spiritual things I attribute to the fact that I once
reveled among books that were filled with fancies,
earth's greatest and grandest event, the putting on
of human flesh by Him who came forth out of the
imagination, the more will be the fruit of faith in
God within the orchard of the matured brain.

But I would not emphasize Santa Claus to the de-
triment of Jesus Christ. Do not put Christ into a
subordinate place at Christmas. Bring Him out of
shadow into light. Too often in our Christmas celebrations Christ is far in the background. Let the
main idea of Christmas be that it is a time in com-
memoration of the birth of a Saviour from sin. There
is no theme that can compare with this one glorious
theme. This is the czar of all themes.

I notice that when the world's master-musicians

wished an inspiring collection of melodies, they chose subjects that were religious. The harmonies of a Mozart, a Mendelssohn, a Haydn, a Handel, and others renowned in the musical world, rose to their highest heaven of excellence when their rhythmic wings beat the air in praise of God. So when the army choirs of the upper world would render their finest chords, they gave the rendition at the hour of the earth's greatest and grandest event, the putting on of human flesh by Him who came forth out of the ivory palaces. The subject of their thrilling notes was that a Saviour was born.

Oh, yes! We need to make prominent the fact of Christ in the festivities of the Christmastide. What if He had never come? This would have been a poor world in which to live. You and I, and millions more, would be at this moment traveling in darkness towards everlasting darkness—a midnight merging into a thousand midnights piled together—solidified gloom around as walls and above as roof, imprisoning forever.

Friend, do you know Christ as your Saviour? Settle that question now. His blood cleanseth from all sin. His righteousness the hammer that strikes off the fetters of sin. His wounded hand the hand that opens the jail of sin into the light and liberty of the sons of God.

IV. Again, I remark, that anthem angelic was an anthem that proclaimed the divinity of Christ. Said the leader of that seraphic choir to the shepherds

on the hill, "Unto you is born a Saviour, who is
Christ the Lord." That settles the fact of Christ's
divinity. I care not what Socinus said, nor what
said Schleiermacher, nor what said Strauss, and Re-
nan, nor what any one has said in denial of this truth.
I would believe an angel rather than any man, even
though the brain of that man should weigh five
pounds. This seraphic messenger declared that
Christ was divine. His statement was reinforced by
thousands of tongues that blossomed with song.
"Suddenly there was with the angel a multitude of
the heavenly host praising God."

In the face of these shining witnesses, offering
their choral testimony to the divine character of
Christ, who will have the hardihood to say that the
Babe whose birth was told to the shepherds of Bethlehem was no more than the babe born last night in
some maternity hospital? What did those angels
praise God for, if Christ was altogether human?

Why, this was the very Saviour for whom the
world had long been looking—looking for Him
through the flashing flames and curling smoke of
numberless sacrifices; looking for Him from the
mountain-tops of prophecy; looking for Him in the
gardens and among the flowers of inspired rhetoric.
Of whom did David speak in poetic phrase when he
said, "The Lord said unto my Lord, Sit thou on my
right hand, till I make thine enemies thy footstool?"
Of whom did Isaiah speak when he said, "Unto us a
child is born, unto us a son is given; and the govern-

ment shall be upon his shoulder; and his name shall
be called Wonderful, Counsellor, The mighty God,
The everlasting Father, The Prince of Peace?"

The fact is that Christ is spoken of on almost every
page of the Old Testament. The brightest similes
and the sweetest metaphors are gathered into bou-
quets for the adornment of sentences that describe
Him. Those who looked for Christ as a Saviour,
looked for Him as a Saviour divine. That there
might be no mistaking the truth of His divinity, a
crowd of angels rushed after Him, as He passed
through the gates of pearl, and crowned Him with
sublime doxologies, their wonderful notes yet echoing
in the air of the earth. "Christ the Lord," said the
leader of those singing hosts. His announcement
was sustained by those who accompanied him with
their voices melodious. Nineteen hundred Christ-
mases have added their testimony to the same glorious certainty. Christmas is in celebration of the
birthday of God manifest in the flesh. If Christ was
not God thus manifested, then let Christmas be struck
off from the calendar of all Christian nations. In its
stead let there be three hundred and sixty-five days
for weeping and wailing and gnashing of teeth. A
merely human Christ could not save this world. If
that is all that Christ was, then all the populations
past of the earth were lost; so are lost all the earth's
present populations; so will be lost all the earth's
future populations. Sound the news among all the
suns and planets of the universe!—a dead world!

Then let Omnipotence swing that dead world out of its orbit and hurry it away to a grave of everlasting darkness. I joyously announce it to-day, and with unmistakable and dogmatic emphasis, "Christ the Lord!" Upon the truth of that announcement I am willing to stake all my hopes for this life and for the life to come. Let the bells of Christmas peal it. Let the organs, with full diapason, roll it. Let every Christian choir voice it in richest carol and anthem. Let holly and pine wreathe it in home and sanctuary. "Christ the Lord!"

V. Once more, I remark, that anthem angelic was an anthem that gave honor to God. Listen to it, as it drops from flaming lips through the radiant air! —"Glory to God in the highest!"

Why was this outburst of praise rendered to God that first Christmas night? Because the giving up of Christ was an act on the part of God that revealed as never before His wondrous love. If you will look closely around that manger in which the infant Jesus was laid, you will find somewhere near a cross. The fact that the announcement of Christ's birth was made to shepherds is more than ordinarily significant. Why did they only hear the sublime melody of that wondrous night? Why not pour that song upon other ears? Christ was to be universal King; why not proclaim Him in the palace of Herod? Christ was to be a Physician; why not proclaim Him among those who practiced the healing art? Christ was to be a Teacher; why not proclaim Him in the schools? The reason why those shepherds were singled out to hear that music of the skies, I think, was that Christ was to be the Lamb of God. This the sole purpose of His coming to earth. He was to die for the sins of the world. No wonder that the angels of heaven flapped their wings in ecstatic flight to the scene of Christ's humble pilgrimage in human flesh, and cleft the air of Bethlehem with their anthem of praise to God!

Oh, the thrilling story! Faith in this Christ means the pardon of sin; means comfort for all sorrow; means sunshine for all gloom; means sweetness for all bitterness; means harmony for all discord; means life for death; means a mansion of glory in a world of glory. Come, let every one of us, in our feeble way, but with glad, exultant hearts, take up the notes of that seraphic choir, singing, "Glory to God in the highest!" By and by, after repeated rehearsals, we shall be able to sing that anthem with more richness of tone than even the angels. Yea, we shall sing a new song. In the Apocalypse John gives us a few bars of that new song. They are these: "Thou hast redeemed us to God by thy blood." When we shall sing yonder that new song, our feet standing upon the shining pavements of the city, that will be heaven's eternal Christmas day. For Christ the songs of that day. For Christ the palms of that day. For Christ the arches of that day. Blessed be His glorious name forever!

I wish you all a merry Christmas. Let it be merry

with Christian joy. Let it be merry with forgiven sin. Let it be merry with the hope of gaining heaven. Looking at the manger of Christ, let us not forget to journey onward and take a look at Christ's Cross. That Cross is the mountain-peak of all human history. That sublime height is all aglow with the light of God's love for a ruined world.

For the New Year

Whatsoever thy hand findeth to do, do it with thy might. Eccles. 9: 10.

IT came last night—a new child of time. The stars chanted its birth-song. The silver-wrought shadows were the garments thrown around its infant form. The winds were the wings of the angels that lovingly flew in attendance around it. Welcome thou fifth babe of the Twentieth Century! Thy life shall be one more sparkling link in the chain that binds the years of earth to the eternity of heaven. Out of thy frost-lined cradle shall spring many a blessing for mankind.

Do you ask me for a motto appropriate for the new year that is now upon us? I find that motto in the text. The life-long motto of the lamented Maltbie Babcock was, "Do it now." In boyhood, in youth, in manhood, he lived by that motto. In his ministerial life he had it constantly before his eyes upon his study desk. That motto was a condensation of the text—"Whatsoever thy hand findeth to do, do it with thy might."

I. I remark, we should obey the injunction of the text because of the shortness of time. How quickly pass the years! Cradles and graves lie close together. It is but a little step from infancy to old age. Our first cry and our last dying gasp soon kiss each other good-bye. What we do, therefore, must be done quickly. Boys and girls to-day at school are to-morrow men of business and matrons in the home. There are no moments that any one can afford to waste. The sands in the hour-glass of life are particles of gold. Let no idler break the glass and scatter its contents. Woe to those who misuse precious hours and days! "Whatsoever thy hand findeth to do, do it with thy might."

Especially should we improve our time as it concerns the soul. It is well to be alert in reference to intellectual attainment and commercial gain. There is no room in this world for a sluggard. It is a world that fairly hums with activity. In the great hive of human existence is no place for drones. But let the interests of the immortal spirit be first considered and settled. Death's coach is always on the go; and it always has a passenger. Its horses are never stabled. Its wheels are never still for long at a time, halting only to take on a new passenger. Its driver stops at no inn for refreshment. Hark! I hear the clatter of hoofs. I hear the grinding of tires among the gravel of the world's highway. I hear the snap of a whip. Death is hurrying on. Let him not call for you, my friend, and find you without a ticket of admission for your soul through the gates of pearl. Such a ticket is red. It takes its color from the blood of Jesus Christ. Be sure of getting that passport through repentance of sin and faith in the Saviour. Get it now. "Whatsoever thy hand findeth to do, do it with thy might; for there is no work, nor device, nor knowledge, nor wisdom, in the grave, whither thou goest."

Procrastination has been termed "the thief of time." It is far more than that. I arraign it here to-day before the bar of human experience, charging it with the murder of innumerable souls. Let me call up from the world of despair the witnesses. Men and women whelmed in the Flood, give in your testimony! "We had one hundred and twenty years of preparation for the awful catastrophe that overtook us, but we put off our safety until it was too late." Felix, what sayest thou? "I waved him away from my governor's chair who sought my everlasting good, silencing his faithful voice with the words, 'Go thy way for this time; when I have a convenient season I will call for thee.'" Agrippa, what sayest thou? "I was almost persuaded to be a Christian, but I never completed the matter." What say the thousands of the lost in all ages? Listen! Like the sigh of the wind on a winter's night, a storm swooping, multitudinous voices whisper their remorse from the depths of hell—"We neglected this great salvation, and we could not escape."

Is it your intention, my unconverted friends, to join these witnesses, and add your hopeless misery to theirs? Be admonished to-day by a new year just begun that time is short. Before yonder cradled child of the century goes tottering to its grave you

2

may be in perdition. Attend to your soul now. This the first business of life. "Whatsoever thy hand findeth to do, do it with thy might."

But for us Christians the time is also short. It is our business to grow in every grace and in the knowledge of Jesus Christ. Yet how many of God's professed children are wasting the precious days of life. Where is the Bible that contains the commandments of their Lord? Often is it a book that is less used than any other book in the home. Frequently is it nothing more than what is styled a "family Bible," an ornament for the parlor table, and never opened, except to record a birth or death, or to press between its ponderous lids a few flowers for preservation. How can a Christian expect to culture his spiritual life when he places but little value upon this divine Book? If you have never done so before, begin this new year and read the Bible through. The same time given to it that is given to the reading of other books will enable you to read it through repeatedly before the year is dead.

Where are the religious papers that should be read by many Christians? Such papers tell of the progress of God's kingdom; they also are stored with a variety of devotional matter for quickening the life of the soul. But where are those papers? They are on the shelves of the publishers, for many Christians do not subscribe for a religious paper. A Christian household without a religious paper is a mill without any grist. What can be expected of the children of a home in which there is no news of the Church of God? No wonder that such children turn away from the preaching services after having attended Sabbath-school or a young people's meeting, considering that their duty is then ended! If parents are not themselves interested in spiritual things, they cannot reasonably think that their children will be interested. One of the saddest sights that ever comes to a pastor's eyes is that of the children of the Church turning away from his voice in the services given to preaching the Gospel.

Where are the majority of Christians on the evening of the mid-week gathering for prayer? They are at home in selfish ease, or at the store, or at the lodge, or at some place of amusement. Anywhere, except in God's house! For feeble health, or infirmity by reason of age, there is, of course, an excuse for absence from the ordinances of the sanctuary. But these two things should be the only excuse for such absence, save in exceptional cases, the providence of God ordering the absence. Should these words of mine reach that class of Christians, let me urge them to turn over a new leaf on this first day of a new year, beginning now to give vigorous attention to the services of the Lord. The time is short. No Christian can afford to misuse God-given time.

At this point let me tell you something. Sometimes complaints are made against pastors in reference to their neglect of certain persons. Such complaints

come from those who are themselves neglectful. That
is invariably the case. It is the sheep beyond the bars
of the pasture-ground that do the most bleating.
Every pastor of any experience at all will confirm
that statement. The sheep that keep themselves
within the field of the Lord have no time to bleat.
They are busy cropping the rich grass of that field
beneath the eyes of the under-shepherd.

II. Again, I remark, we should heed the injunction of the text because of the passing of opportunity.
Among men I find a sagacity that makes them keenly
alive to the furthering of their earthly affairs. This
is a very busy world. Its skies are darkened with the
smoke of mills and factories. Its air rings with
clanging anvil and pounding hammer and clicking
trowel and jingling gold and silver and rustling bank-
notes. Its roads are clattering with wagon wheels
and hurrying feet. Its railways are thundering with
onrushing trains. Oh, yes; it is a busy world. Go
stand on Broadway, New York, or on Chestnut
Street, Philadelphia, and watch the hastening throngs.
Those two cities are types of London and Paris and
St. Petersburg and Pekin, and a host of smaller
towns and villages over all the earth, from the rising
to the setting of the sun. Merchants, bankers, brok-
ers, mechanics, all classes of men are daily busy with
the world's traffic and commerce and labor. Every
opportunity that presents itself for gain is eagerly
seized and made use of to the highest advantage. It
is only in God's business that opportunities are

slighted and allowed to pass on. Christ once said that the children of this world are wiser in their generation than the children of light. What was applicable to His day is applicable to these twentieth century days. In the picture of life religion is too often put in the background.

It seems to be a common impression that religion is something that is born asleep and never wakes up. I was reading not long since of an Indian preacher who preaches while in slumber. It is usually the other way about, the congregation in somnolence while the sermon is going on!

But Christianity ought to be the most thoroughly awake thing in all the world. There should be upon it the stamp of the text, "Whatsoever thy hand findeth to do, do it with thy might." Religion requires fleetness of foot, quickness of fingers, sparkling eyes, acuteness of hearing, alertness of mind and heart. There is no reason that men should be more diligent in worldly things than they are in things spiritual. The fact is that the conditions should be reversed. Said Christ, "Seek first the kingdom of God."

What is Christianity? It is not a hospital, but a recruiting agency for soldiers. It is not a banqueting hall, but a workshop. It is not a picnic, but a forward march against the powers of darkness. But bring back to earth a man like the Apostle Paul, and let him measure the average Christian conduct towards the affairs of God's kingdom. What would be his verdict? As to the Ephesians of his day he said,

"Redeem the time," which means, "Buy up the opportunity," so to all listless spiritual merchants now
he would address the same stirring words, making
them even more emphatic now than then—a very
lightning flash of command.

My friends, I am preaching this sermon to my own
soul as well as to you. We all allow too many opportunities for furthering the cause of God to slip
from our grasp. We suffer ourselves to be too conservative. We exercise too much deliberation. Mean-
while, our chances for doing good are flying off, and
soon we ourselves will be gone forever from these
earthly scenes. Hear we not the footfalls of onward-
moving time to-day. A new year is upon us. What
are we going to do with it? Let the text be heeded.
"Whatsoever thy hand findeth to do, do it with thy
might."

We need especially to be aroused to a sense of the
world's necessity for knowing the Cross of Christ.
If the Bible be true, and to the very bottom of my
heart I believe it true, then without the sacrifice of
the Lamb of God applied to it this is a lost world.
It is a wanderer in the heavens. It has swept off from
the orbit of righteousness. It has for many centuries continued in sin, swinging farther and farther
away from the throne of God. Beautiful world is
it in its physical aspects. Beautiful its mornings and
evenings, one aflame with sunrise, the other ablaze
with sunset and agleam with stars. Beautiful its
oceans and rivers and brooks. Beautiful its hills and

woods and fields and orchards. Beautiful its living
creatures, whether bird, beast or man. But spirit-
ually it is a dead world. Sin in its palaces and hovels.
Sin in its halls of learning and in its workshops. Sin
in its cities and villages. Everywhere is sin. The
only way to quicken this world out of death and send
it hurrying back to God's heart is by means of the
Gospel of Jesus Christ. This is the work that falls to
the hands of every Christian. Therefore, "whatsoever thy hand findeth to do, do it with thy might."

There is one mighty mode of bringing the world
to Christ which affords opportunity to every Christian, and yet that mode is often neglected. What is
it? It is the systematic giving of money into God's
treasury. You may not be able to preach; you may
not be able to instruct a class in the Sabbath-school;
there are many things that you may not be able to
do; but here is a place for the exercise of even the
smallest gifts. You can lay aside systematically a
part of your income for God. It is systematic giving that counts the most. Haphazard giving is of
very little worth, and for the reason that it is haphazard, being dependent upon moods. Systematic
giving develops a mood that is always at fever heat.
With the mercury of beneficence always at that mark
in the thermometer of every Christian life, it would
not be long before the kingdoms of this world would
become the kingdom of Christ. The trouble with the
haphazard giver is that one day he is in the torrid
zone of zeal and the next day in the frigid zone of

apathy. The Apostle Paul's rule was, "Let every one of you lay by him in store, according as God hath prospered him."

What the Church of God needs in these days is to have religion step into the bank and office and store and shop of the Christian and take a definite portion of the income, or profits, or wages for God's service.

I call to mind a story that I have told before, but it will bear repetition. An artist was asked to paint a picture of a dead church. He did not paint a building in decay, its steeple leaning, its walls crumbling, its steps moss-grown, its fences tumbling down. Instead, he painted the interior of a handsome edifice. Frescoed its ceiling. Of stained glass its windows. Its pews richly upholstered. Its floor gorgeously carpeted. Its chandeliers flashing brass, sparkling with prisms. But up by the pulpit he painted a contribution box, that box inscribed with the words, "Foreign Missions;" and over the opening of that box he drew a spider's web.

It was an artist's conception of a dead church. But is it not true? I would go further than that, however, and paint not only that particular box covered with cobwebs, but every box that belongs to the treasury of God. The surest way to have continued interest in the things of the Lord that require to be done with all the might is to be continually giving in a systematic way for their support. "We are laborers together with God." That is a partnership of which to be proud.

III. Again, I remark, we should heed the injunction of the text because it summons us to a business of the greatest importance. There is no other business, in fact, of like importance. This is the most important business that can engage the powers of any human mind, or bring into play the nervous energy of any human body, or bend the muscles of any human hands or feet. If you doubt this, then look at the example of Christ. Here is an example of untiring devotion to it. Into three years of public ministry Christ crowded the service of a lifetime. "He went about doing good." How the winds of the sea smote His face and chilled His frame! How the fierce noonday sun beat upon His head! How the dews of the night wet His locks! He was often hungry and thirsty. Once when pressed to take food His answer was, "I have meat to eat that ye know not of." His meat and drink was the doing of His Father's will. We speak of His sacrifice upon the Cross; but all His life was a sacrifice. The Cross was the final burden that was laid upon His back, breaking His heart. He lived and died for the world.

So might I mention Paul, that man spending himself for his Master—a man who feared not Sanhedrin, nor mobs, nor governor's chair, nor frowning prison gates, nor dangerous journeys, nor shipwreck, nor king's throne, nor martyrdom—a man who toiled and labored and endured hardness as no other man since his day—a man whose last mortal breath, in spite of persecution and suffering and tribulation, his mission

for Christ bringing him finally under the frown of
Nero, was a shout of triumph.

So might I mention Paul's fellow-workers in the
Gospel. So might I mention the names of hundreds
of brave men and women, of whom the world was not
worthy, who gave themselves to the high task of
blessing the world by life and deed. Time would fail
me to call that illustrious roll. But they surround us
to-day in the galleries of light as a "great cloud of
witnesses," looking down at us. With them are the
hosts of God's winged servants, the angels of heaven.
What kind of a spectacle are we making before these
onlooking witnesses?

Oh, no! There is no other business that can rank
with the business of the Christian in importance.
Those who make religious things inferior to secular
things miss the teaching of hundreds of Scripture
passages, those passages setting forth the fact that
the kingdom of God is of supreme interest. Christianity is not an insurance against the fires of hell.
Christianity is not an inscription for a tombstone.
Christianity is not a cordial for a death-bed. Christianity is not a dose of medicine for the hours of life,
a nauseous necessity that must be swallowed with a
wry face. It is the business of the soul. It is the
greatest business this side of the gates of pearl. It
requires earnestness. It must be done with the ut-
most dispatch. The text is its trumpet-call. Listen
to that reverberating blast from the lips of the inspired preacher! Every succeeding year has taken

up its echoes. This new year repeats it with increased emphasis. Do you hear it? "Whatsoever thy hand findeth to do, do it with thy might."

I have given three points to this sermon for the new year. Let me repeat them. We should discharge the obligations that rest upon us because life is short even at its longest length; because opportunities do not tarry, but take wing and fly away; and because this business of the soul is of inestimable importance. Let the whole Church of God be thoroughly alive. As a part of that Church, let us be thus alive.

Let also those who wholly neglect their souls awake from slumber. "What meanest thou, O sleeper? Arise, call upon thy God." Look! I see the old year of 1904 staggering up to the throne of God. Upon its back are the unforgiven sins of all its months, the wasted hours of its days, the broken resolutions of its opening moments—these to be deposited for the final stroke of time along with all the burdens of all the preceding years. Hasten, friend! By the cradle of this newborn year of 1905 kneel, putting up for God's ears the prayer, "Lord, I give myself to Thee. Let this new year be the year of my birth into life eternal!"

The Loftiest Name

(COMMUNION SERMON.)*

A name which is above every name. Philippians 2: 9.

THIS morning I am the pastor of a heap of ashes. But that appalling fact does not weaken my ordination vows and obligations. I am ready to preach Christ again, and Him crucified. No fire can burn out my love for Him.

It was Paul's one ambition to exalt his Lord. What this man did in the service of his Master he did with his whole heart. Many times he termed himself the slave of Christ. But that word "slave" falling from Paul's lips or dropping from Paul's pen was all abloom with the flowers of rhetoric. This was not a man who groaned under bondage. This was not a man who chafed beneath shackles. This was not a man who unwillingly wrought at the tasks that came to his hands. Paul's servitude was a servitude of love. He went from Damascus, on the day of his conversion, clear to Rome, on the day of his martyrdom, proudly bearing the brand-marks of Him who had called him as a herald of the Cross. The scars upon his tumbled corpse outside the gates of the

* This sermon and the two following were preached in the Stevenson M. E. Church, through the kindness of the officials of that church after the loss by fire of the Buckingham Presbyterian Church.

imperial city, when Nero's sword put him to death, were badges of honor. The world never saw a more devoted servant of Christ; the world shall perhaps never look upon his like again. For Christ he lived; for Christ he died. His every breath, until respiration ceased from his mortal body, was charged with the sole purpose of publishing the name of Christ to all mankind. Therefore, we cannot be surprised that Paul here wreathes that name with glory. In the passion of his brain and heart he speaks of it as "a name which is above every name."

On this Sabbath of Communion it is my wish that our thoughts should all cluster around the One who spread for us this table.

Did you ever hear the story of the sculptor whose idea it was to carve a statue of the Christ that should command reverence from all beholding it? Day after day he shut himself within his studio, and assiduously wrought at his artistic work. In every stroke of his mallet and every dig of his chisel there was love. Into the growing figure before him he put his very soul. The hour came when the statue was finished. The sculptor took his little child first into the studio, and bade her look upon the creation of his hands. He asked, "Who is it, daughter?" The child stood before the figure with awe upon her face. She answered, "It is some great man." The sculptor was disappointed, for he knew that his purpose had failed. Again he shut himself within his studio. Again he wrought, his every breath a prayer. Again the task was finished. Once more he led the child into the room. "Who is it, dear?" The girl's eyes lighted with joy, and from her lips rang the joyous answer, "Suffer little children to come unto me." It was enough. The sculptor then knew that he was successful. The statue was placed on exhibition, and crowds of people stood reverently before it.

So this morning I would so preach as to make every heart thrill at the thought of Christ. For this day there can be no other theme. This is the pearl of topics in the golden setting of the days. With Paul, I lift the name of Christ aloft, exclaiming, "A name which is above every name!"

I. I remark, that the name of Christ is a distinguished name. There are many names renowned in the history of the world. The annals of all the nations blossom with such names. They are the names of famous kings and queens and emperors, of famous generals, of famous musicians, of famous orators, of famous men and women of letters. Not only do such names breathe their fragrance from the records of the various peoples of the earth, but they have also been reared on high in graceful shaft, in heroic statuary, and in imposing architecture. To call the roll of the world's illustrious dead would be a long task. Thousands of names are blazing to-day as stars in the firmament of human history.

But the name of Christ has a resplendence that is all its own. All other distinguished names are but ragged beggars in the presence of this imperial name. This is "a name which is above every name."

During the World's Fair at Chicago, in the last century, there was held a congress of religions. Representatives were there of the manifold beliefs of the earth. But when in the addresses made at that congress of religions Christ was placed in comparison with Confucius, with Brahma, with Buddha, and with other gods created by human wisdom and superstitious heathenism, it was a blasphemy. This globe itself, with its twenty-five thousand miles of circumference, is not large enough for the building of a platform for the feet of Jesus Christ to stand beside the feet of other so-called divinities. There is not the slightest likeness between Christ and the gods of India, of China, of Persia, or of any other land of darkness. His is "a name which is above every name."

This distinguished name has been handed down all the centuries. The fact is that this illustrious name was announced even before Christ was born into the world. Away back near the edge of time that name trembled upon the lips of the dying Jacob, the quavering accents of that prince of God giving it pronunciation as the hope of Israel. Isaiah speaks of this same Christ, in one of his rapturous moods exclaiming, "His name shall be called Wonderful, Counsellor, the mighty God, the everlasting Father, the Prince of Peace!" That name is the one flower that perfumes the whole garden of the Old Testa-

ment, greeting the sense as you enter the gate of
Genesis, lingering in the memory after you have
passed out the gate of Malachi.

Other men achieve fame while they live; this divine Man achieved fame long before He had breathed
a single breath out of the world into which He entered. In all the earth to-day there is no other name
that wears so many crowns.

Some names are honored in certain departments of
life. The name of Julius Cæsar is a distinguished
name in the martial world. The name of Demosthenes is a distinguished name in the oratorical world.
The name of Newton is a distinguished name in the
philosophic world. The name of Copernicus is a distinguished name in the astronomical world. So with
the name of Morse in the inventive world. So with
the name of Mozart in the musical world. So with
the name of Tennyson in the literary world. Time
fails me to give even single instances of distinction
among names in the varied realms of human thought
and action.

But look at the name of Christ! What banners are
inscribed with it! What orations give it emphasis!
What wisdom enshrines it! What stars blaze it!
What skill of hand employs it! What melodies ripple
it! What poems sing it! There is no art or science
in which this name is without honor. It is the supreme name of this present age; it will be the one
supreme name of the ages to come; it will be the one
supreme name of the ceaseless ages of eternity.

Paul's statement in the text is not a mere rhetorical flourish. The name of Christ was, and is, and ever shall be, "a name which is above every name."

II. I remark, that the name of Christ is a powerful name. What do I mean by powerful? The ocean is powerful. Look at it, as it hurls its breaking, foaming, writhing billows upon the beach! The force of the impact between those tons of water and the land charges the air with echoes that roll for miles around. You have seen the power of machinery. Look at the huge engines that draw heavily loaded trains over long journeys, climbing with those same trains behind them up the sides of mountains, those engines equipped with immense driving wheels that seem to be the very embodiment of power! I never alight from a railroad train in a terminal station that I do not give the engine a passing glance before going through the gate of exit, looking at both it and the swarthy man whose fingers grasp the controlling lever, not knowing which to admire the more, the hard-breathing machine or its mental master. But what are such exhibitions of power compared with the dynamic force that is in the name of Jesus Christ? These are only physical power; the power in the name of Christ is moral power, that power pulsating through the centuries past and exerting an influence to-day that is world-wide; yea, a power that encircles eternity. This name is a mountain-peak that stands forth in solitary weight of mightiness. "A name which is above every name!"

3

Look at the power of this name! There have been other potent names in the world; there are still such names in the world. But what was a Wellington, or a Shakespeare, or a Plato, or a Socrates, or what are a Morgan and Carnegie, and hosts of others who bear mighty names in their varied spheres, when placed beside the forceful name of Jesus Christ? As well attempt to compare a falling dewdrop with the crash of a Niagara. As well attempt to compare the flight of an arrow with that of an onrushing comet. As well attempt to compare the bursting brilliance of a rocket with the everlasting sheen of the midnight constellations. The name of Christ means more and weighs more and shines more than all other powerful names put together. It is a name that has been the inspiration of thousands of moral victories. It is a name that has hallowed and blessed this sin-cursed world for nineteen centuries. It is a name, as Paul intimates in the paragraph of the text, which is yet to bring into subjection all the powers celestial, all the powers terrestial, all the powers subterranean. Listen to the Apostle's magnificent statement! "Wherefore God also hath highly exalted him, and given him a name which is above every name; that at the name of Jesus every knee should bow, of things in heaven, and things in earth, and things under the earth; and that every tongue should confess that Jesus Christ is Lord, to the glory of God the Father." "A name which is above every name!"

III. I remark, that the name of Christ is a charming name. That name fell in music from the skies upon the ears of the Bethlehem shepherds, as they watched their flocks by night. That name brought under its spell the rugged preacher of the wilderness who proclaimed it on the banks of the Jordan. That name sent its magnetism through the hearts of the Galilee fishermen and called from his toll-booth Matthew, the tax-gatherer. That name touched the innermost soul of Saul of Tarsus and changed him into Paul the missionary. There have been thousands to whom that name was such a charm that they were willing to die for it; those hosts thrown to the teeth and claws of wild beasts in heathen amphitheatres, burnt at the stake, torn upon the rack, whipped and stoned, sawn asunder, of whom the world was not worthy, undergoing such persecution and such martyrdom that one cannot read of without frightening the blood from brow and cheek. There are millions to-day who love that name as they love no other name in heaven and earth. "A name which is above every name!"

Not long since I saw two of the famous generals of the Boer War. As their names were pronounced before a great throng of people, and as they came galloping into the arena upon their fiery steeds, there was displayed an enthusiasm by the assembled multitudes that was grandly thrilling, the clapping of thousands of hands and the huzzas of thousands of throats like the sound of breaking waters on the ocean's strand. But the name of Christ is a name that rouses more fervor to-day than any other name in all the world. Blessed name! There is more music in it than in multiplied orchestras. There is more sweetness in it than in multiplied gardens. There is more grandeur in it than blazes along the walls of autumnal forests. There is more glory in it than in multiplied galaxies. Put together all harmonies, all that is saccharine, all splendors, all sublimities, and they are as nothing compared with the charm of this bewitching name. "A name which is above every name!"

Oh, the charm of that name! It has been the softness of many a pillow of death. It has been the cheer of many a sorrow. It has been the light of many a gloom. It has been the strength of many an hour of weakness. It has been the honey of many a disappointment. It has been the hope of many a despair. It has been the gain of many a loss. It has been the heaven of many a grave. I cannot say it in conversational tone; that would be too tame. I must ring it out from the lowest depths of my heart. "A name which is above every name."

IV. I remark, that the name of Christ is an ever-lasting name. There are names distinguished, names powerful, and names charming that glow upon the printed page and fall from human lips, but they are only historical names, or names that belong to memory. There was a time when the name of Napoleon Bonaparte was able to command thousands of feet to march into battle. Long after the death of that remarkable man the French people held his name in reverence. I do not know how it is now, but once the city of Paris was a veritable museum of Napoleon's life. Everywhere the first initial of his name was inscribed, by day greeting the eye in solid stone, by night flashing forth in the fire of hundreds of lamps. But Napoleon's body is now only a ,handful of dust. So with the bodies of all other mighty ones in the records of the nations. As the centuries roll on, even the names of the illustrious dead dwindle away. Other names come forth and claim attention. But the name of Jesus Christ increases in worth with the growing old of the world. That name is more than historic; it is more than a memory. That name is a living name. It shall endure long after yonder sun has been snuffed out as a candle by the fingers of Omnipotence and the parading stars have halted at their graves of unceasing darkness.

This name has been chiseled upon the rocks of eternity. No vandal hand can obliterate it. No conflagration can burn it. No convulsion of elements can throw it down. While the throne of God endures·it shall endure. Everlasting name! "A name which is above every name!"

But what is the secret of it all? The answer to that question is the climax of my sermon. Yonder table holds the secret. The name of Christ is a distinguished name, a powerful name, a charming name, because of sacrifice. It is the character of Christ as the divine Saviour that places His name above every other name. Christ is infinitely more than a subject of prophecy, infinitely more than a personage of history, infinitely more than a martyr to truth. He is the Lamb of God slain from the foundation of the world. Had there been no Christ coming from heaven to earth to die for human sin, there had been no Old Testament Scriptures to predict Him, or no New Testament Scriptures to record His life and spell out His triumphs. Had there been no such Christ, there had been no Paul, no Augustine, no Chrysostom, no Luther, no Calvin, no Robert Hall, no Wesley, no Guthrie, no Spurgeon, no Moody, to give the Gospel eloquent voice. Had there been no such Christ, the world would have been left lying in wickedness, and you and I to-day, living in this glorious century of the Christian Era, would have been painted savages, with hearts as corrupt as hell itself.

In recent days I have seen many a sight of the progress of Christian nations and those that have been influenced by Christianity; but all that I saw, marvelous architecture, dream-like statuary, poetic paintings, skilful machinery, intricate weavings, the wonderful products of the soil, the witchery of lightning for the driving of wheels and pulleys and the illumination of palaces of art and science, all were the outcome of the sacrificial name of Jesus Christ. In every chiseled marble, in every glowing canvas, in every curling wreath of steam, in every flying shuttle, in every rushing water, in every flash of electric fire, I saw that name. "A name which is above every name!"

Yonder table tells the secret of that blessed name. This broken bread and its blushing companion, the fruit of the vine, take us back to Calvary. They bring to view the Cross. It is the death of Jesus Christ that lends lustre and force and charm and endurance to His name.

O my friends, let that name be enshrined in every breast! Let it be the inspiration of our lives! Let it be the hope of our last moments on earth! Blessed name! It stands for a love that has arms wide enough for the embracing of the globe. Be it our purpose to honor it! Be it our purpose to publish it abroad! Be it our purpose to serve it with undying loyalty! Let it be the concert key of all the music of our souls! Let it be the essence of every joy and pleasure! Let it be the source of all light! Upon the pulsating scroll of the heart write it first, at the very highest point of our affection, so that now and forever it may be to us "a name which is above every name!" Jesus! Saviour!

Beyond the Reach of Fire

Then Shadrach, Meshach and Abed-nego, came forth of the midst of the fire. Daniel 3: 26.

THERE is a proverb which says, "Strike while the iron is hot." Then is the blacksmith's opportunity. Then the strength of his blows gives the metal shape upon the anvil. Then the sparks fly from beneath his ringing hammer. So is this the time for me to enforce useful lessons. I preach to you this morning of those things that are beyond the reach of fire.

The text takes us back to Babylon. Nebuchadnezzar, the king, had been so lifted up with personal vanity as to think that he was the supreme monarch of the earth. It is dangerous business for a man to indulge in pride. Conceit often climbs so high as to become dizzy of brain and fall. The king caused an immense image of gold to be made and set up in the plain of Dura, in the province of Babylon. Perhaps it was a colossal likeness of his own form and features. That is not all improbable. When one becomes unduly impressed with his own importance, he will go to any length to have that same impression take hold of other minds. This golden image was to be worshipped. A decree was made and signed by the king that at the time of the sounding of the cornet, the flute, the harp, the sackbut, the psaltery, the dulcimer, and various other instruments of music, the people should fall down in adoration before the towering image.

Yonder I see that golden image flashing in the sunlight. I see the waiting people assembled. I see the orchestra. At a given signal a burst of melody rends the air. The crowds prostrate themselves. But look! There are three men standing erect. Those men refuse to bow to the image. They are Jews, Shadrach, Meshach and Abed-nego, captives beneath the sceptre of Nebuchadnezzar. They are seized by the police and taken into the presence of the king. Through religious scruples those three men could not worship the king's image. But religious scruples were not regarded in those days. Nebuchadnezzar flew into a rage. He commanded that those foreigners should be cast alive into a furnace of fire. So into such a furnace, heated with sevenfold fury, Shadrach, Meshach and Abed-nego were thrown, that furnace so intensely hot that the men whose office it was to cast these Jews into it were themselves slain by the heat.

But look! The king is astonished beyond measure. He rises from his seat. He speaks excitedly to his courtiers, saying, "Did not we cast three men bound into the midst of the fire?" "True, O king." "But I see four men loose, walking in the midst of the fire, and they have no hurt; and the form of the fourth is like a son of the gods."

Whose form was that fourth form? It was that of

an angel from heaven. Or it may have been that of the Christ, anticipating His incarnation in the later centuries. But whether it was that of an angel or that of Him who is more than an angel, Omnipotence was there to shield those three conscientious servants of God from heathen hate and anger. When God so wills, there is no fire, not even that of hell itself, that can do harm to the least of His saints. With the power of Jehovah around them, those three men were as safe from Nebuchadnezzar's flames as though they were strolling through a garden of roses. When, at the king's command, they stepped out from that fiery furnace, it was found that not a hair of their head was singed; that their clothes were not scorched; and that not even the smell of fire was upon them. "Then Shadrach, Meshach, and Abed-nego, came forth of the midst of the fire."

There is no reason that I should dwell upon the recent calamity that visited this town. The blackened ruins of two churches, of nearly a score of homes, one of them a minister's home, and of places of business, all speak to-day with an eloquence that is far above the touch of my lips and tongue. As intimated at the outset of my sermon, I am to talk to you of those things that are beyond the reach of fire. Be it known to you, my friends, that there are many things which cannot be burned.

I. Among these imperishable things I would place Christian fellowship. There was presented last Sabbath morning the unusual spectacle of a Presbyterian

congregation celebrating the sacrament of the Lord's
Supper within a Methodist church. I do not know
that such a sight was ever before seen. But to me it
was a glorious sight. The bread served in that or-
dinance and the fruit of the vine were sweeter to my
taste than ever before. I am quite sure that this
voices the sentiment of every Presbyterian who sat
down at that Communion table through the hospitality of Christian friends. It was as if that bread
had been mixed and baked by hands angelic, and as
if that juice of grapes had been squeezed from vine-
yards celestial.

This exhibition of Christian fellowship was all the
more striking from the fact that the hospitality of
the day was tendered by hands that had themselves
felt the breath of the flames. They were bandaged
hands, having suffered loss through the destruction
of property belonging to the church. I am not given
much to speaking words of praise; therefore what
I now say will have the more weight. The kindness
of this Methodist people then shown, and still shown,
was beautiful. Their words of invitation were like
"apples of gold in pictures of silver."

Do not tell me that denominational walls need be
so high that they cannot be looked over. Many of
such walls have been lowered for many a day, stone
after stone removed, until now even a child can look
over them. It is well that there should be some
height of wall. Church unity is only a pleasant
dream. In reference to government and modes of

worship it is impossible for all minds to think exactly alike. When men do not all agree in their political views, and when women do not all agree about the best manner of keeping house, it is foolish to expect an agreement among Christians in regard to many non-essential things. Let the walls remain—Methodist walls, Episcopalian walls, Baptist walls, Presbyterian walls, and all other secular walls. But even while such walls are standing, there can be harmony concerning the doctrines of Christianity that are necessary to salvation. Such harmony has long existed. As to those things that belong to the realm of speculation, it is the most bigoted bigotry that makes discord.

Not long since I had a remarkable dream. I need not give it in detail, for if I were so to do, it would make you laugh. Suffice it to say, I dreamed that, for some reason, I was in a Methodist conference for examination, wishing to be admitted as a member of the Conference. Bishop Fowler was presiding. When I made known to him my desire, he said to me, "So you now think that Calvin was wrong and Arminius right, do you?" I answered in a most emphatic manner, my Presbyterian blood stirred within me, that I thought no such thing. But now, if that question should be put to me, I should be apt to say, "Those men are both in heaven; I have no inclination to rake over the ashes of their theological controversies."

Yes, Christian fellowship is one of the things that is beyond the reach of fire. In the calamity that hurt three congregations, the loss of a parsonage and the loss of churches that were loved by many a soul, the pews of those churches sacred with hundreds of precious memories, their pulpits the place where many a beloved minister's voice heralded the Gospel, their organs the tryst of bewitching melodies, their steeples each a landmark, their bells solidified music that was often broken into calls to worship, having summoned successive generations, but now forever silent, there was that displayed which took Christian fellowship out of theory into fact, there crowning it with a glorious crown. Christ walked with us all in the fire. In religious matters there were three of us in that furnace of flames, and with the three was the Son of God. Christian fellowship was not then burned; it was strengthened. Bless the Lord!

II. Among these imperishable things I would place the Word of God. Without doubt, there were some Bibles destroyed in the churches and in the homes during the fire. But there are plenty of Bibles left. What I speak of, however, is the Word of God itself, not single copies of it. This grand old Book has come unscathed through many a fire—through the fires of persecution; through the fires of infidelity; through the fires of heathenish prohibition. It is as fresh and bright and sweet to-day as when it was first gathered together and bound into one volume as a library of books between two covers. Not one of its glowing chapters has ever been dimmed. Not one of its glistening paragraphs has ever been smoked. Not one of its shining verses has ever been charred. There is not even the smell of fire upon its lids. He whom this Book calls the Word of God, the expression of divinity, has ever thrown around the Bible the mightiness of His protection.

After the great fire in Chicago, after the great fire in Baltimore, and after other great fires in other places, safes were opened that contained valuable books and parchments when the conflagration first broke out, and those books and parchments were found in good condition, having successfully passed through flames that were hotter than those into which these three Hebrew captives of the text were thrown. That is but a faint illustration of the preservative guardianship of God in reference to His Word. There is no fire that can burn the Word of God. As well attempt to burn the rocks of the Sierra Nevadas by holding against them a piece of lighted tissue paper, as for earth, or hell, to attempt the annihilation of this Book of books. The same attempts at annihilation directed towards the works of Shakespeare or the writings of a Plato, as have been employed to rid the world of the Bible, would long ago have reduced those works and writings to a heap of ashes.

There have been many times when the people of God feared for the safety of this Book. The Bible declares that there was once a city called Nineveh, that city so large as to require a journey of three days to go around it, prophecy foretelling its destruction by fire and water. Hundreds of infidel voices said that the statement was absurd; that no city of that size was ever built; and that it would be impossible to destroy any place with two such antagonistic elements as are fire and water. Many of God's saints trembled, afraid that the integrity of the Scriptures might be overthrown. But distinguished archæologists went forth, and with pick and shovel those men unearthed the ancient city of Nineveh. Then they measured it, and, according to the old estimate of a day's journey, they announced that it required three days to walk around it. They further assured the world that it was literally wiped out of existence by fire and water, those natural foes uniting in the demolition of Nineveh, a part of the city having been placed under water by an inundation of the river Tigris, another part having been swept by flames, finding the evidences of conflagration in piles of charcoal. That was Shadrach, Meshach and Abed-nego again unharmed in the furnace of infidel thought, the Son of God in the midst.

So might I multiply illustrations of divine protection given to this living Book. Why, if even all the copies of the Bible in the world to-day could be gathered together into one immense heap, and a torch be put to them, the modern printing press having turned off enough copies of the Bible to make a veritable mountain of books, the Word of God could not be destroyed. There are enough inscriptions from it on memorial tablets, on memorial shafts and monuments, on memorial tombstones, and enough quotations from it in thousands of volumes of history and poetry and sermons, in every kind of literature, indeed, to reconstruct it. Besides that; there is enough of this Book for its reproduction lodged in millions of memories. Let every known copy of the Bible be buried in a grave of ashes, and there would be many a saint of God to give those copies resurrection. Yonder is a saint in trouble. Listen to him, as he repeats the precious promises of God's Word! Yonder is a Sabbath-school teacher. Listen to her, as she tells her class of Him who suffered on the Cross for human sin! Yonder is an old, spectacled mother grieving over her absent boy, her white hair a crown of silver upon her head. Listen to her, as she quotes to herself the covenants of God in His Word! Yonder is a death-chamber. Listen to trembling lips, as they pronounce the consolations of God's Word! To destroy this Book, you would have to destroy the world itself. No! I mistake. That would not destroy it. Some day in heaven there would be a group of the saved talking together about the experiences of earth. Then one would say, "The Bible was a pillow beneath my weary head as I lay tossing in a fever. Do you recall that passage which speaks of God as making one's bed in sickness?" Then another would say, "I was once in deep waters of affliction. Do you recall that passage about the faith of the Psalmist when all of God's billows had gone over him? That passage was my stay in that time of anxiety." So from lip to lip would flow the rich music of God's Word, the memory of the redeemed sending forth harmonious strains through the sunny air of heaven. Untold ages in eternity shall not dim the recollection of those saved by the blood of Christ. We shall need no Bible in heaven as a revelation; but we shall carry the treasures of the Bible forever in our hearts.

After the battle of Richmond, a dead soldier was found on the field. His hand was placed upon an open Bible. Insects had eaten off the flesh of that hand, but the bony forefinger pointed to these words: "Yea, though I walk through the valley of the shadow of death, I will fear no evil; for thou art with me; thy rod and thy staff they comfort me." Death itself has no power against this Book.

Friend, you may have lost your home; you may have lost many a keepsake; you may have lost all that you ever owned; but you have not lost the hope, the cheer, the brightness, the sweetness, the comfort of this blessed Volume. No fire can harm God's Word.

III. Among these imperishable things I would place heaven. This world, after all, is a poor world in which to build property or make investments of money. I find no fault with the world in general. Physically it is a beautiful world. Beautiful its over-arching skies by day and by night, those skies the garden in which bloom clouds and sunrise and sunset and rainbows and stars. Beautiful its mountains

4

and plains and valleys. Beautiful the sheen of its forests and orchards and fields. Beautiful the flash of its brooks, and rivers, and lakes, and oceans. Also socially is it largely a kind world. Men jostle each other on the highways of business, apparently caring little for each other, all pushing forward their own schemes or making their own plans. But let trouble come, and thousands of hearts are bared with sympathy and help. Those who sneer at the indifference of this world towards suffering, are owls hooting in the darkness. I have no use for pessimism. This is not altogether an unfriendly world. All of its roses do not have thorns. All of its paths are not rough with stones. All of its winds are not hurricanes.

Yet beautiful as is this world and kind, it is a poor place, I say again, on which to build up all of one's happiness. Many of its elements have been caught and harnessed by man; but those same elements often gain the mastery, and spread desolation and death in their path. A fire on the hearth in autumn days is a pleasant sight; that same fire curling its red tongue among books and pictures and furniture, and devouring roofs and walls, is a sight that strikes the bravest heart with terror. You and I need a better world than this for permanence of health and money and joy and life. Through the blood of Christ, God has provided such a world.

I do not trouble myself about the locality of heaven. The Bible gives no lessons in celestial geography. Enough for me to know that somewhere in the wideness of God's universe there is such a blessed place. Enough also for me to know that *there* no tears shall stain the cheeks; no sighs shall part the lips; no sickness shall pale the brow; no sorrow shall hang weights upon the heart; no disappointment shall cloud the mind; no shadow shall dim the sunlight; no loss shall subtract from the gain; no death shall take down the body.

In that city above no calamities ever come. Never once in all its lustrous history has any one of its mansions been even the least marred by the rude touch of flame or sullied by the noxious breath of smoke. I tell you this morning that the day hastens when this globe on which you and I now live shall be encircled by world-wide conflagration. See it! The mountains on fire! The plains on fire! The continents on fire! A sweep of fire that shall madly race over every sea and ocean! The fire of one hemisphere answering with terrible roar the fire of the other hemisphere! A marriage of fire, the black hands of disaster lifted in the celebration of the awful nuptials, that wedlock of hemispheric flames not to be dissolved until they shall both lie down in ashes and be buried in the hot cinders of a destroyed earth! But heaven shall endure forever. Those who live in that substantial world shall walk in unsullied white; and Christ shall walk with them. Unbroken the life; unbroken the fellowship; unbroken the happiness; unbroken the wealth. "Here we have no continuing city, but we seek one to come." Bless the Lord, we shall find it!   "A city which hath foundations, whose builder and maker is God." O my unconverted friend, be sure to have your final citizenship with the redeemed of Christ! Lose heaven, and you lose all that is good and glorious! The loss of the soul is an irreparable loss!

In Charge of the Angels

He shall give his angels charge over thee. Psalm 91 : 11.

THE Bible is compact sunshine, compact cheerful-
ness, compact strength. There is no human book
so bright, so hopeful, so invigorating. This grand old
Book takes the tears of God's saints and fires them
with the glory of heaven. It takes saintly sorrows
and wreathes them with smiles. It takes even the
heaviest burden laid upon saintly shoulders and les-
sens its weight, removing from the load its iron, and
replacing that iron with feathers. The thought that
the Bible is a book of frowns and scowls is an infidel
thought. Its peals of laughter outnumber its wails
of distress. Its sweetness exceeds its bitterness. Its
hallelujahs burst more frequently than its dirges.

Those who go up into the mountains get away
from the dust and smoke of earth and breathe re-
freshing air. Let us climb one of the mountains of
God's Word to-day and take in a full inspiration of
its tonic atmosphere. Around us flutter the wings
of celestials. "For he shall give his angels charge
over thee."

I. I would remark, that we have angelic guardianship in the smallest affairs of life. I open this door
first into my subject because it is a door seldom entered. The most of us are perfectly willing to be-

lieve that the angels of God are near when we are in sore straits, but unwilling to believe that they are near when the trouble is only slight. For broken limbs plenty of sympathy; for the scratch of a pin no sympathy. For a crushing, grinding, mutilating tribulation the stretching forth of tender hands; for a headache no hands to soothe. For ruined fortunes words of consolation; for the loss of a ten-cent piece oppressive silence. May God deliver us from such paralyzing infidelity! Such thoughts are born and bred in the darkest corner of hell. I want you to know, my brother, my sister, that the guardianship of God's angels touches even the most insignificant things of life.

This very thought was in the mind of the Psalmist. What does he say? Listen! "For he shall give his angels charge over thee, to keep thee in all thy ways." I would place a great deal of emphasis on that word "all." "*All* thy ways." That word is not a straight line; it is a curving line—a circle that wraps itself around your life and my life. But, as if that were not enough to put faith into us, the Psalmist adds, "They shall bear thee up in their hands, lest thou dash thy foot against a stone." There you have the perfection of angelic guardianship. The very pebbles upon which we might bruise ourselves, or over which we might trip, shall offer no impediment to our feet— lifted above them by the strong, loving hands of the angels. Blessed Lord, what comfort is here!

There are no trifles in the Providence of God. During the Spanish-American war, our Government did not think it belittling to place a tax upon the smallest articles of commerce. Neither does it belittle God to give the angels charge over the minutiæ in the lives of His saints. An angel bearing a pair of human feet above sharp stones is engaged in as divine a work as when he is rolling a sun along or kindling an aurora borealis. When I see God building the architecture of the everlasting hills out of grains of sand, or when I see Him making an Atlantic Ocean of drops of water, I know that there is nothing too small in any life to be beyond His notice. "The very hairs of your head are all numbered." It was God Himself, in the person of Jesus Christ, who said that.

What do you call a trifle? Michael Angelo was once visited in his studio by a friend, the sculptor at work upon a statue. After a few days that friend paid another visit to the famous sculptor. He said to the artist, "Why, what have you been doing since I was last here?" Michael Angelo answered, "I have rounded a little more this muscle and given a little more shape to the vein of this hand." "But," said the friend, "these are trifles." "Not at all," answered the sculptor. "It is by such trifles that I make my work perfect; and perfection, sir, is no trifle."

So is it the sum of our daily life that makes up our character. We need the grace of God as much in the sweeping and dusting of a room as in the teaching of a class in a Sabbath-school. We need that grace

as much in driving a nail as in handling thousands
of dollars in a bank, especially if, in driving the nail,
the hammer comes down upon the thumb! We need
that grace as much in mixing bread for a meal at
home as in preparing bread for a table of Communion. It is the common things of every-day life that go
into life itself and make it complete—complete either
for righteousness or unrighteousness. When religion
becomes only the putting on of Sunday clothes, from
Monday to Saturday hung up in closets, or laid away
in bureau drawers, or carefully covered in bandboxes,
it is only so much broadcloth and linen and millinery.
What you and I need is religion that will sustain us
as well while bending over a hot stove in the kitchen
as while sitting in a pew within a sanctuary. The
Psalmist, inspired of God, here offers us that kind of
religion. "He shall give his angels charge over thee,
to keep thee in *all* thy ways."

What a thought that is! Yonder is a man amid
the insectile vexations of business life. "Go, angel,"
commands God, "and help that man!" Yonder is a
woman amid the multiplied annoyances of domestic
life. "Go, angel," commands God, "and help that
woman!" Then I see the flash of wings, those wings
cleaving the air with more swiftness than a bolt of
lightning. Then I see a pair of shining hands outstretched to clear the brow of frowns; to brush away
the clouds of the mind; to quench the angry fire of
the heart. The great question is, Do you and I always accept such ministry? "He shall give his an-

gels charge over thee, to keep thee in *all* thy ways."

II. Again, I remark, that we have angelic guardianship in our journeys. The words of the Psalmist so imply when he says, "They shall bear thee up in their hands, lest thou dash thy foot against a stone."

Does any one doubt the need of such guardianship? There are many doors out of life. One of the doors most frequently opened into death is the door of accident while traveling. How many feet might stumble, if there were no angelic hands stretched forth in protection along the street! How many horses might run away, if there were no stronger hands than ours at the reins! How many steamboats might burst a boiler, if there were no restraining hands upon the safety valve! How many trains might jump the track, if there were no preventing hands at the switches or no governing hands at the throttle of the engine! Angels when we walk! Angels when we drive! Angels when we glide over the river or bay or ocean! Angels when we go rushing like the wind along iron rails!

The fact that you have never seen these angelic guardians is no argument against their presence with us at such times. Neither have you ever seen heat; yet it warms your body and cooks your meals. Neither have you ever seen steam; yet it drives your machinery. That which in common phrase is called steam is naught but vapor—the invisible spirit of steam kissing the air, and the contact of its lips with the atmosphere revealed to the eye. Neither have you ever seen light; yet it blesses the vision with many a picture of beauty. Neither have you ever seen gravitation; yet it takes the world on which you live in wondrous journey among the stars of heaven; and there is no collision, even though millions of other worlds are traveling through space at the same time. All knowledge is not dependent upon the sight. Elisha's servant did not see the horses and chariots of fire that were round about his master; but they were there. When God touched the young man's eyes, he saw them—the mountain full of them—the lustrous legions of the skies drawn up in battle array in defence of the endangered prophet. Elisha knew that they were there, knowing that fact through a keen spiritual sense that was better than outward sight. It is only blind eyes within that need to be helped by quickening the physical vision. "We walk by faith, not by sight."

So are the angels of God with you and me when perils are about us. "For he shall give his angels charge over thee, to keep thee in all thy ways. They shall bear thee up in their hands, lest thou dash thy foot against a stone."

I ask you to note the personal element in the text and its surroundings. "He shall give his angels charge over *thee*, to keep *thee*. They shall bear *thee* up in their hands, lest *thou* dash *thy* foot against a stone." That same personal element runs through the whole of this Psalm. This celestial guardianship is not only over the saints of God collectively, but also individually. You and I may appropriate the promises of this Psalm to ourselves, as if we were the only persons in existence. One is apt to feel his insignificance in a great crowd of people. I have so felt often while traveling in a well-filled railroad train. But looking forth from the window, the steam of the engine flying by has seemed to be the white wings of a host of angels speeding along with the train, their potent hands keeping the train to the tracks, and making the journey safe for every man and woman and child in every coach, all that number of people separated into units. It is then that I have whispered to myself, "He shall give his angels charge over *thee*."

Who will say that this is naught but fancy? I tell you, my friends, that this skeptical age needs a strong infusion of childlike faith into its veins. We are putting the angels of God too far away in the heavens, classing them with the nymphs and dryads of heathen mythology. We are resolving them into mere airy creatures that have no existence except in the imagination, and therefore placing them beyond the touch of human need. But "are they not all ministering spirits sent forth to minister for them who shall be heirs of salvation?" Take from me the thought of angelic guardianship in any journey, even the simple one of walking across my study floor, and you rob me of that which is of more value than the jewels in the crown of a king.

"But," says some one, "accidents often happen.

How do you reconcile that fact with angelic guardianship?" Well, I answer, it is not particular what door of exit from this world a Christian passes through. If I am not tempting Providence, being in danger because of duty, and if it be God's good will to take me home through a door of accidental pain or accidental death, what matters it? P. P. Bliss, the noted minstrel of the Gospel, singing the songs of Zion around the world, was taken home in the disaster of Ashtabula bridge, the train in which he journeyed breaking through that bridge. The passage from that frightful disaster to the gates of pearl was just as swift as though P. P. Bliss had gone to glory from his own bed under his own rooftree. Let no Christian play the infidel in his thoughts about Providence. God's angels are always on guard. Accidents, so-called, but change their opportunities.

III. Again, I remark, that we have angelic guardianship in great difficulties. The troubles of life are not an unbroken plain. They often rise into rugged heights. Look yonder at the children of Israel! Before them the waters of the Red Sea. Beside them the towering hills. Behind them the pursuing army of Pharaoh. When Napoleon Bonaparte was told about the impossibility of taking his troops over the Alps, he said, waving his hand, "There shall be no Alps!" So he built the Simplon Pass, his regiments to march along that pass for the devastation of Italy. But these Israelites could not make any such boast as that. They were seemingly doomed to destruction.

Death frowned upon them from the mountains. Death leered at them from the sea. Death mocked them in the sound of clattering hoofs and grinding chariot wheels behind their backs. But look! One man stands forth and waves a shepherd's rod over the raging waters before that host, his long beard of white snowing in the wind. Behold! The waters divide. A shining path appears. The trembling Hebrews walk safely across to the other shore. Napoleon Bonaparte said, "There shall be no Alps!" But to make his word good he had to spend fifteen million francs and put thousands of men to many days of toil. God said, "There shall be no Red Sea!" and at His command, the tumbling waters halted, pushed back and reared into a crystal wall in a single night by hands angelic.

The angels of that difficulty in the career of God's ancient people, the angels of Abraham and Jacob, the angels of Gethsemane around the Christ, have charge of you and me in every time of special need. If I did not believe that, I should quit the ministry.

I like what I was reading about the faith of a Scotch preacher. In troublous times he and his little flock were climbing a mountain. Suddenly he saw their foes advancing upon them. "Lord!" he cried, "wrap around us the plaid of Thy protection." Then fell a mist upon the mountain, and they were shut out from the view of those who sought their lives. That mist was the drapery of God's angels. Just as a child hides beneath its mother's apron, so that fugitive band of Christians was hidden beneath the skirts of Omnipotence.

I also like what I was reading of Martin Luther. He was summoned to appear before the papal council at Worms. His friends tried to dissuade him from going. He would not yield to them, saying, "I will go, even if there should be as many devils there as there are tiles upon the roofs of the houses!" That has the sound of mere bravado; but it was the utterance of a man of iron faith who firmly believed in the guardianship of God's angels in great emergencies.

My friends, we need to have a vivid sense of divine help just now as a church. Doing what we can ourselves, in reliance upon that help, we shall find, I think, that the flames which leveled yonder beloved structure to the ground were the glistening wings of God's angels, those wings flying abroad and swooping that Saturday afternoon of the first of October to try our faith and test our spirit of self-sacrifice. God will not let His angels desert us now in our extremity, if we have a trust in Him that is willing to work and suffer. God has placed in our hands a diploma of fire, graduating us into broader opportunities of scholarship. Let us use these opportunities for our own spiritual growth and the glory of Him who has given His angels charge over us.

IV. Once more, I remark, that we have angelic guardianship in the hour of death. We commonly speak of death under figures that are dark and forbidding. It is high time that Christian people should

banish such repulsive figures from their vocabulary.
What business has a storm-breeding, black-winged,
starless midnight with a sunrise? Death is not deser-
tion; it is multiplied companionship. If the angels
are with us in the common things of life, if they
travel with us, if they flock around us when we are in
terrible difficulties, then their number is increased
when a Christian soul is about to be liberated from its
prison of clay. Such an hour is a preparation for
bursting grandeur and celestial exaltation. The gates
of the city are flung wide open. The arches have
been sprung over the flashing highways. The orchestra and the choristers are ready. The throne is
set. All heaven waits for the crowning scene. Hosts
of angels are gathered around the dying bed of the
departing saint to escort him to a glorious triumph.
Wings! Wings! Wings! There are wings far
away, hastening on. There are wings fluttering in
air around the home. There are wings folded in the
death-chamber. God sends His angels forth and
gives them charge of His home-coming ones, the redeemed of Christ.

Away with the least poison vine of infidelity that
twists its serpent-like tendrils among the flowers of
our fragrant religion! It has no right to be there.
Away with the smell of varnish and disinfectants
from this subject of Christian death! Away with all
morbid thoughts! Why close the shutters of the
soul and shut out God's sunbeams? Why scald the
cheeks with unceasing tears? Why chase off every

smile from the lips? Why invite all the fiends of despair to come and sit down in a house of bereavement, when we may have angels with us, some of the angels that came to the dying one remaining behind to comfort and help and bless?

I like what I saw not long since upon a calendar that rests upon my study desk. The leaflet gave the date, and beneath the date was the inscription, "Mrs. Moody's Coronation Day." So also do I like what Luke says of Stephen who was battered out of life by rocks hurled from angry, murderous hands, "He fell asleep." So also do I like what Paul said of himself in view of his martyrdom beneath the evil frown of the monster Nero, "The time of my departure is at hand." This whole Bible is full of glowing figures concerning death as it comes to God's saints. So are the histories that record Christian experiences. Why, then, should you and I borrow the sombre rhetoric of heathenism. Why hang up Edgar Allen Poe's croaking raven in the home of the soul, when there are plenty of canaries flying abroad? Why give way to ungovernable grief, when there is music waiting to be swept from the silent strings of the heart? Why not accept the tender ministry of loving angels?

Even when shall come our own hour to "depart and be with Christ, which is far better," the angels of God shall take us in charge. They bore up in their hands the souls of all the saints in the past ages. They bore up in their hands the souls of your sainted

dead and mine. They will likewise bear us up. For
myself, I ask nothing more in the close of life's day
than to have loved ones near, and along with them
the angels of God, their soft fingers filling my dying
pillow with what the Psalmist here calls in bold, yet
fitting imagery, "the feathers of the Lord God Almighty;" then giving their flaming coursers command, and speeding their chariot on and up to the
gates of pearl and the house of many mansions. Angelic guardianship all the way Home!.

The Mission of the Small

Who hath despised the day of small things? Zechariah 4:
10.

THAT question was asked nearly twenty-five hundred years ago. It came from the lips of God upon the ears of His prophet Zechariah. Just as pertinent and just as momentous a question is it now as it was then. Hear me, therefore, while I speak to you this morning of The Mission of the Small.

I. I would remark, that God has much use for small things. We commonly think of God in connection with what is stupendous. We usually have no vision of God except as we see Him working on a large scale. We behold Him only as He comes forth to view in the parade of the stars across the midnight heavens, or in the kindling of an aurora borealis, or in the weaving of a sunrise or a sunset. We stand in awful amazement before Him as He tosses the waves of the ocean, or as He lets loose from His fists the winds of the tempest, or as He pours a Niagara over the rocks, the lightning flash of the waters followed by the thunder of their fall. We are apt to look for God altogether in those things that are mighty and grand and majestic and sublime.

But I wish you to know that God does not confine Himself to those things which we call great. The

fact is that all greatness is but an aggregation of littleness. The storm that comes down like a deluge
from overhanging reservoirs of cloud, flooding the
fields and washing the streets of towns and cities, increasing the volume of mountain streams, and widen-
ing rivers and deepening lakes and seas, is nothing
more than a multiplication of raindrops, each one of
those drops akin to the sweat of a woman's brow as
she stands over a hot stove preparing a meal. Divine
arithmetic! The glory of an autumnal forest, that
glory spreading itself for miles, is nothing more than
the marriage of one lustrous color with another and
the rearing of a numerous family of glowing leaves,
the blush on the faces of those leaves related to the
healthful hue of a laborer's babe asleep in its cradle.
More divine arithmetic! The yellow corn wrapped
up in its pale husks over the broad acres of a Kan-
sas field, millions of grains thus wrapped up, and
like piles of gold in a government vault, is nothing
more than a case of geometrical progression from a
few bushels of corn drilled into the ground in the
early summer, those multitudinous grains bearing
a similarity to the kernels popped into edible snowflakes by a pair of lovers over a fire on a Hallowe'en.
More of the mathematics of God! All greatness in
the physical universe but a union of littleness. That
is how God works. The architecture of the Rocky
Mountains, the Sierra Nevadas, the Alps, the Himalayas, all heaved and upreared and chiseled and tree-
adorned and ice-crowned through the piling together

and the massing of innumerable atoms of matter. God's masonry of mountain systems is but a boy's sand-hill in a dooryard carried higher and extended over a greater length. An Atlantic and a Pacific are but the contents of a tincup filled at a farmhouse pump spread out and deepened. All of God's great things are made from little things.

The trouble is that we get accustomed to looking at God's works through a telescope. We gaze upward, and the skies above us at night seem to be an immense garden abloom with suns and with groups and clusters and constellations and galaxies of worlds. Yet all the while the very small space occupied by our feet is also a garden. In a daily walk from his home to his office or store or shop a man's shoes crush multiplied wonders. I do not know but that the infinitude of God is more plainly in evidence from the eye-piece of a microscope than from the lens of a telescope. The truth is that no human brain has ever yet been able to make a final analysis of God's creations invisible to the naked sight. As the telescope reveals vastness, so also does the microscope reveal vastness. Before both of these instruments God withdraws Himself behind a veil that mortal fingers cannot lift. "Canst thou by searching find out God? Canst thou find out the Almighty unto perfection? It is as high as heaven; what canst thou do? deeper than hell; what canst thou know?" The answer to those questions is silence. God stands back of the upward vision of modern science with more majesty than we can endure. So behind the downward vision of that same science God stands with more greatness than we can imagine. In the shaping of the small, God is, to my mind, more marvelous than in the building of planetary palaces and the rearing of sun-thrones in the heavens beyond.

The same thing is true in the spiritual world. While "the chariots of God are twenty thousand, even thousands of angels," He often uses small means for the accomplishment of His purposes. Just as a traveler's voice has often loosened the accumulated snow of the Alps and sent an avalanche into the valley below with crushing force, so has many an insignificant instrument been the cause of mighty spiritual results. The childish accents of a Hebrew maid, a captive in Syria, directed Naaman the leper to the prophet Elisha for the healing of a frightful disease, Naaman's cure of body the forerunner of divine health within his heathen soul. A baby's tears in an ark of bulrushes afloat upon the Nile were the solvent that melted the chains of slavery from an oppressed people and gave that people glorious liberty. The singing of a boy in the streets of a German town prepared the way for the thunder of the Reformation, the echoes of that thunder yet rumbling in every Protestant church service.

Oh, yes; God can use armies in His providence, if He will, but He also can just as effectively use worms. It seems to me that He prefers the use of what is small. Witness David's sling bringing Goliath with a crash to the earth, the trained regiments of King Saul failing to down the boastful giant. Witness Shamgar's ox-goad in the slaughter of six hundred Philistines. Witness Samson's mowing to death of a thousand men with the jawbone of an ass. Witness Gideon putting the Midianites into disastrous defeat with pitchers and lamps. Witness Hannah's devotion to her child Samuel making that child a priest in Israel whose name glistens with piety. Witness David the shepherd lad mounting the steps of a throne, the harp that he learned to play out in the pasture-field sending its vibrations clear to the end of time. Witness the widow's mite cast into the treasury box of the Temple outringing the gold and silver of the rich contributors whose offerings had preceded her small sum. Witness the basket that let Paul down along the wall of Damascus, giving him descent into illustrious missionary career. Last of all, witness the Cross of Christ, a common instrument of execution, taking on magnetic power for the drawing of untold multitudes into eternal life. God has much use for small things. "Who hath despised the day of small things?"

II. I remark, that there is among men too much of a disposition to disregard small things. By the time that one reaches forty years of life he has come to the realization of the importance of littleness. Success in any calling is the outgrowth of all that has gone before it. Many of the world's men of wealth look back upon poverty. They built up their fortunes upon foundations of pennies. Some of the men whose name scratched upon a check will give that check honor in any reputable bank once hardly had the price of a loaf of bread in their trousers' pocket. By a careful husbandry of small sums of money they prepared the way for a harvest of stocks and bonds and shares and real estate. Where others wasted they saved.

The principle that littles are the seeds of much is true in every department of life. Mozart came to skillful performance of music by spending hours in practicing the scales. Daniel Webster had to begin his training as an orator by learning the alphabet. The architect that designed the Congressional Library at Washington once drew straight lines and curves and angles upon a slate. Michael Angelo spoiled many a piece of marble before he could carve a finished statue.

So with every profession and every trade. Smallness of effort is the herald of greatness of achievement. If that fact could be strongly impressed upon young minds, it would save many a boy and girl in later days a mountain of trouble. Hosts of young people are like the prodigal of Christ's peerless parable. Where he threw away the contents of his purse, they throw away precious moments and shining opportunities and painstaking care, coming up finally against the swine-trough of failure in life. It is by making the most of what lies to hand that more follows. Small things first; then larger things afterwards. Very generally, I think, have those who are near the hilltop of the years learned that lesson. Some learn it earlier.

But why not put that experience into the spiritual life? It is here that there is a wide tendency towards the disparagement of little things. For example, many persons are careful about committing great sins, but lax about inconsistencies of speech and conduct. Some persons would no more be guilty of highway robbery or burglary than a rose-bush would attempt to grow and bloom on the top of an ice-berg; yet those same persons would not hesitate to drive a sharp bargain in trade, that bargain not able to look strict honesty in the face. Some Christians are Christians until they are the principals in a horse-deal! Also would some persons blush to use pro-fane language, but they have no blushes at the es-cape of a so-called "white lie" from the lips. It is the "little foxes that spoil the vines" of character. It is small sins that make large sins, if there be any relative size of sin.

I advance another step, calling attention now to the slighting of little things in Christian work. It is the thought of many that only great deeds count in Christian work. Because they cannot speak like a Phillips Brooks, they will not speak at all. Because they cannot be a Wanamaker in the Sabbath-school, they will teach no class. Because they cannot be a Meyer or a Miller with their pen, they will keep their ink bottle corked. Because they cannot sew like a Dorcas, they will put no garment in a missionary box. Because they cannot give like a Peabody or a Dodge, they will let their purses remain clasped.

It was this disregard of small things that God questioned in the text. Zerubbabel had started the rebuilding of the ruined Temple at Jerusalem. There were many hindrances in the way. For sixteen years was the work delayed. But that man of God, under a fresh inspiration, began the work anew. What did God say? "The hands of Zerubbabel have laid the foundations of this house; his hands shall also finish it. For who hath despised the day of small things?"

It was as if the obstacles thrown up before that man by the enemies of the Jews had assumed gigantic form, rising higher, and higher, and still higher, becoming a veritable mountain of difficulty. Then God said, "Who art thou, O great mountain? Before Zerubbabel thou shalt become a plain: and he shall bring forth the headstone thereof with shoutings, saying, Grace, grace unto it."

God was teaching His people of those days that they should not despise small things. What should not be done then should not be done now. Let those with only a few talents use those few talents for the glory of God. God holds no one responsible for not being largely endowed. If God has not seen fit to bestow upon me the gifts of a Cuyler or a Talmage, that is no reason why I should refuse to preach. Besides that, it is not the possession of great resources only that tells in God's work; it is the energy of divine inspiration behind what one has. So God said to Zerubbabel, "Not by might, nor by power, but by my spirit, saith the Lord."

That same lesson was taught Elijah. That rugged prophet had set too much store by what had taken place on Mt. Carmel, when the priests of Baal had been put to confusion by the fire that fell from heaven in answer to prayer. God reminded Elijah that thousands of souls had not gone after the heathen deity that Ahab and others worshipped. They had been kept from apostasy through the gentle influence of God's Spirit. Elijah had been looking for a general reformation of Israel by means of the dramatic display on Carmel's summit.

Oh, this itching for great things that is characteristic of so many Christians! Let every one know that he has a part in the work of the Lord, however humble and obscure it may be. What if the hopper of a mill should refuse to hold the corn because it could not be the grindstones? What if those stones should refuse to revolve because they could not be the wheel turned by the race? What if the wheel should hang motionless because it could not be the onrushing water? Let the stream and the wheel and the stones and the hopper work together in harmony; then the miller will have his full supply of grist. If you see the force of the parable, apply it. "Who hath despised the day of small things?"

III. I remark, that those who neglect the use of

small means in God's work are guilty of sin. Some one says, "Now you are getting close to the conscience." Well, what is the sense in calling to see a person when you know that he is not at home? That is the fault of too many preachers. They are like the man who aimed at nothing and hit it! Patrick Henry's speech before the Assembly of the State of Virginia was one of the pioneers of the Revolution. It was a stiff breeze that stirred the kindlings of war. A sermon that is pointless is worthless. As well set a hungry beggar down to an empty plate, as to preach without a purpose. So I say again, that those who neglect the use of small means in God's work are guilty of sin.

"But," answers some one, "that is a sweeping statement. How do you prove it?" Well, I prove it by quoting from the very highest authority. You know that when there is a case of litigation in court the attorneys for both the plaintiff and the defendant are apt to cite the opinions of learned judges bearing upon the suit on hand. My source of information upon the point I have named is the Lord Jesus Christ. From His decision there can be no appeal.

Well, what does Christ say about this matter? You will find the answer in His parable concerning talents. The man who had received but one talent did not think it worth while to make any use whatever of such a trifle. I imagine that I hear him one day talking thus to himself: "One talent! Bah!

What is that compared with my fellow-servant's five talents? Or what is it even when compared with the two talents that my other fellow-servant has received? They have put their talents out at interest. I would do the same, if my master had left such sums in my care. But one talent! That is nothing. I will bury it out of sight." "So he went and digged in the earth, and hid his lord's money."

When the employer of those men came back from his journey, the servant with five talents and the servant with two talents had both doubled the money in their possession. The man with only one talent had no increase. His lord said to him, and mark well what he said, "Thou *wicked* and *slothful* servant." Christ's application is, "For unto every one that hath shall be given, and he shall have abundance; but from him that hath not shall be taken away even that which he hath. And cast ye the unprofitable servant into outer darkness."

Have I not established my point? What if the evangelist Philip had failed to preach Christ to the Ethiopian eunuch when the Holy Spirit told him so to do? Suppose he had said, "This is too small an opportunity. Give me a crowd of white men, and I will astonish the people with my eloquence. But I cannot go and speak to yonder negro." That would have been the end of Philip's evangelistic career. God would have had no further use for such a man.

What if Paul and Silas had refused to answer the question of the Philippian jailor, thinking that the occasion was beneath them? What if Dwight L. Moody had heeded his pastor's advice not to open his mouth in public, that advice given him because he stammered in his talk and "murdered the Queen's English?" Ask that question of thousands of instances. What would be the answer? "Neglect not the gift that is in thee" pertains as well to small gifts as to large gifts. "He that is faithful in that which is least is faithful also in much; and he that is unjust in the least is unjust also in much." "Who hath despised the day of small things?"

Therefore, when the Delawares and the Amazons of earth begin their mighty rush to the ocean as tiny rills; when the Andes mountains are built of grains of sand and rock; when the stupendous waterfall of the Yosemite valley is the leap of millions of drops of moisture over a precipice; when God descends with His omnipotence into the infinitesimally minute, even pausing in His work of directing the march of prodigious suns across the fields of space to whiten a lily's cheek, or uphold the wings of a sparrow in their flight, or count the hairs of a man's head, who will have the hardihood to despise the "day of small things?"

Friend, be not guilty of that sin. Have you only a thimble with which to measure your ability? Fill it for the glory of God. Are you slow of speech? Do not keep silent lips because you are not fluent. Have you but little time to spare in the work of the kingdom? Make the best possible use of the time you have at command. Is your income scanty? Out of it set apart whatever you can for the spread of Christianity over the earth. God does not hold a rule in His hand with which to size one's talents. He takes into view only the inches and feet of one's love. A man or woman may have only a fractional talent, and at the same time possess a love that covers acres. Do not despise "the day of small things."

If a new church building is yet to rise above yonder heap of ashes, it will assume shape and beauty, not from the largeness of bank-accounts in the name of millionaires, but from the massing together of little sums of money out of the willing hands of those who are not blessed with much of this world's goods. If you have only dimes or quarters or half-dollars to offer, lay them on top of what others have offered. In this crisis we want addition and multiplication, but no subtraction. Even do we count out division, except as it has to do with dividing the share of responsibility. Give all that you can; only let what you give be given freely and lovingly to God. "God loveth a cheerful giver." The force of that passage in the Greek is even more striking. The idea is that God loves a hilarious giver. Do not frown when you give; laugh; and laugh aloud. "Who hath despised the day of small things?" Out of such a day rose Zerubbabel's majestic and magnificent Temple. So out of such a day let rise a grander Buckingham Church than the one that God blew into a cinder pile with His breath of flame.

The Kicking Jeshurun

But Jeshurun waxed fat, and kicked. Deut. 32: 15.

AFTER forty years in a preparatory school and forty years in college, Moses is ready to graduate. Upon him have come the highest honors. He is the valedictorian of his class. If you have ever closely read his farewell address to the children of Israel, you know that he had well earned distinction. When he was commissioned by the Lord to demand from Pharaoh the release of the Hebrews, this man modestly declined the commission, affirming that he was slow of speech. The duty of the day fell upon his brother Aaron, who was then more gifted than was Moses. But now Moses has outdistanced the fluent Aaron in eloquence. I suppose that Aaron relied too much upon having a pair of lips always ready for utterance, and therefore made no further advance in attainments. I also suppose that Moses was stimulated by his lack of flowing words into untiring efforts at improvement. How well he succeeded is shown in his remarkable address on his commencement day, his time having come to leave earth for heaven. In the fabled race between a tortoise and a hare, the tortoise won the race by keeping on, while the hare lost because it stopped now and then to doze along the way, in its consciousness of superior running ability taking it for granted that any hare could beat a tortoise on its feet. Moses went far ahead of Aaron. That is a picture that has been drawn many times.

Moses fills his valedictory with many figures of speech, the natural language of impassioned oratory. We are to study one of his metaphors to-day and learn its pregnant lessons. That metaphor forms the text—"But Jeshurun waxed fat and kicked."

I. I ask you to note the ingratitude of Jeshurun. Jeshurun signifies supremely happy. It is used by Moses as a poetical name for Israel. The idea of kicking is taken from a pampered ox refusing to draw his load, lifting his hoof, and striking at his driver urging him on. An apt portrayal this of God's ancient people. They were a people highly favored. What blessings were let fall upon them from Jehovah's hands! Witness the battles that were fought for their liberty. Battle of the river Nile turned into blood. Battle of frogs and lice and flies. Battle of murrain and boils and hail. Battle of locusts and darkness. Battle of the death of Egypt's first-born sons and daughters. All of these battles fought for them by the Lord God Almighty.

Witness the miracles that were wrought in their behalf. Miracle of the divided Red Sea, God uprearing the waters into two crystal walls, between which they passed in safety to the other shore; God tumbling those same walls upon the heads of their pursuing foes, the centuries hearing the crash of those overturned walls. Miracle of guiding pillar of cloud by day and guiding pillar of fire by night, that moving equipage of vapor in symbolization of the fact that the Lord, who never slumbers nor sleeps, is always in advance of His chosen ones on the journey of life, for God is ever in His chariot, whether we can see that chariot or not. Miracle of the smitten rock weeping water for the quenching of their thirst. Miracle of bread coming down from heaven like snow, their breakfast and dinner and supper every day, except on the Sabbath, thrown to them from the pantry of the skies, on the sixth day an extra supply given them, enough to last over until the first day. Miracles all the way to Canaan. Miracles!

The blessings of those people were like the sunbeams that kiss the hearts of shower-washed roses and honeysuckle, intended to call from their lips the fragrance of thankfulness. But instead of gratitude, God received from them the noxious exhalations of murmurs and complaints. All the while that Jeshurun was waxing fat upon God's bounty, he was kicking at God's providences. His blessings made him act as a stubborn animal. What a sorry spectacle it is! The blows of Jeshurun's striking foot have echoed clear to the end of time. Hear those echoes!

But let us not be too hasty in condemning these people. It is often the case that we see a speck of dust in another's eye when we have a beam in our own eye. Some persons have a whole lumber yard in their eyes, and yet are caustically critical of the

6

motes that they behold in the eyes of their neighbors. Christ tells us that we should first clear our own vision before we attempt any surgical feat upon the optic orbs of anybody else. The fact is that these people of Israel have had their exact counterparts in every age. They have plenty of them in this magnificent twentieth century of the Christian Era. Look at the blessings we enjoy! Hosts of blessings. They are all about us like an army encamped. For instance, between the hours of six and nine this morning all the people of this town sat down at breakfast. Did everybody bow the head in thankful prayer to Him who thus gave their first instalment of daily bread on this Sabbath? I do not know. Let each one answer for himself. But I fancy that, if the roll were called, there would be many negative responses. Gratitude is a flower that does not naturally grow in the garden of the human heart; it has to be cultivated at great labor and pains.

Widen my thought. Let it take in our county, our state, our country, our continent, our world. How many Jeshuruns are kicking to-day like a spoiled ox? Could we know the sum contained in the answer to that query, it would appall us. The wonder is that God is so patient with mankind. Yet He has been accused of being a cruel, tyrannical taskmaster, ever swinging a whip in air, and lashing and cutting the shoulders of humanity. But the accusation is false. That is one of the blackest lies that ever came up from perdition to soil the lips of infidelity. It is

the Jeshuruns who are at fault, not God. Waxing
fat upon God's benevolences, their very power to
kick is derived from the kindness and love and mercy
of Him against whom they kick. Ingratitude is not
a Niagara cataract belonging to only one hemisphere;
it is an Atlantic, a Pacific, an Indian, an Arctic, and
an Antarctic ocean embracing a globe. Jeshurun's
kick in the wilderness that stretched before Canaan
was practiced long before in Eden. Jeshurun is still
kicking. The habit of kicking is in the blood of the
race. What a set of unthankful creatures we all are!
My friend, blessed with more good things than your
arithmetic can count, more than the stars that smile
at you from midnight skies, are you a Jeshurun?

II. I ask you to note the fact that prosperity often
is a test of personal faithfulness towards God. Jeshurun kicked because he had grown stout under God's
blessings. Not only was he ungrateful for his abundant wealth, but, as the remainder of the passage
states, "he forsook God who made him, and lightly
esteemed the Rock of his salvation." Prosperity;
then apostasy. What a prolific breeder is sin! Itself
a brat of hell, it brings forth other hell-brats of misshapen form and repulsive features. Yet there are
those who treat sin as though it were a mere witti-
cism—one of the jokes that Satan has cracked upon
the ears of mankind. But the Cross of Jesus Christ
tells all the world that human sin is the most seriously serious matter in the whole universe. It leaves
so great a stain upon the soul that nothing less than

the chemistry of infinite blood is able to remove the blot. One sin begets another sin; and so the generation of sin goes on. Says James, "When lust hath conceived, it bringeth forth sin; and when sin is finished, it bringeth forth death." Thus Jeshurun advanced in wickedness, at length forsaking God. His prosperity was the test of faithfulness. He "waxed fat and kicked."

The common impression is that adversity is the only thing that tries a man. Not so. God is not shut up to any one mode of discipline for a human soul. He has varied means for putting one to the proof. In some cases He allows men to gather great riches, in order to bring them to a revelation of themselves. In Jeshurun's case prosperity set Jeshurun to kicking—kicking against a spiritual worship of Jehovah in favor of idolatry; that particular form of kicking characteristic of Israel's history through age after age; that history a series of national relapses into heathenism; and that history persisting until God whipped idolatry out of His chosen people with many a blow from the lash of exile.

What did prosperity do for Abraham? It made him a man of pre-eminent faith. It kept his tent sweet with piety. It ripened his soul for heaven.

Look at Lot in comparison. Where do we find Lot, after he had selfishly chosen what should have been given to his uncle Abraham, the well watered plain of the Jordan? We find him pitching his tent towards Sodom. Then we find him thoroughly tinc-

tured and saturated with Sodom's life. Waxing fat
in that wicked city, Lot had no influence as a religious man. His prosperity almost ruined his soul.

So with Solomon. As his possessions increased,
his spirituality declined. Behold Solomon a wor-
shipper of strange gods! One more Jeshurun who
"waxed fat and kicked."

The past ages are crowded with Jeshuruns. In
some instances prosperity was the sun that brought
forth from the lives of men the flowers of righteousness, the aroma of those flowers yet hovering in the
air of earth. In other instances the sun of prosperity
filled the lives of men with writhing serpents, calling
those serpents up into the light from hearts dark with
evil. Listen to the hiss of Jereboam's abominations,
and Absalom's, and Herod's, and Nero's!

So does God still try men with His abundant blessings. Stocks, and bonds, and houses, and lands,
and luxuries in the home are often the figures that
God places on the blackboard of a man's life, placing
those figures there as a sum to be worked out, and
God standing by to watch the result of the problem.
It is not always in the valley that souls are put to the
test—the valley of sickness, the valley of business reverses, the valley of defeat, the valley of bereavement. As Abraham's faith was proved up the slopes
of Mt. Moriah, so often is it in exaltation that men
meet with discipline—upon the summit of financial
success, the summit of triumph, the summit of unbroken friendship, the summit of health.

Job was tried by prosperity, and not found wanting. He was seen to be full weight in the scales of righteousness. Adversity came upon him at the suggestion of Satan, who thought that Job was a godly man simply because he had been wonderfully blessed of the Lord. But Satan's handcuffs, and chain, and dungeon, that dungeon black with loss and disease and the shadows of ten graves, did not blister Job's tongue with a single curse against God.

Yes, adversity tries; so does prosperity. There are some persons who cannot be trusted with prosperity. Here is a man deeply religious. He is a man who has to struggle hard to gain a livelihood. But he is a praying man, a church-going man, a Bible-reading man, a Sabbath-keeping man. Suddenly the tide of fortune turns from the ebb to the flow. Wealth comes to that man. He moves his family into a larger house. Velvet carpets bloom on the floors. Oil paintings grace the frescoed walls. Silver and cut glass flash upon the sideboard and the table of the dining room. Handsomeness and plenty everywhere. Jeshurun waxes fat, and, alas! he kicks. In that man's heart prayer is silent. He is a stranger in the sanctuary. His Bible gathers dust, exchanged for the newspaper and the sensational novel. The Sabbath is his day for recreation, driving his gold-mounted team through the streets, or boarding an excursion train for God's seashore turned into a recruiting agency for the devil's soldiers of intemperance and lust. I care not what the name of the man

may be, he is a Jeshurun who has forsaken the God
who made him, and lightly esteemed the Rock of his
salvation. It will take the crack of a sheriff's hammer to knock that man into his senses. Prosperity
has made him insane.

How many Jeshuruns there are who thus kick because they have waxed fat! This, perhaps, is the reason that God keeps so many persons growing in the
shade. They thrive better there in a spiritual sense
than they would if transplanted into the open under
the full blaze of the sun. It takes one who has a clear
head to stand upon some great elevation. A dizzy
brain must not attempt the feat of climbing high.
Some persons get spiritual vertigo when they are exalted. It is better to be low for a season in one's
school-room class, if graduation day find you at the
top, than to be first now and last afterwards. So it
is better to be humble on earth and wear a crown in
heaven, than to be proud here and then be cast headlong into hell. If God is blessing your soul with His
grace, do not ask Him for worldly wealth, or worldly
position, or worldly fame. You might become a
kicking Jeshurun.

III. I ask you to note the thought that the fidelity
of nations may become strained by success. It is of
Israel as a nation that Moses here is speaking. It
was this people, supremely happy, a Jeshurun favored of God, who had kicked, forsaking the Lord
who had given them their liberty from Egyptian
bondage. His the hand that had arrested the whip

of the taskmaster. His the hand that had bound up
the wounds of their slavery. But against that benevolent hand, fairly charged with goodness, they had
rebelled. What a terrible indictment Moses brings
against Jeshurun! After describing the triumphs
of the people of Israel, speaking of their waxing fat,
and telling of their proud and wanton behavior under the figure of kicking, he proceeds to specify their
wickedness. Listen! "They sacrificed unto devils,
not unto God; to gods whom they knew not; to new
gods that came newly up, whom your fathers feared
not. Of the Rock that begat thee thou art unmind-
ful, and hast forsaken God that formed thee."

There is a striking similarity between the history
of Israel and our history as a people. The God of
the Red Sea and the wilderness journey to Canaan
was the God who guided the Nina, the Pinta and the
Santa Maria, the ships of Christopher Columbus,
across the Atlantic Ocean to these American shores.
The God who afterwards broke down the walls of
Jericho under the feeble blast of rams' horns was the
same God who stood beside our fathers at Lexing-
ton, and Concord, and Bunker Hill, and Princeton,
and Yorktown. Again stood He with them at New
Orleans in the War of 1812. Again stood He with
them in the late Civil conflict, when brother fought
against brother, God then teaching this nation
through the awful discipline of wasted harvest fields
and the thunder of artillery and the flash of bayonets and swords and a deluge of precious blood, a

lesson that bears fruit to-day in the million-miled orchard of a firmly united commonwealth.   Again stood He with our living kindred on the decks of the fleets that gave their guns voice in Manila Bay and in the harbor of Santiago, those guns putting to silence the tyranny of a worn-out kingdom, and echoing around the world the fact that God had moved our nation to the very front among the governmental powers of the earth.   As a citizen of this country, on this Sabbath that is the golden door of another Independence Day, I am proud to speak of God's providence written in shining letters upon every thread of the Stars and Stripes.

But there is danger that we may become a Jeshurun.   We have already waxed fat.   Alas! if we should kick against Him who has been leading us along the pathway of the years.   It is only righteousness that exalts a nation.   Napoleon Bonaparte was wrong when he said that God is on the side of those who have the strongest battalions, his own inglorious downfall and shattered sceptre proving him to be wrong.   God is on the side of those who are faithful to Him.   Let this nation become a Jeshurun, utterly corrupt in its legislative halls; let bribery altogether stain its courts of justice; let us be a people setting up the golden calf of money as an object of worship; let us be anarchists who put aside divine law in regard to the sacredness of the Sabbath and everything else religious; let us tolerate without indignation that modern uncleanness, Mormonism; let us be a land whose liquor bill far exceeds what it spends for carrying the Cross of Jesus Christ to benighted neighbors beyond the seas, this last woeful thing already a fact, and one before which all true Christians recoil; then must judgment unsheathe its flaming sword against us. There are no national foundations so strong that they cannot be thrown down. Rome stood for twelve centuries. When the time came for its destruction, God hurled that Empire into the dust. Were it not for the millions of God's people who belong to our citizenship, Christ telling us that His disciples are the salt of the earth, acting as a preservative in the midst of rottenness, it is probable that God's hand would already be upon the hilt of the sword of judgment, waiting to draw that sword from its scabbard and cut this nation to pieces, scattering the fragments upon the wind of His anger. "God save the State!" But you and I must help Him save it. As individual members of this Republic, it is incumbent upon you and me to fear God and keep His commandments. If we do not set an example of godliness before our fellowmen, we cannot expect any righteousness from them. Let us be known first in all things as citizens of heaven. While it is not wrong to wax fat it is wrong to kick.

Yes; we are a highly favored people. But our prosperity is of God. To Him, therefore, be dedicated not only our churches, but also our mills and shops, and stores, and banks, every place where industry and commerce are, from banded wheels and clanging anvils and jarring picks and rustling silks and clinking gold and silver, as from a great organ, pouring forth a doxology to Him from whom all blessings flow. As eighty millions of people sit down every day at a table provided by the Lord God Almighty, let there be nowhere under it the kicking feet of a single Jeshurun!

The Triumphs of Christianity

And the disciples were called Christians first in Antioch.
Acts 11 : 26.

SINCE this item of history was recorded nearly
nineteen centuries have passed away. Christianity
then was an infant; now it is a giant. Rocked in a
Jewish cradle, it has outgrown its early culture, and
made for itself an environment that is world-wide.

When once it has learned to fly, an eaglet cannot be
kept in the nest that gave it birth. Yonder is the
sunny air, and beyond is the blue sky; and the sweep
of its pinions carries it forth and upward, till, with
far-reaching vision, it looks down upon the mountains below, and beholds them shrink into mole hills.

Like that is Christianity. The old name applied
to its adherents, that of Galileans and Nazarenes,
was soon exchanged for one that lifted this new
spiritual force from the narrowness of provincialism,
and sent it forth upon a mission that was cosmopoli-
tan in its extent and purpose. First in Antioch, a
Grecian city, were the disciples called Christians.

I would remind you, however, that this new name
given to the disciples was a nickname. The Anti-
ochians were noted for their humor. This term,
therefore, was the outcome of sarcasm, that peculiar
form of wit that hides a sting behind its smile, like

the playfulness of a tiger over its victim, always ending in death by paw and tooth. Seizing upon the
fact that these men preached much about the Christ,
the inventive genius of jesting minds conceived the
name of Christian. There was a sneer in the appel-
lation. It was meant to be a term of reproach.

But, ah! they built better than they knew. That
scornful name, originating in Antioch only a few
years after the cricifixion of ·Christ, has traveled in
triumph through all the following ages. Throwing
off the outward cloak that was jestingly placed upon
it, lo! it speedily stood forth robed in divinity. It
wears to-day a crown that outshines all other crowns
as easily as the sun outshines the light of a glow
worm; for that name Christian is a king that rules
kings. It reigns in absolute supremacy.

Thus, my friends, does God cause the wrath of
men to praise Him. Here is a striking illustration
of that mysterious law by which the will of God and
the will of man, opposed to the higher will, work together in harmony, and produce results that God in-
tends by His decree. With contempt upon their
unhallowed lips, these people of Antioch pronounced
a name that shall endure forever to the honor of
Christ. With hands of hatred they reared to a despised Jew a monument of mud; but the passing
years transformed it into an imposing shaft of marble, which even the dying convulsions of the globe
cannot shake from its granite foundation. My theme
therefore is, The Triumphs of Christianity.

I. Let us glance at the religion of Jesus Christ making its way among the multitudes of mankind. In its infancy, as we have seen, it was a subject of jest. But any condition of babyhood is one of immaturity. No one could have guessed the possibilities that lay in the infantile brain of Daniel Webster. In the cooing of those little lips there was no hint of the eloquence that afterwards thundered its rhetoric at Bunker Hill, or discharged its oratoric artillery in the Senate Chamber of the Capitol at Washington. One may smile at the homely features of a new-born child, and live to see the day when smiles are displaced by admiration.

So could the witty inhabitants of Antioch afford to make merry over the new sect of that time, which had but comparatively a few followers; but who laughs now at Christianity? It has come God's hour to laugh in the heavens, and hold in derision those who despise His royal Son.

It is said that facts are stubborn things. That of Christianity has a special obstinacy that is all its own. From a few thousand converts in its early days it has swollen into the arithmetic of over two hundred million souls. The addition of the first century of its growth has been supplanted by multiplication. But this is only a mere suggestion of the increase that is yet to be. The day is coming when even multiplication will be too slow to enumerate its triumphs. Then the process of growth will have to call geometric progression to its aid. Even that will fail. Looking off upon the throngs of the redeemed, John was unable to count them. He spoke of them as being ten thousand times ten thousand and thousands of thousands. Then he afterwards added, almost holding his breath at the stupendous thought, "a great multitude that no man could number." It was like a view of the heavens at nightfall, here and there a star bursting to sight, then, as the shadows deepen, scores flashing their silvery fires athwart the firmament, then hundreds, then thousands, galaxies and constellations wheeling into line in parade of magnificence, till, with his vision enlarged by the telescope, the astronomer stands in the presence of a universe whose worlds are sown through it with a profusion that staggers the mind and strikes imagination dumb.

Thus, through history, do we behold Christianity to-day as it went forth from Jerusalem, and stepped rapidly onward over the Roman Empire, steadily gathering its recruits, as the army marched, until now we see it swaying the foremost nations of the globe, and still victoriously pushing its conquests upon every inhabited shore.

Alexander the Great and Napoleon Bonaparte both sought for themselves universal dominion; but their ambitious lust was never gratified. The only conqueror of the earth is the Lord Jesus Christ. The only regiments that shall tramp the continents are Christian. The only banner that shall wave in triumph forever is the banner of the Cross. Ride on,

King Jesus! Ride on! Thou art the world's only Sovereign. Europe is Thine. Asia is Thine. Africa is Thine. America is Thine. Thine are the islands of the sea. Ride on! ride on! The heathen are Thy inheritance, and the uttermost parts of the earth are Thy everlasting possession. Therefore, ride on!

I once saw a masterpiece painting of the world's most renowned men of war. Mounted on their spirited chargers, they were in the act of pushing their way to the front, while on both sides of them were stretched the ghastly corpses of the slain; and these extended far into the rear, back to the vanishing point of the vision, row on row of dead bodies, over which these warriors moved into historic fame.

But I show you a grander picture. It is the masterpiece of Inspiration, and it hangs in the gallery of the Apocalypse. Look upon it, as traced by the wrinkled hand of the aged Apostle John! "And I saw heaven opened, and, behold, a white horse; and he that sat upon him was called Faithful and True; and in righteousness doth he judge and make war. His eyes were as a flame of fire, and on his head were many crowns; and he had a name written, that no man knew, but he, himself. And he was clothed in a vesture dipped in blood. And his name is called, the Word of God. And the armies which were in heaven followed him upon white horses, clothed in fine linen, white and clean." It is a picture of the triumphant Christ, whose numberless battalions are Christians.

II. Again, let us glance for a moment at the triumphs of Christianity in the realm of intellect. What a seemingly insignificant beginning Christianity had! Its divine Founder summoned around Him, not those who stood foremost in circles ecclesiastic, neither those who occupied the first rank in the scholarship of the day, but a few fishermen, men of lowly mind, and men of humble life. He chose weakness to overcome strength. He chose humility to remove pride. He chose littleness to match itself against greatness. But He chose wisely and well. To the thought of the world it might have appeared that He was taking the opposite course. God, however, is not dependent upon the forces that are noisy for the carrying out of His purposes. The gravitation that holds the world in space, and that directs the marching of innumerable suns and planets over the infinite field of the universe, works, so far as human ears are concerned, in absolute silence. Also with light, that tremendous power that lifts the forests cloudward, and animates every kingdom of life; it carries on its operations without sound, falling so gently to its tasks, indeed, that no leaf is disturbed by its coming, or no slumbering eyes are awakened. While God "plants His footsteps in the sea and rides upon the storm," He also moves in the quietness of things invisible, like a king that travels incognito, and yet loses thereby none of the power of his sceptre.

I do not mean to say that the apostles of Christ were brainless men. They were far from that. But

7

they were not regarded as being in possession of great intellectual qualities. Under the training which they received from a master Mind, they developed into men of superior mental calibre. Yet, because many of them had followed the sea for a living, and one of their number had been unpatriotic enough to be a collector of taxes from a hated foreign empire, they were by their own countrymen despised; and later on they and those who increased their sect became the subjects of Grecian wit; and in Antioch they were termed fanatics, the partisans of Christ, enthusiasts in an insane cause; for these were all implied in the word Christian.

But out of that small beginning Christianity has widened into an ocean of intellectual influence. Who scorns an Amazon or a Mississippi because of the birth of their mighty waters in tiny springs? Who derides the Alps or the Sierra Nevadas because their mountain masonry is built up of little grains of matter? Who despises yonder sun because its light is the result of countless beams? Who, therefore, can think of no greatness in Christianity because it was nursed at the breast of insignificance?

There are many who think that the religion of Christ is only for those of weak minds. But that same religion has conquered thousands of the finest intellects that ever throbbed beneath the stars. Who, let me ask, was Paul? He is the Demosthenes of the New Testament. Half of that inspired Volume is taken up with his life and writings. What a life that was! Not the life of a man that dribbled a few feeble drops of action, and then was lost to view. His was a life that poured itself forth with torrent strength and velocity. It was a flood-life that broke down every barrier in its way, and swept victoriously on into the ocean of immortality. It was a life that was consecrated to Jesus Christ for the carrying of His Cross before heathen eyes.

One of the Grecian philosophers, it is said, walked the streets of his city with a lighted lantern in hand in the blaze of day. He was in quest of a man. But had he lived in Paul's time, there would have been no need for such parabolic sarcasm. Here was a man, indeed. Every inch of him was a man. Though re-puted to be small of stature, the weight of his brain cannot be estimated. That brain has charged eighteen centuries and more with its influence. Out of it has issued a theology that has shaken the thrones of kings, and produced whole races of intel-lectual giants—a theology, indeed, that has long been hated, which has awakened scorn in rival schools of thought, and at which infidelity has often put out its tongue in jest; but which, nevertheless, under the name of Calvinism, has prominently kept before the world the fact that God reigns in heaven and earth, and whose adherents to-day are like the stars for multitude.

What shall I further say of the eloquence of this man Paul? There never was another such orator. Even his writings are in oratoric form. With him rhetoric was not a matter of the midnight lamp, a laborious polishing of his sentences, but the expression of a soul that was fired with a master passion—love for Christ. That princely voice rang its music upon the ears of philosophers and poets and governors and kings. That majestic pen flashed light through the bars of prisons. Confinement in dungeon walls could not crush Paul's eloquent soul. His body was immured, but his spirit, like that of a caged eagle, soared in the illimitable blue of freedom.

Time fails me to call the roll of the world's immortals who were swayed by the religion of Jesus Christ. I can mention only a few of them. Who was Augustine? Who was Jerome? Who was Martin Luther? Who was John Calvin? Who was John Knox? Who was Sir Isaac Newton, and Oliver Cromwell, and John Milton? Who were the Wesleys? Who was Whitefield? Who was David Livingstone? Who were William Gladstone, and Abraham Lincoln, and Robert Lee, and William McKinley? These are but a fragment of the illustrious dead who were proud of the title of Christian. Yonder stands the monument that bears their fame to the sun. Read for yourselves the shining list of the intellects that bowed at the feet of Jesus Christ. Were these men and women of weak minds? No! I tell you that no other minds have so mightily pulsated in thought within the air of the world. Being dead they yet speak.

And what of the living? Put Christianity on trial

to-day in the court room of Doubt, and there would be throngs on throngs of witnesses to testify in its behalf, and thousands of attorneys ready for its defence, and thousands of physicians to give expert testimony, and thousands of judges to render an opinion in the case, and thousands of jurymen to pass upon the matter, and bring in a verdict.

What has Christianity done in the realm of intellect? It has colored the world's literature, so that the grandest poems are those upon religious themes, and the sublimest oratory is that which pertains to spiritual topics, and the most enduring fiction is that which deals with righteousness. It has inspired the world's richest music, the oratorios of Handel and Beethoven and Mozart, and spread the canvas of the world's most magnificent paintings, and held the mallet and chisel of the world's loftiest architecture and its chastest statuary. It has penetrated every department of the world's intellectuality, and left everywhere its distinctive marks. Its footprints are seen in all the sciences of every name. So will it continue its conquests, until every opposing sword is placed in its hands, and every foeman's banner is furled in its presence. That will be the dawning of the day that shall never end, when the rising Sun of Righteousness shall gild every mountain-top, and flash His flames into every valley, and irradiate every ocean and forest and plain with His undying sheen.

III. Once more, let us glance at the triumphs of this religion in the inner life of humanity. Look, for instance, at its power in the territory of character. By its potent influence lives that were loathsome with sin, covered all over with the scales of a moral leprosy, the very heart itself in the grasp of a deathful corruption, have been transformed into beauteous health. Not the beauty of a snowfall, simply hiding from view a natural ugliness by the art of silently distributing virgin flakes among and upon it; but by a revolution that takes down the old and builds the new. It has breathed upon uncleanness and made it pure. It has opened the eyes of the drunkard to the vision of the serpent in the intoxicating cup and given him lasting sobriety. It has brushed all profanity from the swearer's blistered lips, and caused them to blossom with praises to God. It has exchanged hatred for love, frowns for smiles, cheating for honesty, lies for truth. Do you tell me that miracles are an impossibility? The past ages are crowded with just such miracles as I have mentioned. Do you tell me that the day of miracles is past? Miracles such as I have named are of hourly occurrence. Where the grace of God performs its full work, it gives regeneration to the souls of men. The new birth is one of the greatest of miracles.

Also has this religion shown its power in trouble. The grief, or the reverse of business, or the bitter disappointment, that has for the many stretched the suicide's rope, or mixed the suicide's poison, or loaded the suicide's gun or revolver, has, under the sustaining strength of Christianity, lifted the many into an atmosphere of consolation, charged with the sunbeams of cheer and the oxygen of gladness.

Look again at Paul as an example. Was there ever a man more tried than he? Listen to his count of tribulations in his autobiographic letters. He began his Christian life under a cross; and that cross increased in weight all along the pathway of the years, until, at length, it bore his body down into martyrdom. But in the hatred of his foes, in the public whippings of his persecutors, in the bruises and blood of flagellation, in the dampness and noisomeness of jails, in privations and shipwrecks, in the painfulness and weariness of long journeys, and finally in the Mamertine dungeon at Rome, where he waited for the stroke of Nero's sword, hear his victorious shout: "None of these things move me; neither count I my life dear unto myself!"

Yea, the closing hour has come. A soldier beckons him forth into the day. His execution is about to take place. Yonder I see him. How does he go? Not as a coward that trembles in view of death. In all that prematurely aged frame there is not a single tremor of fear. Upon that wrinkled brow there is not the faintest pallor of dread. His step is that of a prince advancing to his coronation. "Wait, soldier," I hear him say. Taking his pen between finger and thumb, he writes to Timothy, his son in the Gospel, a sentence that has encircled millions of the necks of the dying with gems that flash with a light never seen on sea or land: "I have fought the good fight;

I have finished my course; I have kept the faith; henceforth there is laid up for me a crown of righteousness."

Under the spell of that burst of oratory the soul of this veteran of the Cross mounted the shining hills of immortality, and passed in honor through the uplifted gates of pearl.

That was not an anomalous experience. Multiplied Christians have tasted the sweetness of it. You and I have had its nectarine cup pressed to our lips time and time again. The religion of Jesus Christ has hushed many a sob born in our breast through sorrow, and glorified many a tear, and illumined many a shadow. Even in the deepest gloom the Christian soul that has throbbed in sympathy with the first two stanzas of Longfellow's poem, "The Rainy Day," has echoed the pean of the final stanza in a doxology of triumph:

"Be still, sad heart, and cease repining;
Behind the clouds is the sun still shining!"

Also in the hour of death has this religion scattered its sunbeams over many a tossed and rumpled pillow. Stephen, battered with rocks, what sayest thou? "Lord Jesus, receive my spirit." John Wesley, what sayest thou? "The best of all is, God is with us." John Powson, what sayest thou? "My dying bed is a bed of roses." Alfred Cookman, what sayest thou? "I am sweeping through the gates washed in the blood of the Lamb." Frances Willard, what sayest thou? "How beautiful it is to be with God." William McKinley, what sayest thou? "Nearer, my God to Thee. It is God's way; His will be done."

I seem to hear these voices to-day, and the voices of millions more, like the voices of many waters, the voices of the heroes and heroines of Christianity in past centuries, of recent years also, and of this present hour; the voices, too, of dear ones and friends; and, hark! They mingle, as if a great organ were pealing, and a mighty choir were singing, the thunder of the instrument and the rolling of the anthem breaking forth into this one overwhelming strain of the oratorio of Christianity: "O death, where is thy sting? O grave, where is thy victory?"

My friend, are you a Christian? Know, then, that out of a name that issued from reproach has come forth a title that is prouder than that of any earthly czar or emperor. Wear it in your heart, and show its lustre in your life. Are you not a Christian? Then you are gathering the weeds of earth, and passing the flowers by; or covering yourself with ashes, when you might be adorned with pearls; or languishing in a prison cell, when you might be a prince of God in everlasting freedom of soul.

The Fowls of the Air

Behold the fowls of the air. Matthew 6: 26.

In the springtime or early summer I like to preach a sermon in keeping with those seasons of the year. I am accustomed then to call attention to the flowers or the trees or the grass. But my discourse this morning shall have in it the gloss of bird feathers and the whistle of bird bills.

Flowers are God's thoughts in poetry, some of the flowers blank verse, some lyrics, some pastorals. Trees are God's thoughts gathered into the libraries of the woods and mountains and orchards. Grasses are God's thoughts written over the fields and along the banks of streams, those thoughts punctuated with buttercup and dandelion and daisy. But birds are God's thoughts on the wing, and spilling music through the air. In this mountain sermon from the lips of the Prince of preachers, we are called upon to observe the birds. Christ said, "Behold the fowls."

I. I would remark, that the Bible is full of birds. We hear the rush of their wings upon almost every page of the Bible. In the first chapter of Genesis they fly forth above the earth in obedience to God's command, the same voice that said, "Let there be light," saying, "Let fowl fly in the face of the firmament of heaven." Starting thus in Genesis, birds hop and soar and circle all the way through the Bible to Revelation, in that book the birds summoned by an angel standing in the sun to a great feast, that angel crying with a loud voice, and saying to all the fowls that fly in the midst of heaven, "Come, and gather yourselves together unto the supper of the great God; that ye may eat the flesh of kings, and the flesh of captains, and the flesh of mighty men, and the flesh of horses, and of them that sit on them, and the flesh of all men, both free and bond, both small and great." Birds everywhere in the Bible.

In Exodus we read of quails. In Leviticus a distinction is made between birds clean and birds unclean, one kind for food and another kind not to be eaten—the eagle, the ossifrage, the osprey, the vulture, the kite, the raven, the owl, the nighthawk, the cuckoo, the swan, the pelican, the stork, the heron, the lapwing and the bat, all being an abomination to the mouth of the children of Israel, God prescribing for those people their bill of fare, this accounting for the healthiness of the Hebrew race, that healthiness persisting to this present day.

In Deuteronomy we hear the flapping of eagle pinions, the broad wings of that monarch among birds, as they go sailing in majestic curves through the sunny air, and instructing the eaglets of the nest in the art of flight, used as an illustration of the leadership of God among His people.

So the birds continue flying through every book

of the Bible. The crow, the crane, the dove, the partridge, the pigeon, the stork, the sparrow, the swallow, and many others that I have not the time to mention, all winging their way through this library of inspired volumes, He who made the birds of every name catching some of them in the net of one of His sermons, and saying to the audience gathered around His mountain pulpit, and to the larger congregation of all succeeding time, "Behold the fowls of the air."

In studying this subject I was surprised at the wealth of allusion to birds in the Scriptures. When David wished for an illustration of God's mighty protection and tender care of His children, he found that illustration in the brooding of an eagle over her young, saying, "He shall cover thee with his feathers, and under his wings shalt thou trust." When he wishes that he might leave his troubles and have peace of heart, he exclaims, "Oh, that I had the wings of a dove, that I might fly away and be at rest!" Speaking of the omnipresence of God, he employs one of the sublimest figures of all Biblical rhetoric, saying, "If I take the wings of the morning, and dwell in the uttermost parts of the sea, even there shall thy hand lead me, and thy right hand shall hold me." "The wings of the morning!" Wings of light! Wings of silver flaming into sunrise hues of crimson and purple and emerald and gold! Wings that wheel swiftly over the mountains and flash across the oceans! Wonderful figure!

So when the phrase-maker of the Book of Proverbs would illustrate the uncertainty of earth-born wealth, he says, "Riches make themselves wings; they fly away as an eagle toward heaven." You and I have seen them flying away—stocks and bonds and houses and lands and bank-bills and currency flying, flying, flying!

What multitudes of wings in the Bible! Wings in the Psalms. Wings in Ezekiel. Wings in Isaiah. Wings in Zechariah. Wings in Malachi. Wings! Wings! Wings!

So when Christ would tell of His solicitude for the nation that had rejected Him, standing within view of the Cross of Calvary, He cries out, every word a tear, "O Jerusalem, Jerusalem, thou that killest the prophets, and stonest them which are sent unto thee, how often would I have gathered thy children together, even as a hen gathereth her chickens under her wings, and ye would not!" A lowly metaphor, but transformed by Christ into beauty, a poultry yard becoming a paradise and a barn door the gate of heaven. I have often seen young chicks wander away from the old mother hen in the broad sunshine of the day, but at nightfall they were glad enough to hide under her sheltering wings. At the nightfall of judgment for Jerusalem, forty years after Christ's pathetic outcry, there were no outspread wings of protection for that people. Then was the air darkened with the wings of the Roman eagles—wings of famine; wings of flame; wings of sword—and the Hebrew Commonwealth ceased to be. No

wonder that Christ wept when He spoke of His desire to gather the people under His omnipotence who
would not seek that divine refuge!

The Bible thus having in it so much of bird wings,
we cannot afford to slight the words of Christ when
He says, "Behold the fowls of the air." But as we
have looked at some of the birds of the Scriptures,
let us now come closer and look at them in Nature.

II. In the further opening of the text, I ask you
to notice the anatomical structure of the birds. Man
and the animals allied with him were made for walking, and running, and climbing. Fish were made for
swimming. Birds were made for flying. The same
wisdom that planned the anatomy of life that moves
slowly over the earth, as in walking, or swiftly, as in
running, and the anatomy of life that cleaves the
waters of creek, and river, and ocean with scales and
fins, also planned the anatomy of the creatures of the
air, whether a humming-bird with its marvelous vibration of wing that keeps it poised over a flower,
into which it thrusts its bill and collects therefrom
nectarine food, or an eagle with its pinions bathed
in the clouds and its gaze sunward. The bones of
flying fowl are so constructed as to render such fowl
capable of flight, those bones having cavities that are
much larger in proportion to the size of the fowl than
are in the bones of quadrupeds. Those large cavities
are filled with air. The whole make-up of birds is in
reference to their use of wings. They were designed
to fly. Look at a bird's wing! On the inside con-

cave; on the outside convex; both of those shapes necessary for lifting the bird's body through the resisting atmosphere and steering it, with the aid of the tail, from point to point along the aerial journey. Upon the wing of wren, and robin, and owl, and albatross God has written His autograph, the same hand that pencils that mighty name in stars upon the broad sheet of midnight skies also tracing it along the feathers of every wing that beats the air. Let those who say, "There is no God," not only read the astronomical proofs of God's existence, but also read the proofs that are on the anatomy of all atmospheric creatures. The canary that sings in its prison-cage, the parrot that talks from its perch, the swallow that builds its nest in the chimney, and the saucy blackbird that follows the farmer's furrow in search of food, are all so many living arguments for the being of God. "Behold the fowls of the air."

How do the birds keep their hold at night upon their resting-place? With their heads under their wings, and sound asleep, one would think that they would fall to the ground. But there is a mechanical contrivance in the leg of a bird by which, when it bends its legs to rest, the toes and claws are gripped to the perch, and so remaining as long as the legs are bent in the sitting posture. One of the pastimes of boyhood days is the catching of the tendons in a fowl's severed leg that accomplish this action and pulling them, so as to see the claws move. God giveth the birds safety in sleep.

Oh, the wonders of the bird creation! Feathers and wings and oiling apparatus for the dressing of their coat, and eyes and ears and internal organs, all showing forth the architectural skill of God. I have seen enough ingenuity in the arrangement of a chicken's eye to keep me in admiration for the rest of my life. Two curtains in that eye, one closing upward from the outside, the other closing downward from the inside. No wonder that Christ said, "Behold the fowls." The whole anatomical structure of birds reveals the wisdom and love of God. God's benevolent design seen in the frame of every bird that ever lifted voice in the woods or spread itself to fly, racing with sunbeams. Says that same Christ, "Are ye not much better than they?"

III. Again, behold the birds at their nest-building. Just now they are very busy. As they work, their hearts are overflowing with song, some of which they spill melodiously upon the air. The houses they are rearing will have in them but one room, and that will be a sitting-room, afterwards to be turned into a nursery! The music that now is being woven into the hours of the day, quieting at nightfall into low chirp and subdued whistle, will fade; but there will be other weavings, the wings of younger birds the shuttles that will carry the threads of harmony back and forth through the musical pattern. Since the world began God has not left the world without this aerial minstrelsy. He never will so leave it. The birds of Eden were the capital with which God started the world in song. That capital has been bearing compound interest through all the succeeding centuries. Every nest is the forerunner of three or five nests.

I notice that the birds build their nests high, having in mind the idea that height gives protection. Where did the birds learn that fact? In God's school. Oh, that men would not be such dullards in the same school! It is a shame to be outranked in learning by the birds. The trouble with many persons is that they build their lives too low. Lord Byron was gifted with the wings of imagination; but his nest was in the mire of depravity. Robert Burns was likewise gifted; but his nest was in the bog of sensual appetite. The young man of the parable left the home-nest of lofty principle and righteous living to make a nest for himself. His nest was torn of swines' feet and swines' snout. The only safe nesting-place for any soul is among the branches of the tree of Calvary's Cross.

When I see one loitering around the door of a saloon, giving loose rein to the passions of his nature, or going into bad company, I think, "Another low nest!" When I see one seated at a gaming table, or practicing dishonesty, or false to the truth, I think again, "Another low nest!" When I see a maiden with her eyes wide open consenting in wedlock with one who toys with the serpent of intoxication, I think still again, "Another low nest!"

8

How many marriage-nests have been irretrievably ruined by the foul hoofs of drunkenness! O young woman of pure heart and clean life, fair of feature, and winsome in manner, have high ideals, and keep them high, even if you have to wait forever for the building of a home-nest as lofty as your ideals are! Better one life wrecked than two. Say to him who asks you to join him in building, "Who is your architect? And has he planned a structure equal to my thought? That thought of mine soars where eagles fly!" Oh, never, never, never, occupy with another a nest on the ground! The risk is far greater than you can afford to take.

A bird's nest is to me a poem of wonder. How beautifully it is woven! Sticks and straw and feathers and hair gathered by the industrious birds from varied sources, and constructed into the poetry of a nest that will some day burst into musical chirps, those chirps the prelude to the oratorios and symphonies of the orchards and gardens.

So may we weave into our lives, through the grace of God, the fibres of righteousness, those fibres afterwards breaking out into the unceasing song of praise to God in the chorals of heaven. But if that is to be, now is the time to begin the work—now, while the flowers are blooming, and the trees are full of leaves, and the skies are bright with the siftings of the sun. There is no nest-building in December. Let not death find us without the righteousness of Christ as an everlasting nest.

IV. Again, behold the birds fed by the hand of God. Says Christ, "They sow not, neither do they reap, nor gather into barns; yet your heavenly Father feedeth them."

Now, Christ was not a rhapsodist who indulged in mere sentimentality. The care of God for the fowls of the air is the one point to which Christ invites attention when He asks that we behold the fowls. His argument is that the birds are supplied with food through God. These that Christ refers to are not dead birds, stuffed, and set up within a museum or academy of science. The only thing dead about them is the language in which Matthew reported the Preacher's sermon. These are living birds —birds with fluttering wings, with shining plumage, with song-rippling bills. The birds they are that circled within sight of Christ's mountain auditory. The birds they are that have been flying through all the centuries. The birds they are that hopped over your lawn this morning, or from the branches of the trees that shade your home voiced for your ears a matin carol. "The fowls of the air."

Christ says that God feeds the birds. Did you ever stop to think what great quantities of provision God has to supply for the fowls of the air? Food for the eagles. Food for the ravens. Food for the sparrows. Food for the almost endless varieties of flying life in the atmosphere around the world. Yet none of the birds ever go hungry. God stocks the market where they buy without money and without price. God spreads their table at which they break-fast and dine and sup—table of bare rock under a canopy of cloud; table of tree-branch under a canopy of leaves; table of grass and brown earth under a canopy of orchards. God gives them their meat in due season.

I had often wondered where all the birds get their food; but observing them, I soon learned the sources of their supply. Insects in the air, grubs in the bark of trees, berries on the bushes, worms in the soil—these the birds find every day. A piece of sod turned up by the spade or the plow is a veritable granary and slaughter-house opened to the birds. Out of a shovelful of black earth thrown into their pen chickens will scratch a banquet, afterwards wiping their bills upon a napkin of dry dust. God feeds all the fowls.

Notice the argument of Christ. He rises from the smaller to the greater—from the fowls of the air to men, and women, and children. The irresistible con-clusion of His parabolic logic is that God cares more for His own immortal children than He does for the birds. "Are ye not much better than they?"

Have you come into God's house worried this morning? Anxiety from any cause is mind sickness and heart sickness. Here is a prescription that will cure you, if you have faith. It is from the knowl-edge and skill of the great Physician. That pre-scription is compounded of God's providence. "Be-hold the fowls of the air."

There is a legend which tells about Christ as a boy. While playing one day with His companions, He made some birds out of clay. He stood those clay birds on the ground. An old Pharisee came along, and frowningly looked at the sport. Then he kicked those clay birds and broke them, scattering their fragments with his foot over the ground. But the legend goes on to relate how that Christ the boy waved His hand over those fragments, and how that they were repaired, afterwards taking wing, and flying heavenward in song.

That is only a legend. But Christ can wave His hand over our broken plans, and mend them by His grace of love; and wave His hand over our griefs, over our cares, over our bereavements, and give them tuneful flight to the heaven where tears never fall.

"Behold the fowls of the air." That means, Look up! Get your eyes off the ground! Look away from earth and see the broad expanse of sunshine in which fly the promises of God! The air is full of wings. Behold them! "Are not five sparrows sold for two farthings, and not one of them is forgotten before God? But even the very hairs of your head are all numbered. Fear not, therefore; ye are of more value than many sparrows." All the birds of creation do not equal one human soul. In God's storehouse there is enough for every one of God's children. They shall never want. They shall not want bread. They shall not want clothing. They shall not want shelter. They shall not want grace for the trials of life. God's mouth hath spoken it. That mouth cannot lie. Sooner could the stars of midnight skies fall to earth. The same omnipotent hand that keeps those stars to their orbits also guides the fowls of the air. Shall that hand fail to keep you and me? Never! Never! Not while there is a foundation beneath the throne of God.

Friends, let us more than look up. Let us take eagle wings and mount the skies of faith, leaving dust and cloud far below, soaring with unwearied pinions into the very light of our Father's face.

Green Pastures

He maketh me to lie down in green pastures. Psalm 23 : 2.

THE sweetest and most beautiful of David's poems! This is the canary of all the Psalms. It has been singing through many a century. It warbles its melody in sunshine and rain, in health and sickness, in prosperity and adversity, in joy and sorrow, in pleasure and pain. Even in the darkest night does it sing. When the shadows of evening are stretched out other birds hush their notes. Silence in the gardens. Silence in the orchards. Silence in the woods. But this bird of heaven never ceases its song. Death itself has not sufficient strength of grip to choke its voice.

This Psalm is a cluster of roses plucked from the garden of the Lord. It is a symphony in a concert hall. It is a banquet in a king's palace. It is a breeze from angel wings. It is the fragrant breath of God's love. Rather would I have written it than to have penned all the sonnets of Shakespeare or Mrs. Browning. Among all the poems of all the ages it wears the brightest crown.

Simply as a piece of rhetorical composition this Psalm is superb. The rhythm of it is music. The language of it is music. The thought of it is music. From its opening words to its closing words it is all music. It has been admired by many a literary brain. It has won praise from many a distinguished pair of lips. Better than that; it has soothed many a child of God in anguish of heart, and been a lullaby that has put many a saint gently to sleep. Infancy lisps it in the cradle. Youth chants it in the pauses between games. Manhood repeats it in the noontide of the years. Middle life hums it in the going down of the sun from the zenith. Old age speaks it with trembling tongue in the purple glow of the twilight and under the silvery sheen of the stars before the night hath fully come. The inspiration of the Holy Spirit conceived it and gave it birth.

This Psalm has been the text of many a sermon. But I cannot treat the whole of it in one discourse. There is enough material in it for a volume. I simply call your attention to one little patch of color in this lustrous rainbow of divine rhetoric. "He maketh me to lie down in green pastures."

I. I would remark, we have here set forth the richness of a righteous life. "Green pastures." God's spiritual sheep are not left to browse in some barren waste, with only here and there a spear of grass to relieve the nakedness of the mountainside, or valley, or field. He leads them into pastures that are clothed with an abundance of succulent provision. "Green pastures"; or, as it reads in the margin, following more closely the Hebrew in which the Psalm was originally written, "pastures of tender grass."

I do not know what was in David's mind when he

penned this sentence; but I imagine that he was thinking of God's Word. Here is the richest of pasture for the sheep of the great Shepherd. It is far richer pasture now than it was in David's day. Then the bars of that field enclosed only a few acres called the "Law of the Lord.", But to-day that pasture-ground is greatly enlarged,. God adding to it after David's time, and continuing to add to it, setting the bars farther and farther away, until those bars enclosed a wide sweep of land, beginning at Genesis on one side, ending at Revelation on the other side.

Did you ever stop to think of the thousands upon thousands of sheep that have fed upon the rich pasture of God's Word? Call them up in imagination if you can. Even the strongest imagination fails to call them up. Go number the leaves of autumnal forests in their dying magnificence. Go number the sand-diamonds that have been strewn along the ocean's beach. Go number the star-pearls that are clustered around the breast of midnight skies. Sheep in David's day feeding upon that pasture. Sheep in Isaiah's day. Sheep in Daniel's day. Sheep in Malachi's day. Sheep in Matthew's day, and John's, and Paul's. Sheep in the first century of the Christian Era; in the second century; in the third, and fourth, and fifth; in all the centuries, taking in the millions of this present twentieth century; those sheep in Europe, in Asia, in Africa, in America, and in the islands of the sea. They are like the cloud-sheep that God's hand leads to pasture over summer skies. Uncounted throngs. And yet those pastures of the Word of God still green. Any other pasture would have been long ago reduced to sterility.

But in the very face of this overwhelming argument for the inspiration of the Scriptures, we are told that the Bible is a fallible book. There are forms of scholarship in these days that would mow down this rich pasture-field and leave nothing but stubble behind. There is no human scythe, however, that is keen enough of blade to mow it down. It has always been green; it shall ever be green. I have no fear of God's Word being laid waste.

This Book has also been more written about and spoken about than any other book in all the world. The world's libraries are freighted with volumes that treat of the history contained within this grand old Book; that treat of its ethnology; that treat of its astronomy; that treat of its botany; that treat of its archæology; that treat of its rhetoric; that treat of its syntax; that treat of its texts—innumerable commentaries in Latin, in German, in French, in English, in all languages, both dead and living—books for the scholar; books for the unlearned; books for children; mountains of books. And what multitudes of lips have preached from it and are yet preaching from it! And no two sermons are exactly alike! And enough material here for other mountains of books, though the earthquake of the modern printing press is upheaving books thousands at a time! And sufficient matter here for millions more of sermons! Inexhaustible book! "Green pastures!"

The reason that some Christians are so lean of spiritual life is that they do not suffer God to lead them into the green pastures of His Word. They go browsing very largely upon the husks of the daily newspaper, or the thorn-bushes of periodicals, or the chaff of the popular novel. You cannot fatten sheep upon an exclusive diet of juiceless herbs. Neither can Christians be aught but barren of soul, if they neglect the richness of the Bible. God's finest spiritual sheep take the pasture that He provides; not that which the world, the flesh and the devil have barred in. I plead to-day for more feeding in the green pastures of the Scriptures as a means of developing the life of the immortal spirit.

It may have been, too, that David was thinking of the ordinances of God's house. These, again, were but poor ordinances compared with those that belong to this present age. Yet David calls them "green." For him and all the people of that time those pastures were in the twilight of the early morning. Those pastures now are lying under the risen Sun of righteousness.

Those persons who love the assembly of God's saints are usually those whose life is "rich toward God." When you find a lank, raw-boned, starved lot of sheep among the plump sheep of the Lord, you can be assured that they think they find better pasture at home, or at the card-party, or in the lodge, than within the bars of the Sabbath services or the mid-week meeting for prayer. If more of the professed sheep of God would feed upon the ordinances of God's house, there would be a more abundant spiritual life among the followers of Christ.

God pity the sheep that stray over into the barren acres of the world! Sorry spectacle it is when such sheep are seen herding with the devil's goats and nibbling at the weeds that grow upon the devil's ash-heap! That is why some Christians are not more pronounced in their attitude against the various sins that are pushing this world away from God. That is often why so many are indifferent to the great curse of intemperance. They have forsaken the pasture-ground of church ordinances for forbidden fields. Many a Christian is not known to belong to the Lord's sheep at all, except on Communion day, if he happens then to be present. Some even at that time refuse to lie down in the green pastures of the Lord, preferring to sit in the seat of the scornful.

Also may it have been that David was thinking of the richness of experience that comes to those who are in constant fellowship with God. David had been a shepherd, and through the long hours of the day, while watching his flocks, he had plenty of time for meditation. It was then that he rose to the blessedness of being under the eye of the great Shepherd. In a part of his later life, alas! David lost that fellowship with his Lord which had so enriched the days of his youth. He went pasturing in the rank fields of sin. But through repentance, his heart-throbs of sorrow echoing down the ages, he was led back into the green pastures of righteousness. It was a terrible experience for David, that twin transgression of his, but out of those two black seeds of iniquity God brought the flowers of a piety that were all the more beautiful because of David's crimes. Two of this man's poems have entered into the liturgy of all sincere sorrow for sin and the joy of God's forgiveness. "Green pastures."

Oh, the preciousness of communion with God! I was reading of an old German scholar who was always calm and happy. Some one determined to learn the cause of the man's peacefulness of soul, secreting himself in the scholar's house for that purpose. He saw the old man go to his room at night, and sit down to read his Bible. He read on and on, through many an hour, reading chapter after chapter, until his face was all aglow. When the clock chimed the hour of midnight, the man rose up from his chair, closed his Bible, prepared for bed, saying before he lay down, "Blessed Lord, we are on the same terms yet. Good night! Good night!" That man was one of God's sheep in the green pastures of assurance. He knew whom he believed. There is no pasture so rich as that which God gives to His trusting sheep.

II. I remark, again, that there is in the text a suggestion about the beauty of a righteous life. The common opinion is that religion is associated with an undertaker's establishment and graveyards. The world regards religion with disgust. But what have we here? Not a cemetery with white stones looking ghostly in the moonlight, but an emerald field smiling in the sunshine. "Green pastures!"

The fact is that the Bible is full of figures of speech that set forth the beauty of religion. What does Solomon say? Personifying religion under the name of wisdom, this royal rhetorician declares, "She is more precious than rubies; and all the things thou canst desire are not to be compared unto her. Her ways are ways of pleasantness, and all her paths are peace. She is a tree of life to them that lay hold upon her; and happy is every one that retaineth her." Job says, "The crystal cannot equal it." David elsewhere says, "The righteous shall flourish like the palm tree; he shall grow like a cedar in Lebanon." Hundreds of metaphors and similes are employed to describe the beauty of religion. It is called a lily, a rose, a crown. It is a fountain to which the sun throws kisses of gold. It is a garden. It is a banquet of joy, a city perched upon a hilltop, a blaze of light pouring down from an unclouded sky, a bridegroom taking home his beloved bride. It is a prodigal returning to his father's house to be feasted. I cannot stop to name the many terms of description that set its beauty forth. Go search this blessed Book for yourselves, and you will have both hands full and all

the chambers of your heart and mind of sparkling
rhetorical gems—richer gems than ever flashed in
the coronet of a king.

Oh, no! Ours is not a repulsive religion. That is
one of Satan's gray-haired lies. It is not a tooth-
less witch, as the world portrays it, but a charming
maiden, the blue of the heavens in her eyes, the gold
of the sunshine in her tresses, the glow of the morning upon her cheeks, the symmetry of an artist's
dream upon her form, the gentleness of the south
wind in her step. Come and pay court to her. The
Holy Spirit says, "Come!" We who have found
her beautiful say, "Come!" "Whosoever will, let
him come!"

I sometimes fear that Christian people talk too
much about carrying a cross, and not enough about
wearing a crown. But the Bible speaks more of
crowns than it does of crosses. More sunlight than
shadow. More blue skies than skies storm-tramped.
More roses than thorns. Beautiful religion! "Green
pastures!"

Why, it seems to me that the Christian life is more
radiant every day. Each time I open my Bible I
discover some new beauty. I used to wonder at the
joy of some persons over their experience in spiritual
things. But now I have ceased to wonder. Ask
what religion is. Ask Paul and Silas in prison at
Philippi, and they will answer with a song. Ask
John in exile, and he will answer you with an Apocalypse. Ask Martin Luther, and he will answer you

with a Psalm of David. Ask John Bunyan, and he will answer you with a dream of heaven. There are thousands of witnesses. Ask them. I hear their voices to-day—voices out of pits, voices out of jails, voices out of fire, voices out of death-chambers, voices, voices, voices, and all of them saying, "Beautiful! Beautiful!" "Green pastures."

III. Once more, I remark, that we have here a suggestion in reference to the restfulness of a righteous life. This is a picture of sheep that have had a generous supply of food. Now they are sunning themselves in the verdant mead that forms their pasture-ground. David knew all about it. He had seen his flocks in that attitude times without number. Then his thought rises to Him who shepherds the clouds, shepherds the sun and moon and stars, shepherds the mountains, shepherds the waves of the sea, and who, in the exercise of His omnipotent love, also shepherds all the saints. "He maketh me to lie down in green pastures."

Some one was once asked what he liked the best about this Twenty-third Psalm. His answer was, "I like best the personal pronouns in it. '*My* shepherd.' 'Maketh *me* to lie down.' 'Leadeth *me*.' 'Restoreth *my* soul.' It is a Psalm that every child of God can appropriate to himself."

There is the point. David was resting under the bountifulness and the providence of God. His personal experience of that abundance and constant care is for the saints of the Lord in every age—for you and me. "He maketh *me* to lie down in green pastures."

I have seen sheep driven to the shambles through the streets of cities. Those sheep dusty from their long tramp along country roads; tired from running; dogs barking at their heels. But not so with the Lord's sheep. God is not a drover, but a shepherd. He leads His sheep into green pastures. Shepherd for tender childhood. Shepherd for youth. Shepherd for manhood, Shepherd for middle life. Shepherd for trembling old age. Shepherd for the valley and the shadow of death. "Green pastures."

"Come unto me all ye that labor and are heavy laden, and I will give you rest." Why do you stay out, my friend, upon the barren heath of Satan's world? Come and find rest for your soul in the green pastures of the Christian life. Out there is where swine feed. Why seek to appease your hunger with dry, juiceless, unsatisfying husks? Let the prodigal go home to his Father's house, his Father's outstretched arms, his Father's welcoming kiss, his Father's sparkling ring, his Father's shoes for weary feet, his Father's rich banqueting board. Or keeping to the figure of the text, let the sheep that have wandered far away from the fold, and that now bleat their loneliness upon the frosty air of a mocking world, hear the voice of the Shepherd divine calling them, His voice music, His accents love; and let them go back to the pastures they have forsaken for a life of sin. Those pastures are beautiful with suc-

9

culent grass, and are embroidered with clover and
buttercups. There millions have found rest for the
soul. Oh, what a blessed rest it is! A rest it is
that is typical of the rest that remains above for all
the blood-washed sheep of God. It is a foretaste of
heavenly rest in pastures that never fail. Those pastures parch under no blasting heat. They never dry
beneath blighting winds. They never wither below
brassy skies. "For the Lamb which is in the midst
of the throne shall feed them, and shall lead them
unto living fountains of waters, and God shall wipe
away all tears from their eyes." Evergreen pastures!

Circles.

It is he that sitteth upon the circle of the earth. Isaiah 40 : 22.

In these sublime words the prophet speaks of God. No earthly monarch ever sat upon such a throne. The throne of an Artaxerxes, or Alexander, or Julius Cæsar placed beside this stupendous throne is but as the frothing foam of the ocean compared with the ocean itself, that foam left stranded along the beach by a dying breaker. The rest of the text declares that the inhabitants of the world are but grasshoppers beneath this circle-throne. Only God could occupy such a throne.

The circle of the earth! That looks as if those ancient people knew something of the globular form of the world. There are lost arts. The Egyptians of the past ages embalmed the bodies of their dead with such skill as to make them as enduring as stone. In our museums there are Egyptian mummies that reveal the very features of persons whose souls took their flight from this world thousands of years ago. We pride ourselves upon our superior dentistry for the preservation of the teeth. Those same Egyptians practiced that art when the world was just out of its cradle, some of the mummies exhumed from the pyramids showing the gleam of gold within their parted lips. So it may be that in the bygone centuries the rotundity of the earth was as well known as it is to-day. The text intimates it when it says that God sits upon the earth's circle.

The circle of the earth! What a throne! The clouds are the tessellated pavement around it. The sunbeams are its flashing steps. The blue sky is its canopy. The winds are the fans that sweep before it. Angelic courtiers are in attendance upon Him who sits in majesty upon that throne. It is the throne of God eternal in the heavens.

I. I would remark, that the circle is God's favorite geometrical figure. He uses either the circle or parts of the circle, as curves, which are circles in their infancy. The sun is a circle on fire. The moon is a frozen circle. The stars are silvery circles, the telescope revealing their spherical shape. The earth is a circle. Our world revolves around the sun in an elliptical orbit, an ellipse being a circle pressed in at the sides and elongated into oval form. The revolutions of other planets are along the same kind of lines. There is a theory of science that this whole universe is thus circling around some vast central point. It is not an unreasonable theory. Just like God would it be to have matters so arranged. In connection with this theory is one that makes this one central, stationary point to be heaven. Neither is this unreasonable.

Narrowing our vision, we find but few angles. But there are plenty of curves. Witness the rainbow that banners the heights of a retreating storm. Witness the rolling waves of the ocean, and the curling breakers that rush to their death in spray upon the strand. Witness the raindrops that drum the march of the harvests. Witness the rounding of a snowdrift under the mallet and chisel of the north wind. Witness the outline of a bird's wing, whether wren or albatross. Witness the flowers, whether a dandelion or a century plant. Witness the human form, whether male or female; man's trunk an inverted cone, woman's trunk a cone; so that man, instead of being the lord of creation is only a woman reversed. Witness hundreds of things that I have not the time to mention—God moving His hand in circles when He called the heavens into existence; and His hand yet describing circles in the operation of natural law. We need not therefore be surprised that God sitteth upon the circle of the earth. That circle is a symbol of His eternity, which is a completed circle, being without beginning or end.

II. I would remark, again, that human life moves in a circle. The beginning of that circle, as the pencil of time draws it, is the cradle; the grave is the point where the rounded line is joined to the first stroke. It may be a large circle or a small circle, sweeping far up into the years before it descends along the downward curve and around to the bottom arc, or going but a short distance and then finishing. But large or small, the first breath of life and the last dying gasp meet each other. Birth and death always come together. We are born only to die.

This circular movement of life is often well marked, especially when the circle is prolonged. The only difference between childhood and adult years is that the play of the one is merged into the work of the other. The games and pastimes of boys and girls are a foreshadowing of later toils and cares. The dolls of early girlhood are hints of future nurseries; and the pretended solicitude that brings those dolls through severe cases of imaginary mumps and measles and scarlet fever is the sweet prelude to an after-discord, anxiety that is real then fingering the keys of the organ, and nervousness treading the pedals. The picnic meals under summer trees are types of meals under domestic roofs in monotonous succession three times a day through a period of years. The engineer of to-day, with his hand on the throttle of his wind-racing steed, when he was a boy often made believe that he was driving a locomotive. The doctor on his rounds once dealt in sugar pills and water tinctures. The minister in his pulpit more than one time preached to an audience of chairs. The carpenter at his bench used to plane with a flat block and pound with a stove-lifter. The banker and the merchant wrote checks without ink and passed bills made of newspapers. It is life in a circle, the sports of the morning becoming the trade or profession of the afternoon; and when evening is at hand, and the circle moves on into old age, second childhood comes into view, and death is not far away. Grandfather and grandmother live over again their youthful days in the lives of their children's children. That is why grandparents are often more lenient with children than are the parents themselves. They have gone almost all the way around the circle and reached again the spirit of childhood. Soon afterwards they are undressed for the night by the black nurse, Death, and their bodies put to sleep under the flower-embroidered coverlet of the grave.

But from the death-bed another circle sweeps. The spirit is immortal. It goes forth to fly around the great circle of eternity. Years on earth, though they be fourscore, are but microscopic objects in eternity. We make several respirations in a minute, and in a lifetime of ordinary length these respirations become incalculable in number; but all of them together, condensed into moisture, would not make a single dewdrop in comparison with the waters of eternity's ocean. Even centuries and millenniums are but single grains of sand in the glass that measures the hours of eternity.

Is it a depressing thought or a jubilant thought, that you and I are passing around this little circle of life in preparation for the wider journey around the circle of immortality? It depends upon whether or not our life here is hid with Christ in God. Covered by atoning blood, that thought should rouse up within the soul the most joyous anticipations, like a prospective trip to another continent. Growing old is growing young. The whitening of the hair at the temples is not the gathering of a snowdrift, but the light of eternal youth beginning to dawn. Death will introduce us to endless life in heaven.

But if we are going to the grave with rebellion against God burning within the heart, then we may well shudder at the thought of relaxing our grip upon this present life. "After death the judgment." Heaven is a circle of happiness; hell is a circle of misery. Man, woman, child, where are you going? Answer that question to-day before Him who sitteth upon the circle of the earth.

III. I would remark, again, that the rewards and penalties of Him who sitteth upon the circle of the earth complete circles of well-doing and wickedness. In other words, the providence of God moves in a circle.

Joseph is the favorite son of Jacob's household. That circle of parental favoritism sweeps on until its top arc is above a king's throne, becoming royal favoritism; thence it curves downward to the meeting of father and son in Egypt, and completes the circle of love. God would not let the righteousness of that boy go unrewarded. What mattered it that the curving line that started away from Jacob's tent paused at a hole in the pasture lands of Dothan? What mattered it that it paused again at Potiphar's prison in a strange land after it had swept around an honored slavery? What mattered it that it again paused at Pharaoh's palace, there shining with regal splendor? God's hand held the pencil, and God knows how to draw a circle. Jacob often fancied that he heard the wild beasts rending the body of his beloved son; but at last he heard the rumble of the king's wagons, those wagons bringing him news of the lost one; the tidings so disturbing the action of the old father's heart that he fainted away, but afterwards reviving, and in his old age making pilgrimage to the home and heart of Joseph.

Job is introduced to us as a man of wealth, having not only many possessions, but also many sons and daughters. A little farther on the line of the circle encloses poverty, bereavement, disease. But it does not stop at that point. Still onward it goes, and comes back to where it started. Job is again rich in houses and lands and cattle, and again rich in children, and again rich in health. When God draws a circle it is always a perfect circle.

Paul begins his Christian life as a missionary to the Gentiles. It was his ambition to preach the Gospel in the city of Rome. God takes him around a circuitous route. The line runs from one point to another. It was a wide circle, but God drew it. What mattered it that its line was so far-reaching in its course? What mattered it that it came around at last to martyrdom? The hand of God was sweeping it on to the gates of pearl and the coronation of heaven.

Thus might I continue with illustrations of the fact that God uses the figure of the circle in rewarding His servants. But enough for us to know the fact itself. Let its radiance come down into the griefs and disappointments and darkness of your life and mine. We may not have sufficient strength of vision to follow the majestic sweep of God's curves, but we can trust in His geometrical skill and exactness. The day will come when we shall know that all things wrought together for our good. From the commanding view-point of eternity the providences of God will have a different look from what they appeared to be in time. No angles then, but perfect circles. The crowns that we shall wear will be unfading circles.

.But there is another side to this subject. Evil runs in a circle. Ahab wanted Naboth's vineyard. He murdered Naboth, taking the vineyard by foul means, not being able to secure it through fair means. In the place where the dogs licked Naboth's blood, the dogs licked Ahab's blood. It was a circle of crime and punishment, drawn by Him who sitteth upon the circle of the earth.

Pilate and Christ stand facing each other in the judgment hall of the Roman governor; Christ and Pilate will stand facing each other in the judgment hall of eternity on the last day.

Sometimes this circle of punishment has a larger curve than at other times; but whatever the sweep of the line, it always comes back to the starting point. The hand that draws that circle and the eye that guides the moving hand are both unerring. "Be sure your sin will find you out."

A man holds in his grasp his first glass of liquor. At the bottom of that glass a serpent is coiled in circling folds of poison, that coiled serpent typical of the circle of intoxication in its progressiveness, the curve sweeping on from the first glass to the second, and the third, and the fourth, and dozens and scores and hundreds, describing a rounded line of debauchery that winds on to a drunkard's grave and a drunkard's hell, unless by the grace of God that circle be broken. Around that circle is another circle, enclosing the legislators that licensed the saloon in which the man began his downward career, and enclosing the distiller who manufactured the contents of the glass, and enclosing the wholesaler that sold the vile stuff to the retailer, and enclosing the one who passed the glass over the bar, and enclosing the owner of the property in which the liquor was dispensed, and enclosing the honorable gentlemen who furthered the sale of the hell-broth in the use of their signatures, those signatures giving permission to destroy manhood; to blast the roses in the cheeks of womanhood; to hang rags upon the back of childhood; and to balk all morality and all religion—that circle running on and on, God only knows where; for I cannot trace that circle around the whole sweep of responsibility for the ruination of a human soul by drink. But glad I am that my hands are not holding any part of that fearful line. Are yours? Let each one answer for himself before Him that sitteth upon the circle of the earth.

What a tremendously startling thought that is, that sin and judgment will surely meet! How careful it should make us with our deeds, with our speech, with our feelings, causing us to be honest and truthful and loving! How it should lead us to God and His mercy, and keep us within sight of the Cross of Jesus Christ!

There will be circles described in the world's final scene of trial. Sweeping His hand in circle of gesture, Christ will say to those gathered on His right side, "Come, ye blessed of my Father, inherit the kingdom prepared for you from the foundation of the world." Sweeping His hand in circle of gesture again, Christ will say to those gathered on His left side, "Depart from me, ye cursed, into everlasting fire prepared for the devil and his angels." And those on the right will turn and circle into glory; those on the left will turn and circle into darkness. Two circles at the judgment. Which one will your feet draw?

IV. I remark, once more, that in the circle of God's plan of salvation there is no provision made for defeat. The world started with a garden; heaven will be an everlasting garden. Into that first garden came sin; but for sin God gave the Saviour; so that the line of the circle curved onward to the Cross of Christ; thence it still curves onward, until the paradise lost becomes the paradise regained. The Cross of that almighty Saviour is standing midway between the two gardens, one garden looking at it from one side, the other garden forever looking at it from the other side. Within that circle of redemption are gathered the uncounted multitudes of all the ages yet to come. Sin thought to mar and hinder the purpose of God, but it left out of its calculation of evil the fact of the Cross. What a wonderful circle! It is the circle of God's love.

In the Apocalypse John gives us a glimpse of God's throne. That throne is seen to be circled by a rainbow. We never see a rainbow in its fulness. A complete rainbow is a physical impossibility in the skies of the earth. But around God's throne the seer of Patmos beheld a whole rainbow—a circle of iridescent light. Suggestive is that of God's unbroken plan revealed. Now we catch only partial views of that plan here and there. We see it in fragments. But in eternity all limitations shall be removed. We shall, at least, be much better capable of judging God's purposes, for we shall look at them from the right point of observation. In that sense, if not in others, shall our present limitations be removed. Then the whole rainbow—a full circle.

We need not, therefore, vex ourselves with the metaphysical question, Why did God let sin come into the world? Suffice it to know that God could not be defeated by the presence or the power of sin. It is our business, being sinners by choice, to avail ourselves of God's grace, and thus pass from condemnation to acceptance through the precious blood of Jesus Christ, which blood cleanseth from all sin.

But now I see another circle. The Cross of Christ, while it was in the plan of God, was reared by human hate and wickedness. Christ was crowned with thorns. But around that Cross moves the line of a circle, and beside the Cross is a throne. Who sits upon that throne? He who wore the crown of thorns. All heaven worships Him, standing around His blazing throne in circling ranks of glory—circle of the redeemed in white robes; circle of symbolical living creatures; circle of angels—these circles of splendor within circles of splendor; all of them surrounding the throne of Christ; His throne, therefore, the centre of a trinity of lustrous circumferences. When that coronation scene arrives, it will be the last drawing of the circle of God's eternal plan. As the shining pencil drops from the fingers of Him whose name is Love, the completed circle will be a triumphant answer to all infidelity. Christ forever on the throne! This in vindication of the wisdom and goodness of God! Sin everlastingly repulsed! A magnificent circle of divine victory!

Riddles Musically Interpreted

I will open my dark saying upon the harp. Ps. 49: 4.

THE Emperor Nero played a fiddle while Rome was burning. He was a devil in human flesh who was capable of any crime. The man who could poison the members of his family with less compunction of conscience or revulsion of feeling than you and I could poison a rat was equal to anything wicked. The wonder is that, during the conflagration of the imperial city, that conflagration started by his own hand, he did not lead a whole orchestra in music, instead of simply playing on a fiddle unaccompanied.

But here is a man in an entirely different attitude. He is about to use his harp in the interpretation of a moral riddle. The Psalmist, instead of fiendishly rejoicing over calamity and trouble, is ready to strike the strings of his instrument and soothe all woe and distress with the harmonies of faith. Listen to him! "I will open my dark saying upon the harp."

Human life is an interrogation point. There are many things after which you and I and all our fellow-beings put a question mark. That question mark follows sin, follows sickness, follows disappointment, follows death. We can hardly go in any direction along life's path without coming in contact with what is mysterious and inexplicable. Experience is a stern school master who is ever placing on the blackboard of life sums that we cannot work out and get the right answer.

But the Psalmist declares that the riddles of life can be musically interpreted. He takes down his harp and expounds these enigmas that are common to us all, expounding them in tuneful vibrations. It is not merely an intellectual exposition that is given. Man is a wonderful creature in brain development. His brain is a spark out of God's brain. He can throw the light of reason over many a problem and make it clear. With scientific apparatus he can not only measure the mountains of earth, but also measure far-distant planets and suns. Taking his alpine stock of telescope in hand, he can travel from star to star, stepping from world to world in a single night. Yet there are some things that are beyond him. There are many secrets that he cannot discover. Hundreds of treasures of knowledge there are to which he has no opening key. These are God's providences. But though he may not be able to give any satisfactory philosophical explanation of the government of God, he can sing about it. The Psalmist's exposition of trouble, therefore, is of the heart. He sets the insoluble dealings of the Lord to music. That is better than sulking because they cannot be understood. Let us imitate him in this matter, glancing at a few of life's more prominent mysteries, and then opening them in melodies of trust.

I. The very first question we ask is one in regard to the fact of human sin. Why did God let sin come into the world? That is an old question. It has trembled pathetically upon millions of lips. It has written itself in tears upon millions of cheeks. It has traced itself in wrinkles along millions of brows. It has come forth into the air in long-drawn sighs from millions of hearts. Yea; that question has traveled over sixty centuries of time, starting on the journey with erect form, but gradually bowing its head, like a man growing aged, until it assumed the shape of an interrogation point, as we know that point in these modern days. It is a veritable patriarch among inquiries.

There are those who attempt to answer that question. "Oh," they say, "that is easy. Give us something harder." These smart ones are in the first form in the school of life, at the head of the class. With overweening conceit they tell those of us who are farther down in the list of scholarship that sin is a necessary evil. Perhaps it is. But where did they ascertain the truth? In what text book did they find it? That is what sin seems to be. But what I want is fact, not theory. The fact that I am after is not in the Bible. The Scriptures do not explain the mystery. They simply tell of the coming of sin into the world and narrate its progress over the world. Why God did not build around Eden a wall so high that sin could not climb it is a question that is left in the dark. That dark is the dark of a midnight

10

without stars. It is bounded on all sides and above by an impenetrable gloom.

There are others who declare that God could not prevent sin. That is a bolder step. It is too bold for me. My intellectual legs are not long enough to take a stride like that. If God could not prevent sin, then He is not God. That solution of the mystery is more puzzling than the mystery itself. It discrowns God, snaps His sceptre in twain, and rocks His throne into the dust. When He made the world, and rolled it forth as a new gem in the clusters of worlds that sparkle on the bosom of space, He was omnipotent; but when sin breathed upon that fair jewel the breath of hell, and marred its lustre, God was nothing more than a Napoleon meeting his Waterloo. No, no! I cannot accept that solution of the problem. It does not give the proper result. The figuring is wrong. I take off my hat and bid you good-night, gentlemen. My face is toward the sunrise.

There are others who affirm that God is indifferent towards sin. That is even a bolder step still, and requiring a much longer stride. If I were to attempt to walk with these, I should stumble over the precipice of infidelity and be dashed to pieces upon the rocks of absolute atheism. But you and I know better, or else the Bible is a fraud made up of sixty-six volumes—a whole library of lies. God indifferent towards sin? What then is the meaning of that wonderfully pathetic picture of God seeking His erring children among the trees of Paradise? What means that sobbing query, "Adam, where art thou?" That picture has been reproduced on a smaller scale in unnumbered lives; and that tearful question has been more than a million times repeated by agonized parental lips, inspiring such weeping songs as,

"Where is my wandering boy to-night—
The boy of my tenderest care,
The boy that was once my joy and light,
The child of my love and prayer?"

Is there a father's heart or a mother's heart that does not know something of the pain that took hold of the heart of God when sin stung the innocence of the first man and woman of creation? God indifferent towards sin? Impossible! Do you wish an unanswerable argument against so monstrous a dogma as that? Follow that initial sin of the world; follow it as it engenders more sin; follow it through the darkness of antediluvian days; follow it through the nettles of adultery; follow it through the wilderness of murder; follow it through the jungles of idolatry; follow it through the slime pits of the most stenchful uncleanness; follow it across four thousand years of time. Halt! What is that yonder? A Cross! What means it? Look! Behold its sunbeam inscription! "God so loved the world!" Taking one arm of that Cross as a lever, I pry this rock of blasphemy, that God is indifferent towards sin, out of its place, and send it rolling into the depths of hell! Listen to its far-away fall! Crash!

No human brain knows why God let sin come into the world. It is doubtful that any angelic brain knows. For some inscrutable reason it has God's permission. Like a great, ugly, black cloud of midnight, it has come into being, and spread itself over the sky of human life—over Europe; over Asia; over Africa; over America. But instead of seeking to dissolve that awful darkness, let us patiently wait for the triumphant light to burst through the gloom, adjourning the query until the morning of the Resurrection. Let us open this dark saying upon the harp of faith, and sing of God's redeeming love.

At this point I will tell you what is my own thought about why God let sin come into the world. It is not original with me. I came upon it in my reading upon this subject; and I adopted it as a most comfortable theory. That thought is that God permitted human sin as a preventive of sin in other worlds. We are not to suppose that this is the only inhabited earth of the universe. It would not be like God, reasoning from analogy, to let this earth be the only world-train carrying passengers through the immensity of space. There must be other orbs, and many of them, that are peopled. It may be that God allowed sin here, in this insignificant corner of creation, to spit forth its venom, in order that other worlds, grander worlds, mightier worlds, more stupendous worlds, might learn the terrible story, that story requiring the infinite blood of an infinite Saviour to wipe it out, and those worlds be powerfully deterred from plunging into a like folly. That is deep water, I admit. But I have gone swimming in it, and come back to the shore refreshed and invigorated. Yet, whether this be the solution of the mystery or not, I open my harp this morning, the harp of faith in God, a faith that grows with the passing years, and upon that harp I strike this exultant chord: "Where sin abounded, grace did much more abound!"

II. Another question we ask is in regard to various forms of trouble. In so bright a world as this why should there be any trouble? Why are the flowers in life's garden so often blighted by the frosts of disappointment? Why are the plans that are so often built up into seemingly solid structures of achievement likewise often thrown down flat in the dust by earthquakes of adversity? Why are smiles in sunbeams along the lips so often darkened and chased away by grief, the heart brewing a thunderstorm that sends a rain of tears down the cheeks? Here again is sin. We can readily understand that sin is responsible for the many woes of mankind. If that shadow had not spread its black wings over Eden, there would have been no other black-winged shadows to follow. Sin has written greater tragedies than ever came from the pen of a Shakespeare.

But when we place a question mark after the troubles that befall the children of God, the answer to the inquiry is not so apparent. Why not keep trouble out of a godly life? Why not have every morning roseate with an unclouded sunrise, and every evening golden and purple with an unclouded sunset? Why not have all the day in between the morning and evening overarched with an unclouded sky of blue? Why these oft-recurring sicknesses that make many prisoners in their own homes? Why these agitated nerves? Why do fiery feet of pain go traveling through the head and down the muscles of the trunk and limbs? Why these financial losses? Why these losses of good position? Why these losses of favorable opportunity? Why? Why? Why? A lady once said to me, "There is no word that I oftener use than the word Why?" We all frequently use it. There is no word in our vocabulary that comes oftener upon the lips. It is not a singing word at all. It weeps and sighs. Why does not God brush it from every Christian tongue, filling the throat with laughter?

Well, the Psalmist had been all through this difficulty of trouble. Instead of impugning the love and wisdom of God, he has grasped the truth that God reigns; and that He overrules all sorrow with good. This is the dark saying or riddle that he opens upon his harp. He floods the providences of God with music.

That is what you and I should do. We should take our harps down from the willows and thrum their silent melodies into glad sounds. How can you do that? How did Job do it? Have you ever been so sorely afflicted as he was? Listen to that boil-covered, poverty-stricken, childless man. He has sent a strain of music trembling through all the ages. Listen! "Though he slay me, yet will I trust him." How did Paul do it? Were you ever troubled as he was? Read his epistles. They are portfolios of music. You can turn no page without coming upon notes that are vibrant with joy.

I make no pretence of solving the providences of God. But I can see what appear to be some of the reasons for God's sharpness of dealing with His children. One of these reasons, I think, is that we may have our hearts made tender and sympathetic. Woe to those who are hardened or soured by trouble! Who are those who listen with moist eyes as you tell them of sorrow? Who are those who have a quiver in their voice when they speak of sorrow? Who are those who have great kindness of manner when they come in contact with sorrow? These are those who have taken a full course in the college of sorrow, entering the freshman class, and going clear up to the senior class, from there graduating with a diploma signed by the whole faculty of trouble. What they have themselves suffered! Do you know what made Washington Irving a master of pathetic writing? It was an early loss of love that he kept in the casket of memory, locked up there, far too precious for the vulgar gaze of the world. That love was the love of his sweetheart, Matilda Hoffman, whose beautiful face was shut out from his sight by a coffin-lid, Washington Irving remaining all his life a bachelor. He dipped his pen into his own tearful experience, thus making his books world-wide favorites.

Yes; we need to feel the hand of trouble to make us sympathetic. A rough teacher in a school room, about to punish one of the pupils who had broken the rules, said to the boy, "Take off your coat!" The boy refused to obey. He was a poor, half-starved lad. Again said the teacher, "Take off your coat!" swinging his whip in a threatening manner through the air. The boy still refused. Why? He was not afraid of punishment. He had plenty of that at home. The reason was that he had no undergarment on, so poor were his parents, and he was ashamed to show his poverty. But at the third command from the teacher the lad slowly and reluctantly pulled off his coat, and the whole school room was thrown into sobs and tears, for it was seen that the boy's back was bare, and his sharp shoulder blades had almost cut through the skin. Then a stout, healthy boy rose up and said, "Oh, sir! please don't whip this poor fellow; whip me! Don't you see how thin he is? Whip me!"

That is the kind of sympathy that many need. They get it through the discipline of sorrow. Then the sight of suffering in others appeals to their heart.

So does the discipline of sorrow quicken our Christian graces. What kind of a man would Paul have been, if he had never had a rough, thorny path spread out to his feet? We do not know. But this we do know; that he was a better man because he traveled a hard road. So with David. So with thousands of other saints. The winds of sorrow may be rude musicians, to finger spiritual æolian harps, but they evoke wondrous strains. These harmonious chords that freight the air down here are but the prelude of celestial symphonies. The full orchestration is yet to burst and thrill.

III. Another interrogation point placed over life is that of bereavement and death. Why these early graves out in the churchyard and cemetery? Why are so many of the young and promising stricken down and their usefulness ended? Why these constantly-breaking family ties? Why swathe so many doorbells with crepe? Why halt so many hearses at the threshold of the home? But God knows why. I do not intend to question His acts. If there is any music in bereavement, I am going to strike it. Is there any? Yes! Listen! It comes from a distant land and a distant age. "The Lord gave, and the Lord hath taken away; blessed be the name of the Lord!" Those were the harpnotes of a man who lost seven sons and three daughters at one swoop of the black wings and fierce talons of death. If he could open a dark saying upon a harp under that ten-fisted bereavement, surely we can finger the harp of trust in God when our dear ones go singly home.

So is the fact of death for ourselves a fact for questionings. How many hearts there are that fear death! We go to funerals and see flowers banked around the still form in the casket, and flowers upon the coffin lid, as the mournful procession follows to the cemetery, and flowers strewn over the new grave that closes upon the body of the departed one; but the flowers cannot hide the repulsiveness of death.

It is said that Professor Darwin was accustomed to visit the London Zoological Gardens and stand beside a glass case containing a cobra, the most poisonous of serpents. He would place his forehead against the glass, each time that he did so the venomous reptile striking at him. There was heavy glass between them, the man of science well knowing that he could not be harmed; yet, whenever the snake sprang at him, the professor would dodge. He tried it again and again, each time shrinking as before, his instinct overpowering his will and reason.

So may you and I be instinctively afraid of death; but down in our very heart of hearts we know full well that it cannot do us any hurt. Therefore, even in our fear may we open this dark riddle upon a harp, accompanying a song of triumph. Between every Christian soul and death is the unsealed grave of Him who is the Resurrection and the Life. You and I may go to the tomb with this hallelujah: "O death, where is thy sting?" That music is yet to break into the oratorio of heaven, preluded by the resounding notes of the last trump. God grant that every one of us may have a share in that songful victory!

Christianity vs. Worldliness

Wherefore come out from among them, and be ye separate, saith the Lord. II Cor. 6: 17.

EVERY word in that sentence is emphatic. But the emphasis rises into a climax. The sentence starts on the level and ends in a mountain peak. The mountain peak flames with the presence of God and shakes with the thunder of God's voice. We are standing before another Sinai. Listen! "Thus saith the Lord!"

I am glad that Paul put this important matter in that form. He speaks with divine authority. There cannot be the slightest doubt about his inspiration. His utterance bears the stamp of divinity. The coin that he circulates was not minted in his own brain. It was not counterfeit. What he says is what God Himself says. Hear the text again. "Wherefore come out from among them, and be ye separate, saith the Lord."

Paul was inspired in all of his writings. We must not forget that fact. But lest he should be accused of here giving only his own thought, or simply indulging an orator's taste for rhetoric, he dissipates any fog that gathers around his words with a sunburst—"Saith the Lord!" That settles the matter. He has taken it into the Supreme Court for decision.

Against the opinion rendered there can be no appeal. What God says cannot be set aside. This is no spider web to be brushed away with the broom of human reasoning. It is one of the massive pillars in the great temple of Christian truth. Those who would remove that pillar would bring the whole majestic edifice crashing to the ground.

This passage starts in my mind two inquiries. The first one is, What is the exact import of the text? The second one is, What is the application of the text to the present time?

I. What is the exact import of the text? Paul himself solves the query in the context. His language is unmistakable. He tells those Corinthian Christians to whom he writes that their profession of the religion of Jesus Christ should draw a sharp dividing line between them and the idolatrous world by which they are surrounded. It must be like the line of demarcation between healthy flesh and flesh that is gangrened. He does not beat around the bush. There are no qualifying phrases in his language. He does not mince matters. Listen! "Be ye not unequally yoked together with unbelievers; for what fellowship hath righteousness with unrighteousness? And what communion hath light with darkness? And what concord hath Christ with Belial? Or what part hath he that believeth with an infidel? And what agreement hath the temple of God with idols? For ye are the temple of the living God; as God hath said, "I will dwell in them and walk in them; and I will be their God, and they shall be my people. Wherefore come out from among them and be ye separate, saith the Lord, and touch not the unclean thing; and I will receive you, and will be a Father unto you, and ye shall be my sons and daughters, saith the Lord Almighty."

This is one of the most tremendous paragraphs in the New Testament. There is the weight of mountains in it. There is in it the emphasis of a whirlwind. What does it mean? It seems unnecessary to ask such a question. It means just what it says. Analyze it, take it apart, put it under the microscope of minute criticism, place it on the rack of torture, do what you will with it, and you cannot make it anything less than a clear, clean-cut, straight, positive command to the Christian to turn a cold shoulder to the great evil world that is opposed to him and his regenerated life. To strike friendly hands with that world is to discard the yoke of Christ and work in a yoke that galls. It is to intermingle light and darkness. It is to make Christianity and wickedness harmonious. It is to pollute the sacred precincts of a divine temple with idols. Such things those Corinthian Christians must not even think of doing. "Wherefore come out from among them, and be ye separate." So commands the Apostle in the name of God. That there can be no mistaking his authority in the matter, he adds, "saith the Lord." At the end of the whole paragraph he adds, "saith the Lord Almighty." That makes the command doubly emphatic. It is two trumpet peals in succession, the last one closely following the first, and with increased sound. "Saith the Lord!" "Saith the Lord Almighty." From the final blast is rolled one of God's attributes. When something breaks upon the ear as coming from God, it is well to consider it. When it comes again, charged with God's omnipotence, it is well to give it more earnest heed. That is a lightning flash and its accompanying voice of thunder.

Now, do you suppose that those Corinthian Christians failed to understand what their pastor was driving at? If so, then they must have been dullards of a very pronounced type. There would have been more dunces' heads in that school than dunce caps to fit them. In fact, it would have been necessary to turn the school into an asylum for imbecility. Those who could not comprehend the words of this Christian teacher could not comprehend anything. They would have been hopeless idiots. The Apostle's words might as well have faded from the parchment as soon as they were written. He could not have put the matter more simply or strongly. And if he did not intend to instill into the minds of that people the idea that they must be entirely different from what they were before they began the Christian life, then Paul was doing nothing more than juggling with words. But those to whom he was writing knew what he was writing about. They accepted his command, for it was backed by an unquestioned inspiration. Paul was too serious a man to play with language. The text was a direct, distinct, decided summons to those Corinthian Christians to have no compromising connection with anything in the world that was foreign or obnoxious to the holiness of God. They were to make a clean sweep of worldliness in all its forms from their hearts. Not a single cobweb must be left hanging from the ceiling. Not a single speck of dust must be left griming the walls. Not a single stain of dirt must be left to smirch the floor. "Come out from among them, and be ye separate, saith the Lord." This, and only this, is the exact import of the text—the unconditional surrender of worldliness.

II. What is the application of the text to the present time? This is to be the main part of my sermon. Give me your most earnest attention. May the Lord help me to speak aright!

Now, then, if in Paul's day it was necessary for Christians to be separate from the world, the same necessity exists in our day. It is the very same world, with the very same sins clinging to it, with the very same vices practiced by it, and with the very same boldness of hatred against everything that is pure and good and holy. It is the foe of God.

When I say the world, I do not, of course, mean the physical world. That world I love. Its mountains preach to me of God. Its winds whisper to me of God. Its oceans are to me the glistening pathways on which walk the feet of God. The skies that bend over it are God's picture gallery wherein He exhibits His marvelous paintings of sunrise and sunset, and along which He hangs His matchless drawings of cloud in frame of blue, or in ebony frame of storm gilded with lightning. Those same skies at night are God's book of poems, every star and every galaxy and every constellation God's glowing rhetoric unfolded to the vision, bringing to view the wonderful measures that His infinite mind expresses in silvery planets and blazing suns and whole concourses of grandeur gathered into the Milky Way. Beautiful world! Handsome world! Glorious world! It is one of God's fairest jewels among millions of sparkling gems. I have often looked at this world when I have been entranced by its splendor, at such times of exalted mood wondering if heaven itself could be more lustrous than it. Lift from it the foul touch of human sin, and it would become the suburbs of the celestial city. That is what it was when God first sent it rolling into space as the home of mankind. That is what it shall be again after the second Adam, the Lord Jesus Christ, shall have drawn to His magnetic Cross all that the Father promised Him should be the subjects of His everlasting kingdom. God speed the day!

No, it is not of the physical world that I speak, but of the moral world—the world that is multiplied in human hearts in rebellion against God; the world that openly defies the righteous laws of God; the world that draws its inspiration for evil deeds from the smoky depths of perdition; the world that is influenced and determined and governed by sin. This it is that is the very same world to-day that was in Paul's day. The march of centuries over it has not changed it one particle. The sweep of revolutions has not in the least altered it. The downfall of ancient empires and the rising of new thrones have not disturbed it in its course of wickedness. It remains the same implacable enemy of God that it ever was. To God it has been infernally antagonistic from almost the first stroke of time; and so will it continue to be until the pendulum halts and stands still, when God shall smite it with everlasting death and bury it hell-deep in a grave of everlasting darkness.

It is against those who are enslaved by sin in such a world that the Apostle speaks when he warns Christians to "come out from among them and be separate." As in his day there could be no fellowship between that world and those who had been born anew into a spiritual world, so now can there be no such companionship or alliance. As well attempt to bring the North and the South poles together. As well attempt to raise pansies upon an iceberg. As well attempt to harness a snail with a race-horse. Those two worlds are diametrically opposed to each other. You can no more bring them into harmonious union than you could make the gates of hell the entrance into heaven.

I am by no means inclined to suppress all mirth and pleasure. I do not class myself with those who

11

condemn smiles and praise groans and tears. I have not the least sympathy with a long-faced Christianity that whines and sniffles when it talks religion, and finds its chief delight in haunting graveyards and sitting on tombstones, the thermometer down to sixteen degrees below zero. Some Christians there are who have banished the sugar bowl from their table of life and replaced it with a vinegar cruet and a horseradish jar. I have not so learned Christ. My Bible teaches me that to be a Christian is to be filled with a peace that passes all understanding. My Bible teaches me that to be a Christian is to be possessed of a joy that even the angels do not know. My Bible teaches me that to be a Christian is to be supremely happy. Religion is not a bald-headed monk nor a black-robed nun shut up within stone walls and living on bread and water. Religion is a son or a daughter of God. As a child of God, Religion is blest with both sunshine and liberty. But at the same time my Bible teaches me that the joy and peace and happiness and light and freedom of the Christian life are not drawn from the poisoned well of a world of sin, but that they flow out of the heart of God. The Christian is dead to the world, and the world is dead to him. Paul says that in another place. It is as if the Christian and the world were both hanging lifeless on a cross, side by side, each of them unable to see or hear or touch the other. The world crucified to the Christian; the Christian crucified to the world. Both dead.

Yes, Christianity summons to a crucifixion. That is something that hurts the natural flesh. The nails hurt. The thorns hurt. The rude beams of the cross hurt. I would be false to my trust as a minister of the Lord Jesus Christ, if I were to present religion in any other way. It demands separation from a sinful world. It demands the sacrifice of harmful desires. It demands the surrender of blighting pleasures. There can be no lawful disguising these facts. I let them stand before you to-day in all their austerity of form and feature. They do not wear even the shadow of a mask. What Paul here says in the text is but an echo of what Christ Himself said. Listen! "If any man will come after me, let him deny himself, and take up his cross, and follow me." At the very entrance of the Christian life Christ has placed a cross. He who would tread that path finds a cross waiting for him. That cross he must shoulder, however painful it may be so to do, and carry it clear to the gates of pearl.

I would solemnly say, therefore, to any who are seriously thinking of professing Christ, if you are going to remain on friendly terms with the world, if the cross you are going to bear is nothing more than a florist's cross of wire, filled with roses and twined with smilax, if it is your intention to be a Christian only in name, sporting a heavenly uniform, but still allied with the enemies of God, then, for the sake of the Church of Christ, and for your own sake, stay out where you really belong. This separation of

which Paul speaks is not a fence spun by a spider,
nothing more than gossamer threads floating in the
air. It is a solid wall of granite built around the
soul. The world cannot remove one of its stones,
nor overleap its height. It is a barrier that makes
a complete separation between Christians and the
world.

The fact is that there are too many mere nominal
Christians in the Church of Christ already. There
were such in Paul's day. There were such in all
the following days. There are altogether too many
such in these days. One of the great errors of this
present time among ministers and other officials in
the Church of Christ is a lust for numbers. The multiplication table is considered of more worth than the
Communion table. Persons are urged to join the
Church in order to swell the Church roll. The con-
sequence is that many make a profession of religion
who have no more real piety than there is love in the
sting of a wasp. They are no more separated from
the world than fire is opposed to fire. The line that
divides their spiritual life from the life of the flesh
is like the lines of latitude and longitude over the surface of the earth, altogether imaginary. Such bear
the name of Christian only by courtesy. In their
case the term Christian is a misnomer. Pretending
to be grapevines, they bring forth thistles. Pretending to be honey, they are gall. Pretending to be pure
gold, they are naught but brass. They are the chaff
that will yet fly under the breath of God in the judg-

ment of the last day. Having never been born again,
having never truly repented of their sins, having never
in all sincerity of purpose sought the Cross of Jesus
Christ, their ears shall be smitten with the words,
"Depart from me; I never knew you."

Oh, my friends, I know of no more terrible place
to fall into hell than from a church pew! No one
should join the Church who is not a genuine Christian. Not perfect. I do not mean that. By a genuine Christian I mean one who is prepared to follow
Christ at any cost, come what may, come what will.
By a genuine Christian I mean one who is willing to
turn his back upon sin and face the holiness of God.
By a genuine Christian I mean one who is ready to
respond to what God says through Paul in the text,
and obey it. If these things you cannot do, or will
not do, then I say once more, stay where you are,
and do not add any more weight to the burden already laid upon the overloaded shoulders of the
Church of Christ, that burden made up of inconsis-
tent lives and hypocrisy and utter worldliness. To
follow the example of some so-called Christians
would be to walk into a den of lions, and the lions all
at home!

In his family, in his business, in his pleasures, in
everything that he says and does, the Christian is to
be wholly separate from the world. His whole life
has been revolutionized, turned completely upside
down, changed as entirely as the day that now irradi-
ates the air has been changed from the night that pre-

ceded it. Otherwise he is not a Christian at all. This is the sum and substance of everything that the Bible teaches upon the subject of real religion. If this be not true, then the very air we breathe is a lie to poison the lungs.

The application of the text to the present time is the very same that it was when it first throbbed in Paul's brain, and rushed down Paul's arm to the ends of his fingers, and flashed, a living sentence, from the point of Paul's pen. It is a call to the Christian while he is in the world to be not of the world. It is God's frown upon whatever is harmful to the mind or body or soul. It is God's prohibition against spiritual uncleanness. To forsake the world, to be the foe of the world's evil practices in business and in social life, to be an out-and-out Christian in every particular of conversation and conduct, may be to carry a cross, but that same cross will grow lighter and lighter with the passing days, shrinking, and shrinking, and still shrinking, until finally it shall become the crown that fadeth not away. On the other hand, the crown that is worn by the dupe of Satan here upon the earth shall grow heavier and heavier, enlarging, and still enlarging, until finally it shall become a ponderous cross of iron that shall crush the very soul into an endless perdition. "The wages of sin is death; but the gift of God is eternal life." "Wherefore," and oh, that the words might be heeded! "come out from among them, and be ye separate, saith the Lord."

Friends, this is a call to a higher life than can be lived by the sinner. This is the key that would open the door of a prison. This is the hammer that would shatter the chains of slavery. To come under the power and blessing of these words of the text will be to enjoy the liberty of the children of God. Who would be in captivity when he might be free? The text invites to a life that knows no boundary lines of blessedness, like the blue of the heaven above inviting an eagle let out of its cage to spread wings and fly and fly, the world beneath more and more losing its bulk with every stroke of the exulting pinions along the sunny air. Up, up, to the throne of God, we are summoned to soar, where there are pleasures that never die.

The Father of the Rain

Hath the rain a father? ' Job 38:28.

IF I have any skill of observation, or any skill of thought, or any skill in the art of putting things, I owe that skill very largely to the Bible. I have been studying this Book now for a number of years, finding it a very storehouse of learning. But I have thus far only scratched a little of its surface. In its yielding power to an exploring mind it is inexhaustible. Who thinks of exhausting the Bible? As well attempt to drain the ocean dry with a thimble. I feel sometimes as if my ministry, clear up to this present day, has been nothing more than a preparation for preaching from this wonderful Book—a practicing of the scales to make the fingers of the brain nimble. Perhaps when my life is at its sunset I may be able to play a few simple chords upon this majestic organ of the Scriptures.

What a marvelously beautiful figure is that of the text! It is a figure that strikes the mind like a barb, and sticks there. You cannot forget it. But let us examine it and gather its lessons. I shall treat the text as containing an affirmation and three inferences.

I. I remark, that the question of the text can be answered with an affirmative. A monosyllabic word

answers the query, but that little word having in it
the emphasis of a shot from a cannon. "Hath the
rain a father?" Yes! Who is the father of the rain?
God!

In His mountain sermon Christ tells us that the
flowers have a father. God opens to them the wardrobes of the sun and throws over their shoulders
such garments as even a king cannot afford to wear.
In all his glory Solomon was not arrayed like a single
lily of the field—the splendor of that monarch's royal
attire outrivaled by a daisy or a dandelion or a buttercup or a head of scarlet clover. Christ distinctly
says that God gives the flowers their raiment.
"Wherefore, if God so clothe the grass of the field,
which to-day is, and to-morrow is cast into the oven,
shall he not much more clothe you, O ye of little
faith?"

In that same sermon Christ tells us again that God
is the father of the birds. "Your heavenly Father
feedeth them." The eagle, the pelican, the raven,
the sparrow, the wren, the robin redbreast, the multitudinous fowls of the air are all feathered by Him
who covers the orchards and the gardens and the
wood with garments woven in the loom of light.

If, then, the flowers of the field and the fowl of the
air have God as their Father, so has the rain the same
Father. God is the Father of the rain. Why, in all
the universe there is not a single foundling. The
parentage of the stars is known, for in this Book of
Job they are mentioned as being in company with the

Sons of God at the laying of the foundation stones of the earth, they and the Sons of God singing together and shouting for joy. The parentage of the mountains is known, for God is spoken of as bringing them forth. The parentage of the oceans is known, for God speaks to their waves, and those waves obey. So is known the parentage of the rain. It is born of God. It is wrapped in the swaddling clothes of the clouds. It is rocked in the cradle of the storm. It is sung to sleep by the lullaby of the winds. It is covered with the embroidered counterpane of the grass. The rainbow is the smile of its guardian angel while in slumber. The flash of swollen brooks and mountain torrents is the sparkle of its eyes in waking from repose. The roar of water wheels is its shout of glee. Beautiful rain! Child of God!

II. I remark, again, that if God is the Father of the rain, then is God Nature's King.

"Oh," but say those who are wise in their own conceit, "the rain is the result of natural law." Then they launch out into a learned discussion about the lifting of vapors skyward, and the condensation of moisture, and the discharge of heavy clouds, letting fall their contents upon the surface of the earth, the rain drops pattering down in obedience to natural law.

But law of any kind means a lawgiver. How came the Constitution of the United States? How came the statutes upon the books of Maryland, Delaware, or Pennsylvania, or New York? The very fact that laws exist at all is proof conclusive that they were conceived and framed by living minds. A man commits premeditated murder. He is tried for the crime and convicted of it. Then he is hung by the neck until dead. Some wiseacre comes forth and says, speaking of the execution, "Oh, it was the result of criminal law." Of course it was. But if it should be meant by that statement that criminal law supposes a self-elected and self-written manual of law, the one making so ridiculous an assertion would be laughed into an insane asylum. His very name would be a synonym of foolishness. But when atheistic scientists affirm that rain is simply an expression of natural law, intending by their words to drive God out of being, they are listened to with respect, gaining a wide hearing. Yet it is just as absurd to talk about law in this case without a lawmaker as it would be to so talk in the other case. If anything occurs as the result of natural law, and that only, then write natural law in capital letters and worship it, for natural law must be only another name of God.

I like better the philosophy of the ancient Hebrews, who made Jehovah the King of Nature. The lightning was the flash of His eye, or the fire of His arrows, or the gleam of His sword. The thunder was His voice. The mists of the morning were the smoke that curled and writhed at the touch of His blazing feet upon the hills and the mountains. The clouds were His chariots. The winds were the wings of His swiftly-flying messengers, or the power of His fists, or the treasures of His storehouses. The rain was His child.

With the Bible in hand, I go forth into Nature and get close to God. There are many things to suggest His presence. The Scriptures are full of metaphors and similes that were drawn from Nature. No one can deeply study these numerous figures without becoming a lover of Nature. Going forth into Nature with the spirit of God's Word in the heart, all the sights that bless the eye and all the sounds that bless the ear are so many waymarks that direct the feet of the soul to Him who is the Author of Nature. Looking up at the stars, I hear the scratch of James' pen, and saying, "The Father of lights, from whom cometh down every good and perfect gift, and with whom is no variableness nor shadow of turning." Standing upon the ocean's beach, in the ceaseless crash of the breakers along the strand, and voicing a sublime doxology that will sound clear down to the last heartbeat of the sea, when there shall be no more sea, I hear the thunder of God's command, saying to the collected waters, "Hitherto shalt thou come, but no farther; and here shall thy proud waves be stayed." Opening my eyes in the morning, the night-shadows gone and sunbeams chasing each other in sport across the floor, I see those sunbeams writing with their radiant feet the words, "I am the Light of the world." In fact there is not a scene or sound that fails to call God to mind. The clouds are the tessellated pavement around His throne as He sits upon the circle of the earth. The winds are His servants. The mountains are His audience-chambers wherein He holds converse with His chosen ones. The flowers are His poems. The birds are the shuttles that weave the air with melodies for His ears. The rain is His child—a royal child in robes of flashing silver. God is Nature's King.

III. I remark, again, that if God is the Father of the rain, then He certainly knows when to send the rain and when to withhold it. Born of God, who is the absolute Sovereign of the universe, the rain is under God's full control. That is the same God who once said, "Let there be light!" the light obeying His voice, then spreading its golden wings, then flying over the heavens, flying across the seas, flying over the mountains and down into the valleys and over the plains, and ever afterwards continuing its wonderful flight. That is the same God who orders the lightnings of the storm, bidding them appear before His throne, those lightnings, like obedient children, presenting themselves in God's presence, and with voice of thunder, uttered with tongues of fire, saying to God, "Here we are!" That is the same God who says to the snow, "Be thou on the earth!" the snow going forth and tramping the earth with white feet. In like manner does God command the rain—that rain an army, clad in silver mail, the clouds its banners and plumes. He says to that army, "Forward, march!" and it marches, going forth to overleap the walls of the forests, to scale the heights of the hills, to conquer the wheat fields and the corn fields. He says again to that army, "Halt!" and it halts, its vapory banners furled, its drums hushed, its measured footsteps silent, its guns stacked, then, having broken ranks, encamping beneath the tents of the blue sky.

God knowing when to send the rain and when to withhold the rain, it is becoming in man to trust in God's infinite wisdom. But instead of that, often there goes up into God's ears a million-voiced complaint. There is either too much rain at times or not enough rain. Men know better than God. He that sits in the heavens must laugh at the conceit that presumes to counsel Him!

I am glad that the government of Nature is under God's sceptre. Only He is competent to arrange matters for the best. To provide weather suited always to all classes of humanity would be too great a task for any mortal wisdom. Even God Himself does not attempt the task. He sends rain or withholds it in accordance with His knowledge of what is needed.

I give you two scenes. It is early morning in summer. A farmer is awakened by the music of rain, the falling drops singing their melodies upon the roof to the accompaniment of thunder from the organ of the storm. "Ah!" the farmer exclaims, "that means potatoes, and beans, and full-headed wheat, and plenty of corn!" He falls asleep again, dreaming of harvest-fields reaped by angels, the flash of their scythes answering the flash of the lightnings outside the dwelling in which he slumbers, and those angelic reapers singing songs that answer the song of the rain. When he goes forth to the barn, the falling raindrops kiss his shoulders and lie down at his feet, as though he were a king to whom homage is due.

But in another place a different scene is 'enacted. It is in a great city. A maiden is aroused by the same rain. The lightning that opens its red wings in her bedroom startles her heart. The thunder that rolls its majestic tones over the hills of the clouds sounds to her like the growl of a wild beast. The rain that dashes against the window and patters on the ledge is discord. "Oh!" she exclaims, "there will be no picnic to-day! That horrid rain! I wish that it could have waited until to-morrow." Like the farmer, this maiden falls asleep again and dreams. In her dream she sees a park, and a merry group suddenly overtaken by a shower, that group hastily gathering up the dishes and food that were spread on the grass beneath a broad-branched tree, and beholds a score of ruined hats, and yards of spotted ribbons, and twenty muddied skirts, the party running from the storm, and reaching a place of shelter just as a cloud bursts and whelms the whole landscape with tons of deluging water. The maiden awakes once more, and carries a frown upon her face the rest of the day.

These two scenes are more than imaginary. They have really occurred hundreds of times. The weather that suits one class of people does not at all suit an-

other class. It never did. It never will. So God
sends the kind of weather that suits Him, knowing
what is the best kind to send. He is the Father of
the rain.

"But," says some one, "would you then discourage praying for rain in a season of drought? Or
would you discourage prayer for a cessation of rain
in a time of protracted moisture?" By no means.
I would no more do that than I would discourage
prayer in general. Prayer is a mark of confidence in
God on the part of His children. Prayer to God,
either in drought or flood, is the evidence of faith in
His ability to command the rain. But if you want
rain as an answer to your selfishness, you may pray
until the breath leaves your lungs and never get rain.
So if you want rain to cease in order that you may
indulge your own pleasure, you do not pray under
such circumstances. Let the motive of prayer be
right, and there need be no fear of not obtaining the
right answer.

The fact is, my friends, that God's sovereignty is
God's benevolence. It is not fatalism to say that God
sends rain or withholds rain as He pleases. Fatalism is blindness; sovereignty is light. Fatalism is
the grinding of a heel of iron upon the heart of men;
sovereignty is the touch of a hand of love. Fatalism
is a giant that staggers along the walks of Nature;
sovereignty is the footsteps of a kind father. In
sending rain, or in withholding rain, God acts from
a superior standpoint of knowledge. If you can find

any fatalism in that statement, I wish that I had your power of penetrating vision. As well might one say that he can look through an eighteen inch wall.

IV. I remark, once more, that if God is the Father of the rain, then His providences toward us are the expression of His good-will. The very words of the text were meant to prove that God is good in His dealings with His children. The Lord is here addressing Job. Job's friends, so called, had been weaving their philosophy in an attempt to solve the riddle of that man's woeful afflictions. Out of the whirlwind God answered Job, saying to him, "Who is this that darkeneth counsel by words without knowledge?" That is what much philosophy is—a cloud of gloom over a sound of senseless verbiage. Job's friends had an inexhaustible "gift of gab." They nearly pestered the life of the old man out of him. For once he lost his patience, exclaiming, "Miserable comforters are ye all!" I do not blame him. It takes more than the colored candy of mere philosophy to comfort a heart that has graves in it, or that is pinched by disappointment, or that is under the iron-soled foot of tribulation. What you and I need in trouble is to know that God is near.

The Lord here puts to Job a series of questions, among them the query of the text, "Hath the rain a father?" All of those questions were for the purpose of bringing to Job's mind the fact that God means only good in the exercise of His sovereign will. That

12

is the one great lesson that we all need to learn. Some of us have been puzzling over it for a long time. It is not a hard lesson to master. The difficulty is that we are dull of brain. But when we shall have once fully learned that lesson, we shall be wise men and women, ready for graduation into a higher school. Many, however, have learned it; and the triumph of it has made life sweet and bright and melodious.

"Hath the rain a father?" Yes; God is its Father. Then God will not send forth His child or keep it home except in blessing. Neither will He cause pain or grief in your life or mine without intending thereby to work in us the highest good. The rain that smiles in the sunshower or weeps in the storm, goes alike to the hearts of the flowers, washing those flower hearts with benedictions. So with the rain of trouble. It comes by the grace of Him who is the Father of the physical rain—your Father; my Father.

You know that it is a great risk to sign your name to a blank check, leaving that check in some one's hands to fill in an amount. You would not do that, except for one in whom you had the highest confidence. But that is what God does for His children. The Bible is full of such checks, all of them bearing God's signature, and left for His children to put in any amount they wish. Here is one of those checks awaiting your penmanship in figures: "He that spared not his own Son, but delivered him up for us all, how shall he not with him also freely give us all things."

When I began to think of this sermon, I wondered how I could get the Cross of Christ into it. But yonder that Cross stands. In the shadow of that Cross, name on this almighty check any sum that you please, endorsing it with faith, and the Bank of Heaven will cash it for you. The Father of the rain will give grace for every tear that you shed, for every sob that breaks from your lips, for every burden that weights your shoulders, and for every grave that opens dark and terrible before your feet. Is it hard to trust in God? "Freely give us all things!"

"Hath the rain a father?" Answer, ye clouds of heaven! Answer, ye winds of the air! Answer, ye flowers of field and garden! Then I see those clouds writing the answer, writing it with convoluted pencil upon the blue sheet of the overarching sky. Then I hear the rising winds whisper the answer, afterwards putting more emphasis into their voice. Then I catch the fragrance of the flowers, and I know that the flowers have breathed the answer in perfume. The answer comes, "Yes; the rain hath a Father!" My heart cries out, "Is He my Father?" Behold yonder the glorious answer! See the Cross of Jesus Christ! Read the inscription that glows along the transverse beam of that wondrous Cross!—"He that spared not his own Son." It is enough. He will "freely give all things." In the light of that promise I am willing to walk all the remainder of my days. The Father of the rain is my Father. God pity those who have no glad consciousness of that fact!

The Six Seraphic Wings

Each one had six wings; with twain he covered his face, and with twain he covered his feet, and with twain he did fly. Isaiah 6: 2.

EARTHLY kings sit upon their thrones in great state. Golden crowns, set with sparkling gems, adorn their brow. Splendid robes grace their shoulders. Courtiers surround them in brilliant array. So sat Ahasuerus, reigning over a hundred and twenty-seven provinces, his sceptre stretching its power from India to Ethiopia. So sat Solomon, the most renowned of Hebrew monarchs. So sat Augustus Cæsar, ruling the mighty empire of Rome.

But what, after all, is a human king? His breath is in his nostrils. His lips are dust. He is a creature of flesh and blood. His palace walls, his throne, his coronet, his attendants are but the outward symbols of a perishable splendor. Call the roll of the world's kings and queens of the past centuries, and there is no response. No royal tongue answers. Silence! Dead! All dead!

In exalted vision, however, Isaiah beholds within the Jerusalem Temple a King whose throne is eternal in the heavens. His crown outflashes the sun. His garments are more richly spangled with jewels than are the midnight skies with stars. His atten-

dants breathe the breath of immortality. His sceptre
sways over a universe. He is the King of kings and
Lord of lords. · Compared with the majesty that belongs to Him, the stateliness of earthly monarchs is
like a fading picture of the ocean in comparison with
the ocean itself, as it rolls sublimely between the
shores of the continents.

The text calls upon us to consider the high class
of angels who stand before the august throne of the
Lord God Almighty. We are to observe, in particular, their attitude of reverence and humility, and the
swiftness of their obedience. These angels are the
very brightest angels of all heaven, the seraphim,
that name signifying burners, and that name bestowed
upon them as indicative of their wondrous flaming
beauty. Yet with all their brilliance of face and
figure, they are but sparks out of the conflagration
of God's uncreated glory. Each one of that throng
of heaven's most distinguished angels standing before the throne of God, as the prophet saw them,
had six wings. With two of those wings each one
covered his face. With two wings each one hid his
feet. With two wings each one did fly. Wings as a
veil. Wings as drapery. Wings as instruments of
locomotion.

I. We are to note the reverence of these six-winged
seraphim of Isaiah's vision. "With twain he covered his face." A crowd of dazzling courtiers before the throne of God, and not one daring to gaze
with unshaded eyes upon the effulgent majesty that

blazes from that throne. Posture of reverential awe in the presence of God. Let these seraphim of heaven be examples for mankind. The world to-day needs the lesson they teach.

I would remark that this lesson is needed in regard to the natural world. I do not know how it is in other countries, but here in America we are sacrificing the beauty of our scenery to the spirit of commercialism. Advertisements deface our fields. They splash with paint the rocks of the mountains. They offend the eye at every turn of a railroad journey. Even is the grandeur of the ocean marred by them. I was reading of a wrecked vessel on the coast of New Jersey off Asbury Park. Upon one of the spars of that ship some enterprising agent had fixed a huge sign. The inscription along it urged those who walked the beach to use a certain brand of whiskey! In one sense that sign was appropriately placed. Those who answered its business call would themselves be wrecked, like the ship upon which it was displayed—wrecked in body and soul. But what blasphemous irreverence it was that nailed that sign out where God plants His footsteps, walking the glistening pavement of the waves!

I like what I once read of an old Scotchman among his native hills. He was found one morning at the door of his cottage with his hat in hand. When asked why he stood in that posture, his answer was, "Mon, I stand here ivery day with my bunnit off to the beauty o' the landscape. God is here."

I say that we need to cultivate more reverence for the handiwork of God. We need to behold more His creative genius in the world around us. If the brightest angels of heaven veil their faces in the presence of God, who are we that we should be unmoved under a sunset, or have no emotion when treading beneath the starlit skies, or impiously laugh and chatter when our Maker is riding by in a chariot of storm? The world with all its natural scenery proclaims the glory of God. Let men reverence Him.

Again, this lesson of reverence is needed in regard to the Lord's name. "The Lord will not hold him guiltless who taketh his name in vain." That was one of the thunderbolts that shook Mt. Sinai. Its echoes have not yet died away. They are still rumbling. God's laws are never repealed. Mt. Sinai has not been leveled to the ground. But in spite of God's command, how many violate this moral precept that cannot be annulled! The Mohammedans destroy every piece of paper that they find in the streets or along the road, fearing that it may contain the name of God, and that name on it may be put to some base use. That is superstitious reverence. But thousands in Christian countries go to the other extreme, showing no reverence at all for the name of God. That name is profaned in the home, in the field, in the shop, in the office, in the court-room. Not only does profanity blister the lips of men and women and children, but it stains the pages of the newspaper,

the leaves of the magazine, and the chapters of the
novel. Often in literature the profanity is not made
glaring; but it is profanity nevertheless. A wolf is
a wolf, even when masked by sheep's clothing. As a
servant of the Most High God, I protest against the
ejaculation of such irreverent phrases as, "O God!"
and "My God!" and "Bless the Lord!" by characters
in stories who are shown to have no piety. When
God's name is used in any way whatsoever, with no
reverence in the speech or the writing, that holy name
is blasphemed. God cannot hold him guiltless who
sins against Him either with tongue or pen.

Again, this lesson of reverence is needed in regard
to the Lord's Sabbath. That lesson was never more
needed than in these boasted days of the twentieth
century. We may laugh at the unbending rigidity of
our Puritan fathers in reference to the keeping of the
Sabbath; but we cannot afford to laugh. Plymouth
Rock is a better foothold for the feet than the willowy
foundation of extreme liberalism. If they of New
England were wrong in their strict observance of the
Sabbath, we of the United States are more wrong in
our lax observance of the Sabbath. Their Sabbath
was rocked in the cradle of reverence toward God;
ours is being laid out in funeral robes in the coffin
of irreverence. Where is the Sabbath of former
days? For response, I hear the voice of the news-
boy hawking papers through the streets of our cities.
I hear the roar and rattle of excursion trains along
the railroads. I hear the tramp of moving throngs

on pleasure bent. I hear the whistle of steamboats on the rivers. I hear the splash of oars in the creeks and on the lakes. I hear the multiplied sounds that bring an ache to the heart and a pain to the soul, and extort from the lips a mournful cry, those lips saying, "God's holy day is forgotten!" And the bells that ring their invitations to deserted sanctuaries echo it—"Forgotten!" And breathing organs sigh it in minor key—"Forgotten!" And from faithful lips that voice the praise of the Lord issues a tone of sadness that intensifies the word, these trembling lips saying, "Forgotten!" But hark! I hear another sound. It drops from the heavens like an angel's song. It is both a command and an entreaty. It speaks with emphatic pathos. Hear it!—"Remember the Sabbath day to keep it holy!" Let all Christians see to it that they reverence the Lord's day. It is God's gift to the world. Like all of His gifts, it is charged and surcharged with blessing.

II. We are to note the humility of these six-winged seraphim of Isaiah's vision. "With twain he covered his feet." "That attitude was in token," says Albert Barnes, "of their nothingness and unworthiness in the presence of the Holy One." These bright seraphim veiled their feet with two of their wings to denote how far beneath God they were. It was the hiding of their lower extremities under the vision of their King. Seraphic modesty.

Now, if the brightest and noblest and most exalted of heaven's angels, privileged to be the cour-

tiers of the Lord God Almighty, are thus accustomed to an attitude of humility, what should be the
mind of man towards God? While in one sense this
world is the palace of God, in another sense it is
naught but His footstool. There are mightier worlds.
In fact, this world is one of the meanest and most insignificant of all worlds—a mere mote that swims in
the radiance of millions of suns. Compared with
God, what are the inhabitants of such a world? Isaiah says, "All nations before him are as nothing; and
they are counted to him less than nothing, and vanity." This same Isaiah, in one of his marvelous paragraphs, tries to give some idea of the greatness of
God. He speaks of God as measuring the waters in
the hollow of His hand. Just as you might hold a
few drops of water in the palm of your hand, so God
holds the Atlantic, the Pacific, the Mediterranean,
and all the other oceans and seas of the earth. Isaiah again speaks of God as weighing the mountains
in scales, and the hills in a balance. Just as a merchant weighs the goods in his store, so God takes up
the Alps, the Andes, and the Sierra Nevadas, accur-
ately estimating the number of their pounds avoir-
dupois. Isaiah still again speaks of God as sitting
upon the circle of the earth, before whom earth's inhabitants are as grasshoppers, and who spreads out
the blue heavens as a tent in which to dwell, stretching that azure canvas of the sky as easily as a boy
lifts up and outward a play tent for summer pastimes.
He is the Lord God Almighty. No wonder that the

angels around His throne hide their limbs and feet
beneath a veil of wings!

But that seraphic humility, alas! is often sadly
lacking in men. Often we do not fear to run in before God with thoughtless pride. Nadab and Abihu,
the sons of Aaron, offered strange fire before the
Lord, which He commanded them not to do, and they
were smitten by God's avenging glory—struck dead
for their want of humility. Uzzah touched the Ark
of God when it was in danger of falling, and for failing to recognize the infinite distance between him and
his Lord, God felled him to the earth in his tracks. It
is dangerous business to play with sacred things. How
does that passage read from one of the sermons of
Ecclesiastes? "Keep thy foot when thou goest to the
house of God, and be more ready to hear, than to give
the sacrifice of fools; for they consider not that they
do evil. Be not rash with thy mouth, and let not thy
heart be hasty to utter anything before God; for God
is in heaven, and thou upon earth."

"Keep thy foot when thou goest to the house of
God." Yes, Solomon, that is a reminder of humility
that is needed by all worshipers, not only in thy time,
but in all times. With two wings the seraphs covered
their feet before God. Who then are we that so often
engage in the services of the sanctuary in anything
but a reverentially humble spirit? God's house is no
place for merriment or idle gossip.

I remember hearing once a story of one being taken
in vision to a certain church on the Sabbath day. An

angel was his guide. The organist was vigorously
playing his instrument, but there was no sound from
the pipes. The choir and congregation were lustily
singing, but their voices were not heard. Then the
minister offered prayer, but though his lips moved,
no tones issued from them. The man in his dream
greatly wondered at what he saw, and asked the angel what it all meant. His guide answered, "You
hear nothing because there is nothing to hear. These
are not engaged in the worship of God at all, for
there is no heart in their worship. This is naught
but proud formality. God hears only that service
which honors Him. This silence is the silence that
is around God's ears when no humility is in the
hearts of those who sing and pray. But listen now!"
And listening, the man heard a child's treble voice
ringing out clear in the silence of the building, as the
minister seemed to pray and the people seemed to
join his petition, that child's voice saying, "Our
Father, who art in heaven; hallowed be thy name."
"That," said the angel, "is the only true worship in
this great temple to-day. Man looketh on the outward appearance, but God looketh on the heart.
The prayer of that child is rising to God's throne."

Would that the same angel, not in vision only, but
in reality, would open the eyes of all Christendom!
If we could all see ourselves as God sees us, there
would be many an unhallowed thought put away
while we are professedly worshiping the Lord in
His sanctuary. Then, like the seraphim of the text

covering their feet with two wings, we should wear the robes of reverential humility. What blasphemous attitudes are often assumed in the presence of God!

III. We are to note the swiftness of obedience characteristic of the seraphim of Isaiah's vision. "With twain he did fly." Not only reverent and abased before the Lord of glory, but instantly and with alacrity giving heed to His commands. "With twain he did fly."

This remarkable chapter blossoms with wings. I am as much impressed with these flying wings of that seraphic host as I am with the wings folded. What a rustling of wings when the King gives His orders! Mercury, the fabled messenger of the gods of Greece, was represented as having wings on his feet, those wings increasing his speed, as he rushed forth on errands for superior divinities. But Mercury would be a snail in comparison with a modern express train when placed beside one of these six-winged seraphim of Jehovah. The idea here is that these bright beings used all their wings for flight when they went forth from God's immediate presence, the twain with which they did fly, while before God, simply keeping them poised around Him, the other four wings covering face and lower extremities as they attended God's court. When told to go forth on some behest, six broad wings carried them like a lightning flash to distant worlds.

I believe that such is the right interpretation. Six wings for flight upon the errands of the Lord. Yes;

they come very swiftly in obedience to God. If our eyes could be opened, as were the eyes of Elisha's servant, we should see them. Angels in our homes. Angels in our business. Angels along our streets. Angels as we journey along the rail or over the waters. Angels crowding the air. The highways of the heavens on fire with angels. "Are they not all ministering spirits, sent forth to minister for them who shall be heirs of salvation?"

That is the only kind of spiritualism in which I believe—the triune God a spirit, and His angels spirits. If there are spirits that rap on tables, and open doors that are fastened, and ring bells, and perform other circus feats, they must be bad spirits. God sends His angels only upon errands of love and mercy. There are crosses laid on feeble shoulders; the angels of God lighten the weight. There are broken hearts; the angels of God bind up those hearts with divine surgery. There are tears of sorrow that write anguish upon the cheek; the angels of God breathe upon those tears and crystallize them into gems of joy. Wings! Wings! Wings! With twain they fly around the throne of God, these angels, two wings covering the face, two wings covering the feet; but with six wings they hasten to Christian souls in trouble.

Let there be a like promptness of obedience on our part in the service of God. You and I lack wings, but that is no excuse for listlessness or inactivity. We need to put more swiftness into our feet in working for the Lord. There are many feet so laggard that they seldom get to the sanctuary on the Sabbath, and never reach the prayer-meeting at all. Those same feet are quick enough along the street for business or pleasure. One is tempted to look at such feet, closely examining them, to see if they have Mercury's little wings fastened to them, so quickly do they move in selfish interests. But for the culture of the soul those same feet seem to be dead. For the service of God they seem to be loaded with iron.

But who is this I see? A Stranger is walking up yonder aisle. There are sandals on His feet; but beneath the leather thongs that bind those sandals fast I see on each foot a scar. Bow in His presence! It is He of Calvary. He speaks! Listen! "With these feet I walked for you into humiliation and poverty and death. What are you doing for Me?"

Let us go to our homes, bearing in mind the fact that Christ has been with us in the sanctuary, not in imagination only, but in the fact. Wherever His disciples are, there He is. And let the question that He asked of both you and me nestle in our hearts, that question being the inspiration of our feet, our hands, our eyes and ears, and our lips. Hear it again, that plaintive question from Him who died for us! "What are you doing for Me?" Ye six-winged seraphim hovering over this scene, fly swiftly back to the throne of the glorified Christ with the news of our consecration! "The Lord our God will we serve, and His voice will we obey."

Words Fitly Spoken

A word fitly spoken is like apples of gold in pictures of silver. Prov. 25: 11.

DIFFERENT commentators give different interpretations of this flashing simile from Solomon's pen. Some think that the apples here referred to are real fruit, a rich yellow in color, and showing their beauty of hue upon plates with a network of silver around the rim. Others think that the royal author was making his poetic simile from embroideries of golden fruit wrought into a background of silvery material, those embroideries hung upon the walls of a palace for purposes of adornment, and thus appearing as pictures. But we need not stop to inquire further into the matter. Solomon's kingly pen has long since been laid aside and gone into dust, and he himself, as a being of earth, is no more. Not being able to interview him, we shall have to remain in doubt as to the real meaning of the comparison here used. But whatever is meant by it, this one thing is certain, that Solomon intended to set forth the possibilities of well chosen words. The literal translation of the Hebrew phrase, "A word fitly spoken," is, "A word spoken on its wheels." The American Revised Version gives it in the margin, "A word spoken in due season." That brings in the thought of opportunity and appropriateness in regard to words. So does the English Revision render it in the same way, but making the simile read, "Like apples of gold in baskets of silver," while the American Revision says, "Like apples of gold in network of silver." But as all versions agree in reference to the kind of words described, and do not materially disagree in their translation of the simile, I shall treat the text as it stands in all three of the versions. In whatever way rendered, it is one of Solomon's gems, and its scintillations awaken in my mind a multitude of thoughts.

I. A thought about the beauty of words. It is probable that Solomon had that same thought in mind. A word fitly spoken is suggestive of such beauty as is seen in a collection of fruit served in baskets of silver, or fruits showing their mellowness upon the table in platters that have a network of silver around their edges; and whether in baskets or plates, those fruits making pictures that please the eye. Solomon's phrase is itself a choice word-picture.

What is more beautiful than ripe fruit? Beautiful the cherries that blush against the embracing hands of the leaves in the month of June! Beautiful the pears that hang like ear-rings from the orchards in autumn! Beautiful the apples that glow like embers from the setting sun amid the radiance of October's fading foliage! All ripe fruits are like fruits of gold in pictures of silver. I do not know which I admire the most, God's paintings of rainbows in ebony frame of storm, God's paintings of clouds in frame of blue sky or frame of sunrise, God's paintings of forests in frame of emerald or frame of fire, God's paintings of light in frame of ocean, or God's paintings of fruit in frame of boughs and leaves. All are beautiful.

You will notice that the point of the text is in regard to words fitly spoken, not simply words in general. There are many words that are not beautiful. Lord Byron wrote some poems whose words have in them much of beauty; he wrote many more whose words are lepers hidden beneath an embroidered mantle of rhetoric. So wrote Robert Burns. So wrote Thomas Moore. So wrote Shakespeare. So have written others among the world's masters of expression. But it is only words fitly spoken, whether by voice or pen, that can lay any claim to beauty.

Among the words that are not beautiful I would place all those words that throw discredit upon the inspiration of the Scriptures. Be on your guard against all such words. They crawl like sneaking serpents over the columns of the daily newspaper, over the pages of the monthly periodicals, over the chapters of the popular novel. Hardly a week passes that I do not catch the gleam of their wicked eyes and hear the hiss of their poisonous throats. The inspiration of the Scriptures is not a mere dogma of theology, but God's truth. That doctrine is the very foundation of the Christian faith. Whatever weakens it tends to destroy it altogether. Once let doubts enter the mind as to the historic authenticity of Biblical events and persons, and it will not be a great while before the whole brain will be tramped with murderous feet. If Adam and Eve were only mythical beings, if Abraham was a fictitious character, if Jonah never existed, except in the fancy of the one who wrote of him, then what warrant have we for believing in the reality of any of the names given in the Scriptures? The scholarship that uses its battering ram of words to make a single breach in the walls of Inspiration will not hesitate to lay every stone of the structure in ruins, going on with its destructive criticism until it has leveled the Cross of Christ to the ground and rocked the very throne of God into the dust. Talk about anarchy! I do not know which anarchy is the worse, the anarchy that throws bombs at kings and shoots presidents, or the anarchy that seeks the overthrow of God's Holy Word. Yes! I have it. This last named anarchy is the worse. There may be new rulers to take the place of those set aside; but the death of the Scriptures would make a funeral of hopeless sorrow. Whenever in your reading or hearing you come upon words that speak disparagingly of the Bible, even if they be words that wear crowns of gold and robes of purple, regard them as ugly words, misshapen words, hypocritical words, all beautiful without, but within full of rottenness. Instead of being "like apples of gold in pictures of silver," they are like toadstools growing from the decayed stump of a fallen tree.

Also among words that are not beautiful I would place all those words that are caricatures of good language. These are profane words, filthy words, slang words. One may not be sufficiently educated to speak with grammatical exactness every time he gives expression to a thought, but there is no excuse whatever for using words that are bad. It is possible always to speak well chosen words. John Bunyan was not a man who had been trained in the schools of his day, yet he wrote a book that has been the admiration of scholars ever since his pen gave it birth in Bedford jail more than two centuries ago. Thomas Macaulay, the English historian accorded it the very highest praise. Its words are nearly all Anglo-Saxon words, many of them words of one syllable, the whole book a powerful argument for beautiful speech, words fitly spoken, "like apples of gold in pictures of silver," without the aid of a liberal education. While there are hosts of words in our language that have upon them no taint or odor of corruption, why should one load his speech with words that are an insult to his mother tongue? Yet there are hundreds of persons in every community who seldom open their mouths without giving voice to some kind of abuse of language, either that of profanity or that of slang. They need to make David's prayer, "Set a watch, O Lord, before my mouth; keep the door of my lips." They need to practice Paul's injunction, "Let your speech be alway with grace, seasoned with salt." They need to tremble at

Christ's statement, "I say unto you that for every idle word that men shall speak, they shall give account thereof in the day of judgment. For by thy words thou shalt be justified, and by thy words thou shalt be condemned."

II. A thought about the music of words. I speak not now of the rhythm of poetry, nor of the measured tread of an orator's words, as they march in stately ranks across the field of his speech, words on parade, with flying banners and beating drums and blowing trumpets; nor of the words that flow like a brook through the flowery pages of some George Eliot, or Charles Dickens, or Nathaniel Hawthorne; nor of words sounded from the golden cornet of such princely essayists as Thomas Macaulay, or Ralph Waldo Emerson, or John Ruskin. If you wish to learn the music of words, you can do no better than to listen day and night to the canaries that sing in the cage of the Bible. This grand old Book is itself the very richest of music. But I am not now thinking of words that breathe with the graces of rhetoric. Of what then do I speak? Why, of words uttered in every-day life—words common; words simple; words with their working clothes on; yet words that are as musical as a bar of melody in the score of a Mozart, or a John Sebastian Bach; words fitly spoken, and that are "like apples of gold in pictures of silver."

Among such words I place the words of thanksgiving in prayer. These are words fitly spoken, and they rise to God's ears with all the sweetness of an angel's song. Thankful words for the ordinary blessings of life; for home and dear ones; for raiment and food; for vision and hearing; for mental faculties unimpaired and use of limbs; for life itself. We all know the harmony struck out of words of gratitude following the bestowal of a gift. The very nerves vibrate in unison with such words. Is God different from us? Think you that He carries a heart of stone within His breast? If it gives us pleasure to hear the music of thankfulness, such pleasure also belongs to Him. We are each a miniature of God. His image is impressed upon our souls. The question is, Are we all accustomed to thankfulness for the gifts of God? It is comparatively easy to take part in some grand anthem of thanksgiving, when there are many voices, and when the theme of the choral is the large mercies of God. But I am speaking now of secret solos in the silence of one's closet or heart, the individual soul lifting music words to the ears of God for those things that come every day, and of which thousands of minds never stop to think. These are the words that I term melodious. These are the words that are fitly spoken, and that are "like apples of gold in pictures of silver."

Also among such words I place words of sympathy with those who are in trouble. This is a world of trouble. The skies that bend over us are not always blue, but often storm-tramped. The paths we tread are not always smooth and easy, but often rough with stones that cut the feet. The seas we sail are not always sun-glinted, but often shadowed. The cups we drink are not always sweet, but often bitter. We need often to hear the music of sympathy breaking harmoniously upon our hearing. Those around us have the same need. Then it is that Love sweeps her harp with the most thrilling melodies. Then it is that words fitly spoken are words on wheels, coming swiftly and surely to their destination. Then it is that appropriate words are "like apples of gold in pictures of silver." Let no Christian heart seal itself against the tuneful chords of such words, refusing to sound them.

Among words that are not musical I would place angry words. The common ground for letting loose such words is in the home circle. There are men who in their business relations are the most urbane of men, but who under their own roof-tree are like a locomotive whistle in their tone of voice. The same kind of utterance elsewhere would bring the blow of a fist upon their face every hour of the day. There are women who are abroad the very soul of sweetness, but who around their own fireside speak like exploding torpedoes, the parlor, the dining-room, the kitchen the scene of a perpetual Fourth of July. But why should music words be reserved for strangers, and the ears of dear ones and servants be hammered with dissonant words? Let the tunefulness of speech be everywhere sounded. But let the richest notes of the tongue be heard among those who are closest to us in life and service.

There were two sisters in a fable. One was gentle of speech; the other spoke as if her tongue was a file. A fairy gave to each of them a gift appropriate to the habits of utterance of each. One girl thereafter, whenever she spoke, dropped pearls and diamonds from her lips; her sister let fall toads and serpents.

What this world needs is more jewel-words. Let reptilian words sneak their way back to the perdition from which they came. Says Paul in the only sonnet he ever wrote, "Though I speak with the tongues of men and of angels, but have not love, I am become sounding brass, or a clanging cymbal."

III. A thought about the power of words. What are words? It depends upon the words themselves. Words spoken by a Demosthenes can call a nation to arms. Words spoken by a Gladstone can influence a parliament. Words spoken by a Wendell Phillips, or a Henry Grady can thrill a continent. Words fitly spoken are the lightning flashes of great minds— thunderbolts. Moses once spoke, and filled the centuries with echoes. David spoke, and caught the ears of an audience of many generations. Paul spoke, and his words were embalmed in theologies. Luther spoke, and shook all Europe out of ecclesiastic bondage. John Knox spoke, and made a government tremble. The Wesleys spoke, and George Whitfield, and Jonathan Edwards, and Finney, and Moody, and swayed multitudes with revivals of religion. What are words? They are thought on the wing; thought on swift errands; thought linked with Omnipotence. A breath expresses them; a dash of the pen gives them being on paper; but simple as they are, they are akin to divinity—the sparks of Wisdom supreme.

What are words when God utters them? Words upon His lips spoke worlds into existence. Words from His lips created light. Words from His lips, as He walked incarnate among men, unstopped deaf ears, straightened crooked limbs, hushed storms on the sea, and, rocked graves as though they were shaken by an earthquake. Words from His lips shall yet halt the march of time, roll back the heavens as a curtain, and summon a world's inhabitants of every age of history to judgment, those same lips afterward speaking words that shall enwrap the earth in conflagration—Europe on fire; Asia on fire; Africa on fire; America on fire—those wide-spreading flames the winding sheet of a dead globe of sin, from which death is to rise in resurrection a new earth in which dwelleth righteousness.

Oh, the power of words fitly spoken! Words may be misused, as when a Thomas Paine writes his "Age of Reason"; as when a Hume sneers at Christianity; as when a Voltaire derides Jesus of Nazareth; as when a Robert Ingersoll makes the Bible a subject of jest and flings the coarseness of his wit into the very face of God. But when they are rightly used words are imperial. They are packed with dynamite.

Some say that they have no learning or eloquence, and that they are thereby excused from the use of

powerful words. It was a few words fitly spoken by
a plain man that turned John B. Gough from drunkenness to sobriety. The echoes of those words were
afterwards heard on the platform of hundreds of lec-
ture halls in sublime oratory for the cause of temperance. It was a few words fitly spoken by another plain man that inclined the heart of Dwight L.
Moody to God. How those same words, not many
years following, reverberated in Great Britain and
the United States! It was a few words fitly spoken
by still another plain man, a warm-hearted, evangelist, that made T. DeWitt Talmage a preacher of
the Gospel, by means of the press millions of people
his audience every week through a long period of
time.

Say not that you have no force of words. Use
whatever words you have, words of voice or pen, that
voice and that pen consecrated to the service of
Christ, and the Holy Spirit will give them power.
Let them be such words as Solomon describes in the
text, words "on wheels," words "fitly spoken," words
"in due season," and they shall be "like apples of gold
in pictures of silver."

IV. But I come now to speak, in the last place, of
the greatest of all words. This thought I have reserved as the climax of my sermon. Whatever else
you may forget of what I have thus far said, I pray
you to give your earnest attention now, so as to be
able to recall this final thought.

Words are the dress of thought. That dress may

be slovenly or elegant, but it is what thought wears upon its emergence from the cells of the brain. Turn now to the first chapter and first verse of John's Gospel, and you will learn of this greatest of all words. Listen! "In the beginning was the Word, and the Word was with God, and the Word was God."

Here is a thought out of the mind of the Almighty. Jesus Christ was the manifestation of God. He came speaking God's love for a ruined world. Yea, He was God Himself who could no longer keep His thoughts from mankind, but who must needs clothe Himself in human flesh and reveal His very heart. There were tokens of His love in the past ages; but His coming into the world was the embodiment of His love. He is the Word that has filled this old earth with more beauty and more music and more power than were ever in it before. His birth under angelic minstrelsy and stellar magnificence, His toil in the Nazareth carpenter shop, His life of poverty and persecution, His blood-sweating agony in the garden, His arrest and false trials, His painful journey to Calvary, His uplifted Cross, with its shame, with its cruel nails, with its crown of thorns, with its last heart-breaking cry, were all one word, and that word Love. And that Word is yet to conquer all nations.

The practical question remains, Do you know Christ? Have you gone to school and learned this Word? If not, then let the Holy Spirit be your

Teacher. Frame this Word within your soul, and you will find Him to be a word fitly spoken, indeed, and more glorious than any fruit that ever glowed in any baskets of silver, even though those fruits were plucked by angel hands from the gardens of heaven, and those flashing baskets were wrought into beauty by silversmiths celestial. "He is the chiefest among ten thousand."

> "Sweetest note in seraph song,
> Sweetest name on mortal tongue,
> Sweetest carol ever sung,
> Jesus, blessed Jesus."

Do not Fret

Fret not thyself. Psalms 37 : 1.

On dark mental days, when in need of good cheer, I am apt to turn my heart into the sunshine of the Book of Psalms. Like the ancient forests that stored many a ray of light for the farther centuries of time, the pick of the miner now releasing those treasured beams for the dwellings of men, the Psalms are the experience of God's children of ages ago lending radiance to the children of God in this era of the world's history. They are the accumulated sparks of comfort that grieving souls may uncover and kindle into flame, sitting in their glow and warmth.

To my mind, this Thirty-seventh Psalm is a masterpiece of blessedness. It ought to be written in letters of gold and hung upon the wall of every home in Christendom. A most eloquent orator is it of faith. Changing the figure, it is a whole orchestra of trust in God, opening with soft melody, rising into bolder notes, and closing with a grand burst of music.

Listen to the first strain of this inspired symphony! "Fret not thyself." I take that breathing of harmony as my text this morning.

Does any one say that this is a message only for a day long since faded into the night of oblivion? That is not true. Just as pertinent is this message

now as if it had this moment fallen upon your ears
from the lips of an angel out of heaven. There is no
mouldy bread in the pantry of the Bible.

I. I apply the words of the text to those who make
their life discordant through trifling annoyances.
"Fret not thyself." That means do not give way to
thoughts that tease, that irritate, that vex, that make
anger boil within the heart. Do you ever study
words? Here is a most interesting word to study.
I have often found pictures in words as delightful as
any that ever flamed out before my vision from a
fire on the hearth. A dictionary has more etchings
and pastels and engravings and paintings within its
covers than hang upon the walls of the finest palaces
of art. This word "fret" is a veritable panorama.
Look at it as defined by Noah Webster! It signifies
"to rub; to eat away; to wear away by friction; to
corrode; to chafe." Varying definitions, but all of
them conveying the same idea; when applied to men
and women picturing a soul thrown out of its normal
condition, and exhausting itself and killing itself
with unnatural excitement. The Hebrew word here
translated "fret" means to heat, portraying a mind
inflamed with impatience.

Well, that is exactly what thousands of persons are
doing. They are burning themselves into worthless-
ness, and burning themselves to death, their fretfulness called into being by circumstances that do not
warrant the least expenditure of energy. How much
force is wasted in that way! If half of the power

that is thus squandered upon useless things were applied to righteousness, this world would soon be rolled into the Millennium.

Did you ever scan the faces that you daily meet? Upon many of them is fretfulness written in unmistakable lines. That word is as deeply cut into them as though a chisel had left it in enduring stone.

I do not refer to the faces along which real sorrow has traced its autograph. There are many such faces. But these have been sculptured into beauty. A charming grace is upon them that arrests the attention and impresses itself upon the memory. Some of the most radiant faces I have ever seen have been those of God's aged saints who have passed through hundreds of troubles, those faces framed with white hair. Sanctified sorrow leaves no disfiguring marks on cheek or brow. It lights up the face with the shining of heaven.

The faces I mean are those faces that have been grooved and puckered and wrinkled into a scowl by constant fretting. Such faces are common sights.

Many of our drug stores and department stores have their counters loaded with various lotions for the preservation of female facial loveliness. But the very best preservative of beauty for both women and men of which I know is the avoidance of fretfulness. Make constant use of this prescription given by the Psalmist, and it will keep any face from growing ugly. Apply this divine ointment when you go to bed at night, apply it when you rise in the morning, continue the application throughout the day. Thus applied, it will keep you as young in soul features and as fresh of countenance as though the whole of life were the month of May, with no hint in it of December or January.

Fretfulness is a malady that frequently requires heroic measures for its elimination from the soul. Many persons fall into the habit of worrying over little things, that habit developing a typhoid fever of anxiety. My advice to all such is, Beware of placing yourselves in favorable condition for becoming thus terribly afflicted with consuming fretfulness. Once let that poison run riot through the blood of the soul, and you will need the strongest kind of divine medicament before you can recover your spiritual health.

This fretfulness over trifles of which I speak is a very common soul disorder. Ministers fret about little matters in their parishes—you see I am firing a gun that kicks! Merchants fret about little matters in their stores. Mechanics fret about little matters in their shops. Housewives fret about little matters in their homes. Fretfulness blazes in every form of human life. But what is the use of it? If fretting did any good, it would be well to fret. On the contrary, it does mischief. Therefore it is wrong to fret. To all fretful persons Paul's advice to the Philippian jailor is most appropriate—"Do thyself no harm." Fretfulness is slow suicide.

I know that we all have our crooked days—days

when nothing seems to be straight; days when every-thing appears to be awry and out of joint; days when the chimney will not draw and the oven will not bake; days when customers before the counter are like porcupines with outspread quills; days when the sermon does not flow freely from the pen; days when the very air seems to be loaded with disagreeableness. On such days one's regular duties, usually light and pleasant, are dull and irksome. If you are a man, you go through such a day as one with a body full of sores, and all the passing moments are fingers dip-ped in vinegar, those fingers touching your rawness with their acid impressions. If you are a woman, the broom that you handle has the weight of a crow-bar. Your pie-crust gets the shortening into it the wrong way. The apple-dumplings turn out like balls of lead. The bread sours. Your servant moves among her tasks like a caterpillar afflicted with rheu-matism. It is one of your crooked days. But do not fret. If you do, you will open yourself to the habit of fretting. Then the least thing will tend to annoy you, each day adding to the discord set up within your soul, and making all the rest of life out of tune. Beware of chronic fretfulness.

I am well aware that these thoughts were not in the Psalmist's mind when he wrote the text. But that does not make fretting over trifling matters ex-cusable. What I am preaching is a religion that places its helping hand upon the common things of life. Therefore, "fret not thyself." Better is it to

14

take one's cares to the Lord, for He careth for you. I once heard of a woman who was thrown into momentary trouble by the thought of having to entertain guests at an inopportune time. She prayed for strength. That was the right thing to do. What is religion worth, if it is not an iron with which to smooth out the wrinkles of a crooked day?

II. I apply the words of the text to those who call into question the operation of God's providences in the world. This is a form of fretfulness that takes on a deeper tone than the one I have dwelt upon. The fact is that we all wear spectacles. Some persons look at life from a financial standpoint; these wear spectacles of silver and gold. Other persons look at life from the side of distrust in their fellow-men; these wear cynical spectacles. Still other persons look at life with the vision of a sunrise before their eyes; these wear optimistic spectacles. Others, again, look at life in the dark; these wear spectacles that magnify the surrounding gloom and fill the soul with the morbidness of pessimism. These last named optical instruments are the worst spectacles that any man or woman ever places astride the nose.

It is to such a class of people that David here addresses himself. One of the prominent causes for railing at God's providences is the prosperity of the wicked. That was true in David's day; it is true in our day. In fact, it has been true of every age. I suppose that the same discordant tone will be sounded from human lips clear down to the first note of the final trump. The prosperity of the wicked is an enigma that many have tried to solve, fretting at their inability to make it clear.

I show you two pictures. Picture the first: The home of a godly man. Every-day is heard beneath that roof the voice of prayer. Among the small collection of books within those walls the Bible holds the chiefest place. The home itself is comfortable, but humble. There is an entire absence of luxuries. The head of the household is in very moderate circumstances. Measured by the wealth of those who count their riches with six ciphers after the first figure of the enumeration, he would be pronounced poor. Yet he is a square man, an honest man, an upright man.

Picture the second: A mansion of imposing architecture, that handsome edifice surrounded by a park. Carpets of the finest weaving abloom on its floors. Masterpieces of painting aglow upon its walls. White statuary gracing its halls. Cut glass and polished silver flashing upon the sideboards of the dining-room. The softest down within its bed-chambers. Curtains draped and festooned at its windows that are like woven frost. Everything that heart could wish within that palatial home. But the man who lives there made his money by fraud. He is a polite rascal, a veneered thief, a leper in broadcloth. There is not an honest penny in his purse, nor an unsoiled bill in his wallet, nor an honest bond in his bank vault.

These are not fancy sketches. They are found in

real life. Looking upon these living pictures, many persons heat themselves into doubts of the goodness of God, those doubts kindled by comparing the lot of many a righteous man with the lot of many a wicked man. Their thought is that the providences of God are not perfectly adjusted. Then their conclusion is that piety has but poor show in this world.

But who is fully competent to pass judgment upon such cases? It is this very thing against which David here warns. He says, "Fret not thyself because of evil doers, neither be thou envious against the workers of iniquity."

The Psalmist has also drawn some pictures. Look at them! In one picture a wicked man is in great power; and he spreads himself like a green bay tree; but soon that picture fades completely away, vanishing under the withering breath of divine justice. On the other hand, the perfect, or well rounded man, ends his days in peace, the picture remaining and growing brighter. One picture closes with darkness; the other has its shadows chased off by the dawn of everlasting day.

Like a breath from woods of pine into lungs long filled with foul air, David here inspires patience in those who question God's permission of iniquitous prosperity. The time of blooming for the wicked is short. "For they shall soon be cut down like the grass, and wither as the green herb." Therefore, no reason can any child of God have for being mentally disturbed by the prosperity of evil men. "Fret not thyself" because of them. Leave everything in God's hands. In due season the scythe of judgment will sweep the fields of sin.

But let no one make the mistake of supposing that righteousness is always down and unrighteousness always up. That is a false supposition. Religion is not a taskmaster; it is sin that flourishes a whip. Religion does not put handcuffs upon the wrists and chains around the ankles; it is sin that enslaves. Religion does not blow out the lights of happiness from the soul; it is sin that creates gloom. Because here and there we see a wicked man apparently enjoying life, drinking sweetness from a cup of gold, eating pleasant fruits from a platter of silver, and wearing the finest raiment, we are not to infer that it pays to serve the devil. "The wages of sin is death." Do not study logic from the textbooks of hell. Too many do that. Take full views of truth.

A frog leaps out upon a piece of rotten board to sun himself, and because he sees nothing but swamp around him, he reasons that the whole world is a swamp, and built expressly for frogs. But the frog's vision is narrow and circumscribed. It is well for us to climb high and view the whole landscape of a religious life. Over that life play the sunbeams of Paul's inspired statement—"Godliness is profitable unto all things, having promise of the life that now is, and of that which is to come." Therefore, "fret not thyself."

You and I are not to worry ourselves about any

of God's providences. When there comes something into the life that you cannot understand, do with it what you do with bones when you are eating fish. Too many persons choke themselves with seeming mysteries. Let what you cannot understand go. There is no use trying to masticate every hard thing that presents itself to the teeth. Instead of fretting about losses and disappointments and graves, try the effect of trusting in the wisdom and goodness of God.

Some persons throw themselves into a fever of anxiety over so-called providences that they have themselves brought about. They wonder, for example, why they are often sick, when if they would pay more attention to the laws of health, they could avoid frequent illness. We often blame God for what we ought to blame no one but ourselves. If one eats unwholesome food, he must expect to have an attack of indigestion. The only connection that God has with such an attack is that He has ordained suffering to follow a violation of the simple rules of living. If one sleeps in a room with the windows closed down tight, shutting out every breath of circulating air, why should he hold Providence responsible for poisoned lungs? If one sits down upon a cake of ice, why should he murmur at Providence for giving him pneumonia? Many a casket has been carried out to the graveyard and lowered into an ugly hole that might have been delayed perhaps for a few years, if there had been the exercise of good sense for preserving the life.

I· say these things for two reasons; because I like to get away from the beaten paths of sermonizing; and because I wish you to think of things that are not commonly considered. Instead of fretting ourselves over what we could probably avoid, if we·were to try, let us do the best we can, and do that in reliance upon God's help. Old Putnam's advice to/his soldiers in the Revolutionary War was the very richest philosophy. He said to his men, "Trust in God, and keep your powder dry!" Faith and works can never be successfully divorced.

III. I apply the words of the text to those who fail to look on to the ultimate triumph of God's purposes. I like the optimism of this Psalm. Its prevailing tone is that of a bugle. You never hear any dirges in David's Psalms. Though now and then you listen to a note pitched in a minor key, it is soon changed into more stirring harmony. So with all the Bible. The Scriptures open the windows of the soul towards the sunrise. The Word of God is full of hope and cheer from lid to lid. It is so filled because it *is* the Word of God. This fact, to my mind, is a strong proof of the inspiration of the Bible. If men had written this book without divine help, it would have been written with a pen of iron; the Holy Spirit breathing upon those who traced its paragraphs, it has been written with pens of gold, the points of those pens flashing with the glory of God.

"Fret not thyself." You and I, of course, are to be concerned for the redemption of the world. The text does not teach that we should sit down in idleness, simply expecting that all wrongs will eventually be righted. God and we are in partnership. But we are not to chafe ourselves because the world is not redeemed in a day. Too many are doing that very thing, failing to look on to the victory that is surely awaiting the vision. This world, long under the tyranny of sin, is to be gloriously emancipated. That is an inspiration to earnest fighting.

God often seems to move slowly in the execution of His plans, but He moves surely, nevertheless. Men are sometimes impatient. They are like a boy at school pushing on the hands of his watch to bring a coming holiday. But he does not bring it. The great sun in the heavens beyond keeps on its appointed way, measuring time as it has been accustomed to measure it. We cannot hasten God. It is for us to wait on Him, working while we wait. It is useless to fret.

At the World's Fair in St. Louis I saw an immense clock. Its large hands mark the minutes and the hours over a dial of variegated plants. I afterwards thought of that floral clock as an emblem of God's decrees. Although its dial is three hundred feet in circumference and one hundred feet in diameter, it perfectly shows the time of day. Its slow-moving indicators are cumbrous in form compared with those that travel around the face of a lady's chatelaine watch; but they march majestically on over a blooming field of numerals, and reach every hour of the day with undeviating precision, each hour and half hour announced by a bell weighing five thousand pounds, the heavy tones of that bell sounding for miles.

Far greater is the clock of God's decrees. It is vast beyond comprehension. The sweep of its hands is over the circle of eternity. You and I catch only a glimpse of those hands as they pause at the little points of our lives. With God centuries and millenniums are but single pulse-beats of being. With Him human time itself, though it should be extended to untold ages, is no more than a spider's web floating out from one small section of the arc of everlastingness. But the stupendous hands on that clock of decrees are steadily climbing on to the hour that is yet to strike the moment of heaven's daybreak upon the night of the world's sin and shame. When that hour peals forth its sonorous strokes, wickedness will flee, and hide itself in unending darkness. Therefore, O child of God, whoever thou art, "fret not thyself."

The Serpent's Subtlety

The serpent was more subtle than any beast of the field.
Genesis 3: 1.

IN the beginning God made a beautiful world and gave it a beautiful king and queen. That king and queen were created in the image of the King of kings and Lord of lords. This royal pair lived in a garden palace. Everything pleasing to the eye. Everything pleasing to the ear. Everything pleasing to the taste. No intense heat to smite the head. No chilling blasts to send a shiver through the frame. No driving storms to lay waste the trees. By day the skies blue and the air shining with sunbeams; by night the same skies aglow with dazzling brilliance and that same air agleam with flashes of silver darting through its shadows. No sickness; no pain; no death. Sorrow unknown. The subjects of these jointly-reigning monarchs were the birds that fly above the earth, the fish that swim in the waters, the harmless insects that flutter on diamond-dusted wings among the flowers, and all the animals of various names, the lions, and tigers, and wolves, and hyenas that now roam the forests and jungles and wooded hills wild and ferocious, then tame and gentle, often coming up to lick the hands of the ones who ruled them in love. As made by the Almighty, that world was not far from heaven. Angels walked it in companionship with those who were its king and queen. God Himself pressed its paths with His glorious feet. That first man and woman were given a fair start, and there was before them the prospect of unending happiness. They were like a ship launched upon a smooth sea and with favoring winds filling the sails.

But one day that garden palace was entered by a foe, his feet black with the smut of perdition. A serpent, naturally wise and cunning, was used by Satan as a tool of temptation. With its fangs it injected the poison of unbelief into the minds of that king and queen. It was their first step along a road that was alive with serpents. Sin uncrowned them. Avenging Justice banished them. They went forth from their first blessed home into a wilderness world.

I once had a strange dream. In boyhood days I had read in the "Arabian Nights' Entertainments" a story of a fisherman who one day drew up from the sea upon his hook a heavy vase of copper. He broke the seal of the vessel, supposing that it contained something of great value, perhaps gold or silver, perhaps diamonds, perhaps pearls. But when he had thus broken the seal, there issued from the vase a thick smoke, that smoke afterwards solidifying and taking on the shape of a gigantic genie, the monster threatening to kill the fisherman for giving him liberty. With that tale impressed upon my mind, I dreamed one night that I opened a vase out in a field. From that opened vase rose a wreath of black vapor, curling and twisting and writhing in air like a serpent, and then mounting to the skies. Up there it spread itself, and became a funnel-shaped cloud that swooped down and then went sweeping over the land as an agent of terrible destruction. I had let loose from that vase an imprisoned tornado!

Something like this was the result of the serpent's temptation in Paradise. From that first act of sin followed all the sins that have since cursed the world for six thousand years or more. The world that once swung near heaven, now swings near hell. The history of mankind is the trail of a serpent.

I imagine that when Satan had accomplished his diabolical purpose of ruin, he lifted his grimy wings, and sped quickly back to his den of darkness, there summoning a conference of his fallen companions. Seating himself upon his throne of fire, he exclaimed, "Hear me, ye fellow-outcasts from the brightness of God's face! I have marred Heaven's new work of creation. In yonder world there is a palace of beauty destroyed. It is the work of these hands of mine in obedience to the thought of my subtle brain. Those who lived in that palace are now in disgrace, exiles forever from all that once was theirs to enjoy. They have sinned through a brilliant temptation from my wicked tongue. Made in the image of God, they have lost their beauty of soul. Behold the one who defeated the purpose of Him who turned us into this vile abode! How sweet is this revenge! Join me at this hour in tasting that sweetness!"

Then I hear the rustling of thousands of wings, like the sound of a tempest blowing from the sea, and from thousands of burning lips I hear hoarse huzzas. like the breaking of storm-lashed waves upon a rocky coast. It is the applause of hell over the broken sceptre and tarnished crown and demolished throne of the world's first king and queen.

"Order!" cries Satan. "Hear me again! The work is not yet complete. You and I must poison man and woman with other temptations. There is a possibility that they may recover from their fall. They may regain what they have lost. I heard the Lord who created them speak of One who should bruise the serpent's head. It is for us now to prevent them from returning to their original state. Let the ruins of their palace remain forever. We must make devils like ourselves of this sinful pair. Listen to me, as I unfold my plans!"

Then, in my fancy, I see the arch-fiend rise to his feet. His throne of fire behind his erect form flames forth with a more sullen brightness. His wicked face takes on a more wicked look. His audience of lost spirits gives silent attention. Satan continues:

"This man and woman are to be the father and mother of uncounted hosts of descendants. Through all the centuries of time these populations of the earth are to be taught every evil thing that my infernal brain can invent. I promised that man and woman that they should be gods. By all the iniquity of my depraved heart, I will keep my promise. My purpose is to fill the world with violence and blood-shed. You are to help me. So soon as children are born to that fallen pair, let one of you go to the child whom you think to be a likely subject, carrying in your hand from these flames of hell an ember of jealousy. Place that ember in that one's heart; then with your foul breath blow it, until it snaps and sparkles and leaps up into a blaze. Then stand off and watch the effect of your work. Why, I already see it! Behold, devils, the first murder! See that brother lying along the ground slain by a brother!"

There is deep silence for a moment, broken finally by another round of applause. Then one in that auditory of fiends drowns the applause with stentorian voice, shouting, "Long live Apollyon!" That cry is taken up by multiplied flaming lips, and the sound of it echoes and reechoes among the deepest caverns of hell. It roars like an earthquake.

"Listen!" exclaims the speaker. "Do not think that my imagination is carrying me away from my-self, but I see yet more. Yonder outstretched form is bleeding from the blow that fell upon it. I see that blood flowing out over the ground. It writhes. Be-hold, it is a red serpent! I see it creeping on. I fol-low its trail. It is joined by other serpents. Lo, there is a great multiplication of serpents! Men are beginning to murder each other by wholesale. They call that wholesale murder war. Families fight against each other. Tribes fight against each other. Nations fight against each other. Inspired by me, ingenious minds invent many instruments for spilling blood. They war against each other with bows and arrows. By and by they tip their arrows with poison. They war against each other with swords and spears. They war against each other with guns and cannon. I hear the tramp of great armies. I see those armies marching on. Their banners fly in gorgeous colors in the winds. Their helmets sparkle in the sunlight. Their uniforms flash. Men achieve fame on the fields of battle. The most distinguished men are those who have slain the largest number of their fellow-men. Their names are written large in history. Then I see fleets of armored vessels riding the waves of the seas. Those vessels are floating volcanoes. Day and night men plan and think, seeking to make ships more destructive. Chemistry teaches them the art of forming new explosives for the hurling of the thunderbolts of war. By mechanical skill they devise more powerful engines of warfare. Cities are thrown down. Strong fortifications are toppled into the dust. The very bed of the lakes and oceans is laid with hidden hells of death. All around its mighty circumference the world is stained with blood! Stained with blood! That blood the outcome of envy, and pride, and greed, and ambition."

In my fancy I hear the applause that again greets the speech of Satan, and I hear thousands of cries that say, "Let us go up to earth and begin this direful work!"

Then Satan responds, "Not yet. I have not done. Hear me further in the unfolding of my plans. Men's hearts are to be filled with hatred of God, with jealousy, with selfishness, with murder, with lust, and with every form of wickedness. Their hearts are to become fountains of iniquity, spitting forth rottenness. But I have yet to name one thing that shall shadow, and curse, and blast, and destroy the world. This one thing is to outrival war in its effects of evil. It will take a man of good disposition and change him into a devil. It will separate husbands and wives. It will batter down happy homes and divide families. It will forge and cut the screws of many a coffin lid. It will dig many a grave. It will break many a heart. It will ruin many a soul. Yonder I see gardens of joy in full bloom; this invention of my brain will frost and kill every flower within them. Yonder I see blue skies that smile with prosperity; this invention of my brain will cloud them, and tear them with lightnings, and shake them with thunder. Yonder I see thousands of sunbeams of happiness; this invention of my brain will scatter them. Those sunbeams are like troops of visiting angels; they shall give place to shadows that are like the furies of hell. Everything lovely and beautiful and glorious in the lives of men will this one invention of my brain bring to ashes. Like war, men will praise it, the minds of poets praising it in metric phrase, the minds of orators praising it in language exalted, the minds of musicians praising it in wondrous tunes, the minds of artists praising it in glowing colors upon the canvas, the minds of sculptors praising it in creations of marble. Great palaces will be erected in its honor. It will have the chief place at all worldly banquets, clothing the tongues of those who speak with eloquence. It will have full sway at many a wedding feast, prompting the wishes of those who gather around the wedded pair. It will be the principal guest at the launching of many a ship. But wherever the feet of this thing shall go, they will leave behind them desolation, and woe, and the blackness of darkness. Under the withering touch of its hands, kings and queens, emperors and czars, and presidents and legislators, and judges and attorneys and juries will lose all sense of righteousness and receive bribes. Beneath its bewitching spell politics will be corrupted. By reason of its blandishments all classes and conditions of men will put forth their grasping fingers to clutch within them corroding gold and silver, blistering their palms with dishonesty and miserliness."

Then, in my fancy, I see Satan draw himself to his full height of wickedness, as he proceeds with his narration of plans for peopling hell with lost souls through his invention of evil. Satan continues:

"Listen, fiends! I have not done. My brain is in a whirl of imagination. Yonder are Adam and Eve just beginning their fallen life. But I see their descendants. Among them are many who are not

15

wholly given to badness. But there is something in
their veins that is like a smouldering fire. They have
inherited from their forefathers a tendency towards
self-destruction. See them yonder hanging dead
from swinging ropes! See them yonder lying dead
from wounds inflicted by pistols and knives! See
them yonder stretched dead from eating poison!
See them yonder floating dead upon the bosom of
the rivers, having drowned themselves in their mad-
ness of mind! One of you fanned that smouldering
fire in their veins into a blaze and it consumed them.
Yonder I see mighty men falling under the influence
of this infernal invention of mine. High in the
world's seats of fame, they are down in the mire.
Yonder I see a funeral of a prodigal son who went
off from his rural home to wallow with human swine
in the gutters of a large city. There is a streamer of
black blown by the winds from the door of the farmhouse. A long line of carriages wheeling slowly up
the lane. Crowds of mourners. Look at the corpse
within the casket! The undertaker has tried to hide
a cut across the brow, but he was not wholly successful. Here come the old gray-haired father and
mother to take their last look at the form of the re-
creant one. The friends respectfully stand back to
give them room. Heart-breaking sobs, the father
bending his head down at the rigid feet, his beard
snowing into the coffin, the mother at the head, her
blinding tears falling upon the face of her dead boy.
Oh, how it fills my foul heart with joy to behold that

scene! Those tears are nectar. Those sobs and that
wail from a mother's lips are music to my ears. But
there is more than one such scene. There are millions of them. Look yonder! A happy home. A
loving husband. A smiling wife. A group of rosy-
faced and golden-curled children. But look now!
An unhappy home. A growling, fist-brandishing
husband. A grief-stricken wife. A throng of af-
frighted children. Multiply that picture changed,
and you, my fellow-fiends, will know something of
the work that is yet to be accomplished by this in·
vention of mine."

Again applause rings out in hell. But Satan
checks it as before, proceeding with his plans for
blighting further the world that he first blighted
with a serpent temptation. Satan continues:

"This thing that I shall teach men to learn will
have a powerful influence in every century. I will
teach them, as the ages roll on, more of its forceful
energy. They will add to its strength, as their knowledge increases. It will take on more virulence. It
will often be the inspiration of family feuds. It will
often be the inspiration of tribal disputes. It will
often be the inspiration that will unchain the wolves
of war among the nations. By means of it riches
shall become poverty, wisdom shall become foolishness, learning shall become idiocy, pride shall become indifference, and religion shall become hypocrisy. There will be many means devised by godly
men and women to stay the influence of this invention

of mine, but they will for a long time fail. I shall
so arrange matters that the majority of the earth's
populations will not listen to the protests of the
feeble few who shall work against me, that majority
calling those few hair-brained, calling them insane
enthusiasts, calling them fanatics, calling them
cranks. Even ministers who shall preach of the One
who is to bruise my head, will, in many cases, be
afraid to speak out what they really believe, fearing
loss of position, or loss of money, or loss of popu-
larity. Men in business will hide their real senti-
ments for fear of suffering in trade. Those holding
office will be silent lest they be unseated. I will so
lengthen this serpent that I am to send abroad over
the face of the earth as to make it long enough to
twist its folds throughout the whole of human life.
There shall be no form of life untouched by it. Sermons against it will be of no avail. Lectures against
it will die as soon as their echoes die. Scientific dem-
onstration of the virulence of my invention will fade
from the memory like a dream. I will have my
agents in every church aisle, in every court of justice, in every hall of medicine. I see many rising
up in righteous anger against this infernal invention
of mine for ruining the earth, but I see many more
aiding in its spread. Laws will sanction it, and make
it respectable by means of their seal. Those high in
society will embrace it, becoming examples for the
low and vicious. In some cases it shall have ecclesiastic approval. For thousands of years the world

shall be held close in the folds of this serpent of iniquity born and reared within my burning heart of wickedness. Oh, yes; it will poison mankind with a poison for which only the superior power of God shall be able to provide an antidote. What I see before my eyes thrills me with delight. God's world shall be turned into a hell by this invention of mine!"

Then Satan's assembled auditors cry, "Give us the name of this supreme evil, that we may baptize it with everlasting darkness!" "I have no name for it," is Satan's answer. "I will leave it to men to give it a name."

It seems to me, my friends, that I, your pastor, have just awakened from a nightmare. Like Dante, the Italian poet, I have been in the depths of perdition. I wish that I had his gift of words. But I am reminded that this is the World's Temperance Sabbath. The name of the invention about which Satan has discoursed to-day in this allegorical sermon of mine is ALCOHOL!

The Frost

By the breath of God frost is given. Job 37: 10.

WHILE there are scholarly men searching the Bible to find flaws in it, picking it with pins of destructive criticism, it is a part of my mission as a preacher to turn over its leaves in quest of unfamiliar texts with which to enforce fresh and helpful lessons. Instead of finding this Book, as some do, covered with the dust and cobwebs of a past usefulness, I find it to be the most wonderful book that was ever penned and printed. It has withstood many a skeptical assault. It will withstand many more. In one single year of recent date, the year that was a brother to this present year, over eleven million copies of the Bible were sold in England and the United States, those enormous sales in evidence of the fact that the Bible is the most popular of all books with us and our cousins over the sea. In these same countries, during five years of time, the total sales of thirty of the most popular novels amounted to less than one year's sale of the Bible. What can infidelity do with a book like the Bible? Can such a book be destroyed? As well attempt to catch the lightnings of an August storm with a butterfly net! As well attempt to draw off the tides of the Atlantic Ocean with a teaspoon!

As well attempt to stop the flow of Niagara's waters with a mud-dam thrown up by a child's spade!

Out of this treasure-house of divinity I bring you to-day a handful of sparkling gems, those gems crystallized by the breath of God, and those gems being the frost that covers the ground in the evenings and mornings of the winter season now upon us. "By the breath of God frost is given."

I. I inquire, What is frost? It is the dew with its winter clothes on. It is the first cousin of hailstones and snowflakes. It belongs to God's royal family of evaporation and condensation. The raindrops of an April shower are its brothers and sisters. The frost hath kingly birth; and it always wears a crown. It is a prince of the household of the Lord God Almighty.

There are just seven references to frost in all the Bible from lid to lid. In fact, there are but six references to it, one out of the seven spoken of being really a reference to hailstones, the original Hebrew word being so translated in the margin. You know the reason, of course, for this paucity of reference to what is to us so common a sight. Frost was not so frequently seen in the lands described in the Bible. Plenty of references to other things in Nature; to clouds and thunders and lightnings; to grass and trees and flowers; to iron and gold and silver; to birds and beasts; but to frost only here and there a reference.

But this scarcity of reference to frost in the Bible

does not do away with the fact that frost is of divine origin. My text declares that it is given by the breath of God. What a thought that is! How near it brings God to us in the winter season that is now upon us! It is not hard to realize that God is close to us in the glad, bright days of the summer. When the trees are full-foliaged, their leafy banners keeping time in their waving under the wind to the melody of the birds; when the grass is greening the fields and the meadows, that grass embroidered with buttercups and daisies; when the brooks are singing, as they run on silver feet to their betrothal to the river; when the gardens are all abloom with pansies, with geraniums, with ragged-robin, with all classes of roses, white roses, pink roses, deep crimson roses, their cheeks kissed by the sunbeams of May and June, it is not a difficult matter then to see everywhere the footprints of God, and know that He is not far away. But here is a reminder of God's proximity in the bleakness and barrenness of December, of January, of February, of all the months when frost is abundant. Listen to the text again! "By the breath of God frost is given."

"The breath of God!" One of the pastimes of boyhood days was that of breathing upon a window-pane, and watching the moisture of the lungs freeze, when there was biting cold on the outside of the glass. On a grander scale God breathes upon the landscape on a winter's night, and when we awaken in the morning and look forth, lo, all the ground is white with flashing jewels fired into brilliance by the sun! It is the frost given by the breath of God.

Another pastime of childhood was that of scratching one's name upon the frosted window-glass of the home. I have seen boys and girls of a larger growth do that same thing upon the windows of a passenger coach while traveling. So upon the frost along the paths of the woods, and in field and orchard, you may find the autograph of God. That signature is just as much written in the frost as upon lichened rocks, as upon the snowy crests of the mountains, as in letters of stars upon the black page of midnight skies. What is the use in looking for God only in great things? He is not only the God of the stupendous, but also of the small, a spider's eye constructed by Him with as much care as a flaming constellation, the path of a minnow through the waters as unerring as the roadway of a planet circling around the sun, the frost of a winter's night as carefully arranged as the drapery of clouds around the ebony cradle of a rainbow born of a storm.

I once read of a man who went away from home in search of diamonds, going a long distance. He was gone a great while. In his absence a stranger stopped one day at the home, the stranger observing that the children were playing on the floor with peculiar looking pebbles. The visitor examined one of those pebbles, afterwards exclaiming to the children, "Where did you get these stones?" "Down in the brook that belongs to our farm." The stranger hastened to the brook, finding it paved with the same kind of pebbles with which the children were playing. Those pebbles were diamonds. The father of the household had gone to far-away lands in quest of diamonds, and there were acres of diamonds within sight of the smoke of his own chimney!

So there are many who take a telescope with which to see God, when He may be seen on the ground beneath their feet. The frost proclaims Him near. The frost is the gems that sparkle on His hand. The frost is the product of His breath.

It strikes me that the most of people need to know the nearness of the Lord in the sharp, freezing weather of life. There are so many pangs of disappointment that hurt the heart, so many business reverses that blight our prospects, so many difficulties that make the path of life hard to the feet, so many white tombstones that stand at the head of graves where sleeps beloved dust, those stones appearing as if covered with tears that have congealed in the winter of bereavement, the grief-dew of love turned into frost, that we need to know just how close our Father in heaven is to us. Who would have thought that consolation could be pressed out of this icy text? But it is there, waiting for the warm hand of faith to melt it down into blessed comfort. "By the breath of God frost is given." That means that God sends our wintry trials. If then He sends them, they are sent in token of His love. Frost is the breath of God.

II. I remark, again, that the frost is an evidence of God's artistic skill. We are accustomed to the pictures that God paints along the walls of autumnal forests, or hangs with cords of fire from the two horizons of the day, or the frescoes that God's brush traces upon the canvas of evening skies, so accustomed to great conflagrations of color on land and sea and sky, that we forget to look for the more delicate skill which God everywhere displays. The frost of the winter season bears witness to that skill. Look over the ground in the early morning! The earth is covered with white. It is not snow, for it is not piled so high as snow often is. The Psalmist said that it reminded him of ashes everywhere scattered. "He scattereth the hoarfrost like ashes." That is a beautiful figure, but, like all other figures, it must not be dissected. Ashes are the refuse of combustion. What the inspired poet referred to was not that the frost was a waste product. He was probably thinking of the hue of the frost, and of its abundance. In these respects it was like ashes thrown out. But I like to think of the frost as lace-work, its white-flowered meshes woven by the same Will that weaves the rainbow as a scarf for the dark shoulders of the storm. The loom in which the frost is woven is the breath of God.

Then, too, look at the frost on the window-panes! There is no human engraving that can equal the engraving of the frost by the breath of God given. The rich adorn their mansions with the masterpieces of famous artists. But the frost, under the direction of divine inspiration, makes even a poor man's windows a marvelous combination of artistic forms; gardens impressed upon those windows, and in full bloom of foliage; ferns of rost, daffodils of frost, hydrangeas of frost, crysanthemums of frost, great clustering roses of frost; and when the sun kisses these frosted leaves and blossoms, it is as if every kiss were a diamond. Along with the gardens are other scenes; scene of hunting, a fox on the run, hounds and horsemen in pursuit; scene of palaces and thrones and crowns; scene of battle; scene of victorious processions; scene of cities with imposing architecture, as the sun strikes those cities, setting them on fire, until they look like a picture of the last judgment, flames in the heavens, men and women and children and beasts rushing to find a place of safety, angels flying through the air with the vials of God's wrath; the whole scene melting away, as if the judgment had passed. Grandeurs and sublimities etched in frost upon the commonest piece of window glass that ever came from a glass-making establishment. Those scenes one day rubbed out, the next morning repeated; no one but the infinite God, whose breath gives the frost, being able to afford such an expenditure of genius. How wonderful is God!

What do we learn from God's artistic work of frost? This is the work that He displays in the winter. So it seems to me that it takes the freezing temperature of adversity often to develop beauty in the

human soul. Paul in prison; John Bunyon in prison.
Do you see the frost on the window-pane? Read
Paul's glowing epistles that came out of the winter of
his incarceration in Rome; read John Bunyan's immortal dream that came out of the winter of his incarceration in Bedford jail. David in exile; John the
apostle in exile. Do you see the frost on the ground?
Read David's superb Psalms; read John's Apocalypse. John Milton blind; Fanny Crosby blind. Do
you see the frost in those lives? One life that was
dark writing "Paradise Lost"; the other life that was
dark writing hymns that have sung themselves in
thousands of hearts, one of the best hymns of those
shaded eyes the hymn that speaks of the rapture of
seeing Christ face to face in the glory of God's night-
less city.

Oh, yes; the frost is a most wonderful artificer,
producing scenes that the pencil of smiling June
cannot draw; also tracing in another realm, the spiritual realm, lines of beauty upon the soul that no summer time of prosperity has ever yet attempted even
to imitate. "By the breath of God frost is given."
Bless God for frost in the physical world! Bless
God for frost in the world of the soul!

III. I speak again of the frost as medicine. In
the science of medicine there are remedies classed
as prophylactic, remedies that prevent disease. Vac-
cination is a prophylactic against the scourge of
small-pox. The frost is a divine prophylactic. It is
made in heaven's laboratory. You know that there

are various germicides used to kill the many germs that assault human life and threaten its destruction. So uses God the frost. The summer season loads the air with impurities, and for the health of mankind God gives the frost the mission of removing these impurities. The frost is one of the greatest, if not the very greatest, prophylactic measure of our temperate zone. Whatever may be your opinion of rival schools of medicine, you must admit that God believes in allopathic doses of this medicine of the frost! Frost on the hills. Frost in the valleys. Frost over the fields. Frost in the woods. Frost upon the gardens and orchards. An abundance of frost. All of it given by the breath of God. It is God's prophylactic, God's germicide.

We sometimes complain of the chilliness that rides down the atmosphere and lays its cold hands upon our bodies. Complaining is one of the common habits of the race. There are many who complain under all circumstances. Nothing is ever exactly right. But let us cease complaining about the frost. Let us find in it cause for thanksgiving. It is a tonic. How a low temperature whips the lazy blood into activity! In the summer season many persons become almost too languid to talk. But what a change when the frosts arrive! How the eyes brighten! What briskness in the step! What animation in the whole frame! Better than alcoholic stimulants, such stimulants always reacting, calling for a larger draught the next time used; better than any medicine known to human science, is this that God gives when His breath fills the air with frost. Instead of scolding the frost, and frowning at it, we ought to be stirred by it into words of thankfulness, making it the subject of a doxology.

Also ought the frost to be an inspiration to the life of the soul, correcting the indolence of summer months, and sending sluggish spiritual blood in quickened tides along the arteries. If cold weather would drive men and women to church on the Sabbath and to the prayer-meeting through the week, gathering them to the warmth of the ordinances of God's house, there would be many a pastor with a glad heart. There is no more dispiriting sight than that of a long line of empty pews, or row after row of vacant chairs in the sanctuary. Talmage once said that such things are non-conductors of Gospel electricity. More than that; they are the juniper trees under which heartbroken Elijahs sob and weep. O thou Breath of God, breathe upon Thy Church everywhere, not frosts that kill, but the frosts that will so tingle and smart as to draw Thy people to the fires of renewed interest in themselves and others! Let those fires be revival fires!

IV. Once more, I remark, that the frost is a preacher. It is an inspired preacher, God's breath upon it. I have seen many a time other preachers of God in the pulpits of Nature—the white-robed ministers of the springtide orchards; the rainbow-gowned ministers of the gardens; the ministers that smile in sunbeams, and the ministers that weep in summer showers. God has many preachers in Nature; and they belong to many sects—ministers that are classed with ritualism, wearing sacerdotal garments and chanting liturgies; ministers that shout in the winds; ministers that baptize in the waters; and ministers that come of good Presbyterian stock. But this white-haired and white-bearded preacher of the frost is more of a Quaker than anything else, though given to the wearing of jewelry, especially when the sun is up, but relying altogether upon God for utterance, and in quiet tones declaring the counsel of God.

The message that the frost brings us is of God's love. What is the frost? It is not the poisonous breath of a foe, but the beneficent breath of a beneficent God. "By the breath of God frost is given."

Listen to this one message spoken by this patriarchal preacher, that one message outranking all others in force and eloquence! The frost is the white blanket that God by His breath spreads over the sleeping wheat and plants and bulbs—spreading that blanket in the first falling of the shadows of winter over all that slumbering life, like a mother caring for her little ones, and then kissing them good-night. In the golden morning of the springtide that life beneath the frost shall again awake and laugh and romp and play through all the hours of the summer's day. A picture that of God's love for this frosted world of ours—frosted by sin. Out of death to come life. Out of curse to come blessing. Out of darkness to come

radiance. Out of frost to come bloom and fragrance.
Then no more winter, but one long, everlasting summer of joy and gladness.

But how shall this transformation be accomplished? By the manger of Christ around which
gathered the frosts of a December night more than
eighteen centuries ago. By the carpenter bench of
Christ around which gathered the frosts of exile and
poverty. By the persecution of Christ around which
gathered the frosts of ecclesiastic bigotry and scorn.
By the Cross of Christ around which gathered the
frosts of human hate and devilishness, those frosts
killing frosts, sending their lancets into the body of
Christ until the blood spurted, and leaving that body
in the pallor of death. All these frosts permitted by
the Lord for the carrying out of His purposes—the
provision of salvation for ruined mankind; the lifting of the despair; the dawning of hope; the pushing
back of heaven's gates for the entrance of uncounted
redeemed souls, those gates twelve in number, and
each one a solid pearl; and the resurrection of the
blighted flowers of righteousness into beauty.

O wonderful love of God by whose breath frost is
given! The question that springs out of the closing
of my sermon is this, Are you taking home to your
heart, my friend, this last point? Would that every
unconverted soul in this room to-day might answer,
"Yes!"—the same breath divine that gives the frost
of winter melting the hard frost of impenitence
around every heart into the dew of contrition and
faith!

16

Spiritual Compulsion

Compel them to come in.—Luke 14 : 23.

THAT sounds like a command to use force. But that is not what it means. In the spiritual world God has very little use for either battering rams or thunderbolts. Men are not to be pushed into the kingdom of heaven at the point of a sword, nor driven in by a fixed bayonet, nor blown in from the mouth of a cannon. Neither are they to be dragged in by the hair of the head. Some of the mightiest powers in the physical realm are so gentle in their touch and influence that we do not notice them. The light that rushes earthward from the skies travels faster than sound. If there were an explosion in the sun that could be both seen and heard on the earth, we should see it eight minutes before the noise of it would reach our ears. Yet swift-traveling light, moving on its flashing wings so quickly that an express train seems like a crawling caterpillar in comparison, descends upon our globe so silently as not to shake an aspen leaf or disturb the sleep of an infant. A Niagara cataract tumbling over the rocks awakes many an echo; but the soft snowflakes of a winter's day build themselves without noise into walls that stop the march of armies and halt trade and commerce. Bluster and effectiveness of result do not always go together. There is more sound in the lighting of a match than in the kindling of a sunrise.

Let us study for a little while the parable from which the text is drawn, and then we can determine what the words of the text really mean. A great deal of false interpretation of Scripture comes from a failure to view Scripture on all sides.

It is like some blind men of whom I once read. They tried to describe an elephant. One felt the elephant's side, and said that an elephant is like a wall. Another one felt of its legs, and said that an elephant is like a column of a building. Another felt its trunk, and said that an elephant is like a serpent. If they could have seen an elephant with their eyes they would have known what an elephant is. Like that, I repeat, are some interpretations of certain passages in the Bible. Those passages are blindly examined, and wrong conclusions are drawn from them.

In this parable it is said that a certain man made a great supper, and sent out a large number of invitations. Now, there is nothing more embarrassing and mortifying than to prepare for the coming of guests to one's house and have those guests fail to put in an appearance. That is what happened to the man of the parable. When the servant went to tell those who had been bidden that the supper was all ready to serve, they each offered an excuse, declining to give their presence to the meal. What a

deep student of human nature Christ was! This is no
mere fancy sketch. Such things had many times happened. They are still happening. The fact was
that those invited ones did not wish to sit down at
that man's hospitable table. But rather than to seem
wholly lacking in politeness, they offered pretended
regrets. I wonder how many regrets are real? One
man had bought a piece of ground, and he must
needs go and see it. Why, that man had already
seen the land that he had bought. Men are not such
fools as that in matters of business. The man's excuse was as thin as a spider's web. It let the daylight
through it.

Another man had been guilty of the same folly.
He had bought five yoke of oxen, and he was under
the necessity of proving the animals. That was a
reversal of the true order of things. The usual rule,
as everybody well knows, is to prove a thing before
purchase, not after the money has been laid down
or a check for the amount drawn and handed over.
Another spider-web excuse. Even coated thickly
with the dust of falsehood, it could not shut out the
daylight.

Another man urged that he had taken himself a
wife, and for that reason he could not attend the
banquet. But that could not have been a real hin-
drance. In that case, the one who made the supper
would have included the wife in the invitation, the
more especially as she was a bride. What could have
been more natural than for the husband to have said,

"My dear, we have been asked to a supper this evening. The invitation comes from one of high standing in society. If we go, we shall gain recognition
at the very beginning of our married life among the
upper classes. Get yourself ready, and we will go."
Under those circumstances, the honeymoon being in
its first quarter, the bride would have sweetly and
gracefully yielded to the wishes of her husband and
gone with him to the banquet. That would have
been too great an opportunity to be missed.

There were other excuses offered that are not mentioned in the parable. These three are representatives of all the rest. They were all of the same kind,
Their prominent characteristic is flimsiness. A blind
man could almost see through them.

Now, before we proceed further in this study, I
wish you to notice that Christ uses these excuses as
types of the excuses that many hearts offer for not
accepting God's rich provision of grace in the Gospel. I do not care what excuse you give, my friend,
for not being a Christian, whether it be the inconsistencies of those who are already in the Church, or the
seeming hardness of some Bible doctrines, or lack of
time, or what not, your excuse is not sincere. It will
not stand the scrutiny of truth. You have wrapped
it up in tissue paper. You cannot hide your heart
from the eyes of God. Even if that heart of yours
were placed in the middle of a piece of granite ten
feet square, those lightning eyes would reach it in
its concealment. Whatever be your excuse, God

knows that your real reason for not accepting His
grace is that *you do not want it.* That makes your
excuse all the more hypocritical. Aye, it brings upon
you the crime of murder. At the judgment-seat of
God you will lift up a pair of hands all stained with
the Saviour's blood. Rejecting God's grace is a
much more serious matter than that of declining an
invitation to a banquet. It is to turn from the door
of your heart your very best Friend. It is to crucify
the Son of God afresh and put Him to an open
shame.

When the servant returned with his adverse re-
port, the man who had made the supper was ruffled
in mind. The parable puts it even more strongly
than that, saying that he was angry. Who would not
have been? I can see him yonder, as he listens to
his servant's recital. "What!" he exclaims. "Am I
awake or dreaming? Here I have gone to this ex-
pense for those whom I counted my friends, and on
all sides I am met by rude, discourteous rebuffs.
Well, I am not going to be defeated by a few fools.
Here, man, go out quickly into the streets and lanes
of the city, and bring in hither the poor, and the
maimed, and the halt, and the blind. I am not
going to be made a laughing-stock by a set of num-
skulls."

Let us pause again in the unfolding of the parable
for a lesson that suggests itself by the way. What
do we learn? Why, it does not require any unusual
depth of brain to understand that the grace of God

is something that puts joy into human life. From Christ's own lips we have the statement that religion is a banquet. Some consider it to be a funeral, as if it is a possession of the soul that kills a man's gladness, leaving a downward curve of the lips, and the dampness of grief coming out from the eyes. The common impression is that to become a Christian is to move out of the sunlight into everlasting shadow; that it is to make a change in one's residence from a thronged highway into a graveyard; that it is to leave the temperate zone for the frigid; that it is to pour into the sweetness of life's cup a gill or more of vinegar, the acidity of the mixture turning the whole draught sour. But that is one of Satan's blackest lies, wrapped up in the folds of ten midnights. The more persons the devil can get to believe such a dense falsehood, the more laughter rings out in hell. Which one will you believe, Satan or Christ? Christ says that becoming a Christian is to sit down to a table loaded with good things. Religion is a banquet.

Where is there a brighter place than at a scene of festivity? Sometimes such a scene is on the occasion of a birthday anniversary. Friend greets friend. One warm hand clasps another warm hand. One smiling face looks into another smiling face. The guests seat themselves at the festal board. Flashing lights. Through the air steals the fragrance of flowers. To the nostril ascends the odor of palatable food. Upon the table the orchards have thrown kisses of fruit. Sparkling silver. Glistening cut glass. Pleasant conversation. Brilliant repartee. Happy intercourse. Or sometimes such a scene is on the occasion of a wedding. A few tears perhaps from one pair of eyes, those of the mother of the bride, the father keeping his tears back, vigorously using his handkerchief, and complaining of a sudden cold, but those tears like an April shower with the sun shining through the raindrops, the mother remembering her own joy of thirty or forty years before. Plenty of parted lips in the facial gesture of delight. Congratulations offered. The bride's cake cut with merriment. Good wishes sent across the table. Gladness written along every face. And if now and then a tear comes out again upon the mother's cheek, it is only a comma or semicolon of pearl punctuating the happiness.

Yes; religion is a banquet. Christ Himself so describes it. I do not care to hear anybody talk about religion as though it were anything else than joyous. Away with whining prayers! Away with lugubrious tones when speaking of the kingdom of God! Away with sanctimonious rolling of the eyes in inviting men and women to Christ! Our God has a great many beautiful daughters. He is the Father of a large family. The sunrise is one of those daughters. The sunset is another one. The rainbow is another. The spring is another. The autumn is another. They live in earth and air and sea and sky. Glorious daughters of God! But the sweetest-lipped and the fairest faced daughter of all is religion. Solomon says, and he knew, for he had formed an intimate acquaintanceship with both her and that child of hell, worldly pleasure, and is therefore competent to give an unbiased opinion— Solomon says, "Her ways are ways of pleasantness, and all her paths are peace." A greater than Solomon here to-day declares that this daughter of God is so radiantly handsome that it takes a banquet to describe her.

O, my friend why will you stay out upon the ash-heaps of this world when you might be a happy guest at the table of the King? Religion is good for the body; it is good for the mind; it is infinitely good for the soul. Balm for wounds. Knowledge for ignorance. Everlasting blessedness for misery and despair. To become a Christian is to stop feeding on husks and satisfy one's self with the sweet, nourishing bread of heaven. To become a Christian is to leave the swine-pens of beggary for the wardrobes of the Father's house. To become a Christian is to take the feet from sin's hard and thorny road and place them under the banqueting table of God's love.

Resuming the narrative of the parable, after the servant had followed his master's directions, bringing in to the supper the various classes described, he said, "Lord, it is done as thou hast commanded, and yet there is room." Then said the master to his servant, "Go out into the highways and hedges and compel them to come in, that my house may be filled."

Do you not see the meaning of that, dear friend? In your stubbornness of will and hardness of heart you may persistently refuse the offers of God's grace, but your attitude of indifference is not going to frustrate that grace in other directions. Even after large numbers have been gathered to the banquet of God's love, there will be found an abundance of room for many more. More than human arithmetic can reckon. Ten thousand times ten thousand and thousands of thousands. What stupendous figures! A great multitude that no man can number. The highways and hedges of the world are already being searched for guests to sit down at that table of the Gospel. God's servants are abroad upon all the continents with invitations to the people. At the deluge there was only one family of eight persons saved from the wrathful waters that rose above the mountain-tops; all the rest of the world lost. But in the final count of heaven's census by means of the mathematics of God's infinite brain, it will be found that there will be far more of the redeemed than of the damned. Oh, yes; you may oppose God's invitation to His supper of grace; but you cannot balk His purposes. That banquet shall yet have many a table provided with guests, and there will be no flush of embarrassment upon the cheeks of the Host. Oh, come to-day to the Christ! Be numbered with the throngs of the redeemed! Yet there is room!

But what now is the meaning of the phrase, "Compel them to come in?" That, I take it, is a divine direction to ministers of the Gospel and other servants of God. Are men and women then to be forced into the kingdom of God? I will answer that question by asking another one. How much force would it require to make a crowd of poor people go to a dinner or supper provided by the long purse of a man of wealth? In some cities, in the winter season, soup-houses are provided, to which those in want may go for a substantial meal of soup and bread. One of the vivid recollections of my very early boyhood days is that of the sight of such persons going to establishments of that kind in Philadelphia. I had the time and the opportunity for sights of that character, that being one of my pleasures during convalescence from a severe attack of scarlet fever. They passed the windows of my home every day. I saw them going with bowls, with kettles, and with tin cans. No policeman's club drove them along the street. No bayonets pushed them on. No pistols were pointed at them. Their want and hunger compelled them to go.

So, says the rich man of the parable, "Compel them to come in. Go out into the highways and hedges, and let the famishing multitudes know that there is a place and plenty of room in my house, and that I have prepared a supper to which they are welcome, and their very necessity will urge them to come in and satisfy themselves with my generosity."

Under such circumstances there would be no occasion for the use of violence. The fact is that Christian work requires gentle tact in making it effective. We are to be careful how we give invitations to the banquet of the Gospel. The main thing is to compel men and women to attend to the needs of the soul by showing them their need. Many sermons are a dead failure because they are so clouded with metaphysics or the technicalities of theology that those who listen cannot see their meaning. About the poorest place in all the world to build a fog-bank is in a pulpit. We ministers should come down from off our scholastic stilts and address the people in the language with which they are familiar. Christ stood on a level with His audiences. It is safe to follow His example. Him the common people heard gladly.

So is a great deal of what passes for Sabbath-school instruction a failure, and for the reason that it is lifelessly presented. So do many exhortations in evangelistic meetings fall to the ground, and because they are made up of pious platitudes. I can imagine the servant of the parable going out to the beggars of the road, and by his earnest and hearty manner persuading them of the reality of the feast provided for them. In that way he compelled them to go in.

There is a work for all of us to do in compelling sinners. Ministers and missionaries and Sabbath-school teachers and other special helpers cannot do all the work. It was never intended that they should do it all. In fact, every Christian is a servant of the King, and is charged with the responsibility of trying to save souls. Some are gifted in one way, and some are gifted in other ways. Whatever your gift, my friend, you are to use it in this gently compulsory way suggested by the text. Some can sing. Let them do that. Some can write letters. Let them wield a consecrated pen. Some have a magnetism of person that makes them influential in other directions. Let them employ their persuasive manner for Christ.

But there is one thing we can all do, and that is lead a life that is so thoroughly Christ-like that it will compel assent to the reality of religion. The very best argument in all the world in behalf of Christianity is a clean, square, honest, blameless life. That is an argument that weighs more than a thousand treatises on apologetics; and for the reason that only a few persons ever read works on theological science. But everybody reads a Christian.

I also believe in the power of prayer for compelling the salvation of the lost. We do not make enough of this spiritual power. Yet that is the very power that has frequently been employed in bringing about revivals of religion. It was prayer that took hold of three thousand souls on the day of Pentecost and moved them irresistibly into righteousness. It is the prayers of God's people that will yet shake this world of ours out of sin into salvation. The prayer "Thy kingdom come" is bound to be answered. Behind the stars is the dawn. Back of the dawn is the sunrise.

How many of you will regard yourselves as the

servants of the King, and serve Him in the very best way that you can in filling His banqueting house of the Gospel. Millions have been brought in during all the ages. But there is room for millions more. No fear of overcrowding that festal hall. It has a wide doorway. Even a multitude thronging it at one time could not overcharge its space. One of the door posts of that entrance on one side is "Whosoever," and the other door post on the opposite side is "Will." "Whosoever will!" That is an entrance wide enough for the admission of the whole world at one time.

Oh, let us feel upon us now, as never before, the obligation of helping to save the lost! Let us by words of invitation through the mouth or pen, by example, by public and private prayer, compel the sinners around us to press into the feast of the Lord. To see them coming, and to see them seating themselves at the Lord's table—that will be itself a banquet for our own souls. There could be no grander sight on earth for either pastor or people. There could be no richer banquet, even though the viands that graced the feast of an Ahasuerus, or a Belshazzar, or a Solomon were upon the board. At such banquets the angels of God fold their wings and sit down. They are banquets of joy.

Nine-Tenths

(THANKSGIVING SERMON.)

Were there not ten cleansed? but where are the nine? Luke 17: 17.

It was a day of thanksgiving on the outskirts of a little village between Samaria and Galilee. No emperor's edict or no governor's proclamation had appointed it. That day of thanksgiving was for ten men who had been miraculously cured of leprosy. But only one of those men saw fit to observe it. This single man was one of whom, according to the popular thought of the times, much was not to be expected. He was a Samaritan. Yet he was the only one who opened his heart and poured out its treasures at the feet of Him who had wrought his wondrous cure. The other nine were Jews.

That day of thanksgiving had been ordered from a higher source than from beneath the pen of one who sat upon Cæsar's throne or occupied a gubernatorial chair. It had been fixed by what should be a regnant principle within every human soul—Gratitude. Nine of those men deliberately chose to despise the mandate of that royal principle and hush its kingly voice. When only one of the group came back to speak his thanks upon the ears of his divine Benefactor, Christ asked the pathetic question of the text, "Were there not ten cleansed? but where are the nine?"

No argument against ingratitude, however well reasoned or skillfully worded, could surpass this living illustration of that theme. For myself I always prefer a picture to logic. Many have the same preference. Often a cartoon in a newspaper outweighs the thoughts heavily expressed upon its editorial page. To the wizard pen of Thomas Nast must be given the credit of bringing to judgment the notorious Tweed gang of years ago in the city of New York. So this breathing, palpitating, walking portrayal of selfish unthankfulness is of more worth than a whole library on the same subject. Let us study it this morning.

I. We learn from this incident that ingratitude is a common fault among mankind. That small group of healed lepers is representative of the human race. It is the whole world sifted. Nine-tenths of the earth's mighty populations have but little or no spirit of real thankfulness.

Do you say that this is a sweeping statement? So it is. I do not deny the fact. But look for the proof of that assertion in the conduct of those nine Jews back there in the first century of this present era.

Those men had been cured of a most terrible disease. Their bodies were the tramping ground of leprosy. What is leprosy? It is a most virulent ailment. It begins to show itself first upon the skin, white patches gathering there, those patches afterwards developing into running sores. The man afflicted with leprosy becomes a mass of living rottenness, all the surface of his body covered with putrid eruptions. These pustular excrescences then eat their way into the innermost tissues, attacking the joints, the blood vessels, the muscles, the nerves, everything on the inside and outside of its victim, until finally every part of the frame is literally consumed by gangrene. Leprosy is an enemy that shows no quarter. It is a pirate that does not rest content until it lays its wasting hand upon every precious thing belonging to one's vitality, and floats its black flag in triumph over ruin, afterwards burning its prize clear to the water's edge, and leaving it as the sport of the winds and waves. In plain words, leprosy is sure death, a horrible death, a ghastly death.

That was the loathsome disease of which those nine men had been cleansed. They had been walking to the grave; by a word from the Saviour's lips they turned and walked into roseate health, postponing their funeral.

Besides that; leprosy made a man in those days a social nuisance. Afflicted with a highly infectious disease, he had to be quarantined. Lepers were an isolated class of people, and by everybody shunned. As misery is said to love company, lepers often lived together in communities of their own. They had the freedom of the roads, but when approaching anyone the law compelled them to give warning of their presence by crying out, "Unclean! Unclean!" They were to be avoided, contact with them being a menace to one's personal safety. To be a leper was to be

17

a venomous snake. He was an outcast from society, often pitied, but pitied with disgust.

Out of that dreadful state Christ delivered ten men all at once. On the outskirts of a little village by the way He saw them. They "stood afar off," as they were forced to do by the stern law of the day. Upon the Saviour's ears rang their plaintive cry, "Jesus, Master, have mercy on us!" that cry issuing from cracked tongues and ulcered lips, and the very breath that sent it through the air loaded with pestilence. Christ's answer was immediate and powerful. He simply said to them, "Go show yourselves unto the priests." That meant that they were cured, the scrutiny of the priest being a provision of the Levitical law governing such cases, the law requiring the scrutiny before they could return to the liberty of citizenship. In no other way could their quarantine be lifted. "Go shew yourselves unto the priests," was therefore the prescription with which this divine Physician wrought the cure of those men. As they passed on in obedience to the Master's command, they found that they were healed. At once, before seeking his priest, one of them "turned back, and with a loud voice glorified God, and fell down on his face, giving him thanks." But the other nine hurried on, seemingly with not a single spark of gratitude within their hearts. "And Jesus answering said, Were there not ten cleansed? but where are the nine?"

"Well," says some one, "how does this prove the statement so sweepingly made, that nine-tenths of humanity are ungrateful?" Why, in this fact, that those nine men did not think it worth their while to show even common decency in the matter of giving voice to thankfulness. They went back to their business, to the pleasures of social life, to their families, and to the rights of citizenship, as if they deemed their wondrous cure to be no more than what they ought to have received at the hands of Christ. If that is not the attitude of nine-tenths of earth's throngs towards the blessings of God, then I am a poor student of human nature and a loose observer of the habits of men. On that day of thanksgiving long ago gratitude was a scarce article. The proportion of it was one against nine. There is the same rarity of the same article now. Let Jesus Christ come down into the United States on this annual Thanksgiving Day of the nation, and visit the various churches opened in response to Presidential proclamation, and there would come from His quivering lips the lament of the text, "Where are the nine?" In the cities the custom on Thanksgiving Day is for several congregations to unite in service. Why? Because of the nine, the majority, who have no incense of thankfulness to burn upon the altar of their hearts. It takes several churches to make one respectable group of worshipers on that day. Nine-tenths of the people are elsewhere.

II. Again, we learn from the text, that we should be thankful for daily blessings. Where did those nine ingrates get their health? It came to them through the power of Christ, that Christ being God manifest in the flesh. The same God is the source of all benefits.

I was reading of the famous musician Haydn. Sick and weary and worn, he was carried for the last time into a hall of music. There he listened to the rendering of his own oratorio, the "Creation." When the orchestra came to the noted passage in the score which harmoniously says, "Let there be light!" it is said that the whole audience rose up and cheered and cheered. Then Haydn waved his hand toward heaven, and exclaimed, "It comes from there! It comes from there!"

That great genius of melody had the right thought. The inspiration with which he wrote his masterpiece was God-given. It came from above. That is where everything good comes from. God is the fountain of every gift that flows into every life.

The trouble with nine-tenths of humanity is that they do not perceive the divinity of what are called the common blessings of life. Many become so accustomed to receiving favors at the hands of God that, like those nine lepers healed, they fail of gratitude. Who thanks God for the air he breathes with every rising of his lungs? Who thanks God for the water he drinks? Who thanks God for sunrise and sunset and the starry pomp of the night, and the eyes with which he beholds such splendor of color and such an aggregation of flashing magnificence? Who thanks God for woodland pictures painted by the fiery brush of autumn? Who thanks God for the thousands of every-day beauties that come within the sweep of the vision? Who thanks God for the multitudinous sounds that greet the ear with music? Why, there is enough in one's own body to awaken thankfulness, if he would but stop to consider the blessings that God has there stored. Here and there a soul is vibrant with gratitude for daily gifts; but many souls, alas! are silent, their harp-strings untouched by the fingers of a single thanksgiving.

But let God withdraw His daily blessings. Let Him banish the sunbeams; let Him dry up the brooks and rivers and lakes and oceans; let Him take off His care from these frames in which we live, frames that need much attention, food for renewing their tissues, oxygen for supplying the blood with the elements of life, sleep for repairing the waste of hours passed in activity; let God sit yonder upon His throne, and be stolidly indifferent towards the world; what would follow? What would have followed, if Christ had been unresponsive to the prayer of those lepers? They would have gone on as they were, the vise of death pressing them more and more, and finally pinching their diseased hearts into a little lump of rottenness for the grave. So would we die, were it not for the constant and unremitting goodness of God. From our first cry as a babe down to our last respiration as a man or woman we are the subjects of God's care. Blessings daily; blessings hourly; blessings with every beat of the pulse of life.

I find no fault with a national day of thanksgiving. Such a day is appropriate. I wish that it might be more widely observed. But every day ought to be a thanksgiving day. In a world in which there is so much of ingratitude, let not you and me be numbered with the unthankful nine-tenths.

III. Again, we learn here that we should be thankful for many things that we do not have. Reading about those poor outcasts in this incident, I am deeply thankful that I have no such disease as leprosy in my body. The fact is, the most of persons do not think enough of their negative blessings. But such blessings are just as real and beneficent as are the blessings that are positive. If our hearts were in proper tune, we should be thankful with almost every breath for hundreds of things that do not touch us. Some years ago I saw a man in a railroad station who was afflicted with paralysis agitans, or shaking palsy. As I saw his trembling form, I lifted my heart to God, saying, "Father, I thank Thee for sound nerves!"

So we may thank God, if we are not blind or deaf. So may we thank God, if we have never been in an accident on the rails or on the waters. So may we thank God, if we have never been burned out of house and home; or if that has been our experience, we may thank Him that we were not ourselves hurt by the flames. So may we thank God, if we have no taint of alcoholism in our veins. Plenty of things for which to be thankful. If nine-tenths of humanity would stop grumbling because they are unblessed with what they imagine would increase their happiness, and pause to think of all that they ever escaped, they would find that they have abundant subjects of praise. I suppose that those nine men of this narrative had many a murmur upon their ulcerated lips against what they considered to be the partiality of Providence; but when God stepped in and freed them from their loathsome disease, they had no gratitude for exemption from leprosy, that exemption making them like the multitudes whom they before envied. Christ's question, "Where are the nine?" is yet vibrating its pathos in the air of earth.

Thanksgiving, my friends, is something more than a national affair for once a year. It is well to be grateful for a big country on whose possessions the sun never sets, for untold wealth in our hills, for millions of acres that bring forth wheat and corn and potatoes in unstinted measure, and for a marvelous prosperity that dazzles the eyes of all the world. I fear that there is not enough of real thankfulness for our unrivalled privileges as a people. But there are other things for which to be thankful. Our God has given us much stock in His stupendous enterprises, and He declares dividends every moment of our lives. Among these dividends are numerous blessings that are not ordinarily estimated at their true value.

Negative blessings can be viewed as positive blessings. The plate upon which a photographer takes a portrait, when developed is called a negative. With that negative he prints his pictures, the camera reversing the true, black things being white and white things black; but in the process of printing from that reversed negative the paper shows the reality. So may our negative blessings be made to impress themselves upon the heart as matters for which to be thankful. When so impressed they become the opposites of negatives. My advice to everybody is that they take down their negatives from the shelves of life, brush the dust from them, and put them out in the sunlight of God's grace, printing from them pictures of beauty. This would be a fine exercise for those who think that they have but little or nothing at all for which to be thankful.

IV. Again, we may learn that we should be grateful for our trials. I do not know why those nine men had been afflicted with leprosy. Often that disease was the direct outcome of sin. Miriam, the sister of Moses, was thus visited. So was Gehazi, Elisha's covetous servant. Leprosy in the Bible is a graphic illustration of the virulence and deathfulness of sin. But whatever was the cause of their affliction, those nine men were given many an opportunity to show patience and resignation under suffering. I have no reason for believing that they used those opportunities, their conduct afterwards revealing the fact that they were far from being in a high state of spiritual development. But that does not alter the truth that they had the means for rising Godward.

If, my friend, you have met with loss, or been in frequent pain, or shed many a tear of grief or bereavement, and if these things have made you better, is not that sufficient cause for praising the Lord? In that case your loss was gain; pangs of body were pleasures; griefs were joys; opened graves were doors thrown back that let the glory of a deathless city stream in upon your soul.

What illustrious company you are in to-day! You are sitting down at God's banqueting table of love with such distinguished persons as Abraham, and Jacob, and Job, and David, and Peter, and Paul, and Luther, and Calvin, and Knox, and Wesley, and a whole shining host whose names I have not the time to mention. As you lift the chalice of thanksgiving to your lips from that board, can you not say, as some of its contents of mercy spill upon the snowy cloth, "My cup runneth over?"

Oh, yes; you and I have much to be thankful for, if our trials have been the rungs of a ladder by which we have mounted closer to God. Woe to those whom trouble sours! Woe to those whom trouble pitches headlong into darkness! Woe to the ungrateful nine!

Why, even our trials might have been worse. That is something for gratitude, I am sure. I once read of an old lady, who had only two teeth. She said she was thankful that those two remaining teeth were opposite each other, one in the upper jaw, the other directly underneath. That was the right spirit. Two teeth were better than none at all; and their position, favorable for chewing, was an added blessing. Nothing so bad that it might not be worse. A night without any stars silvering its shadows is worse than a night that heaven illuminates with sun-lamps and world-tapers. Plenty of reasons for thankfulness, if we have the mind to search for them. Those nine men deserved to have their leprosy returned to them. What would nine-tenths of humanity deserve, if they should get justice instead of mercy from God?

V. Once more, we may learn that we should be thankful for eternal life. That one grateful man of the narrative I now place in the foreground of the picture we are studying. I think we are warranted in believing that he received that day, not only a cleansed body, but also a cleansed soul. I gather that from what Jesus said to him, the Master's words being, "Arise, go thy way; thy faith hath made thee whole."

That was not the mere pronunciation of physical wholeness. The other nine who did not come back had the same blessing. Christ's words went in and found the man's soul. Those words opened to this Samaritan the gates of pearl.

Friends, you and I should have full gratitude for the blessings of the Gospel. Even if there were nothing else for which to be thankful, which is not the case, I bless God to-day for the sky-song of angelic choristers announcing Jesus born in Bethlehem, and the swinging lantern of star that guided Gentiles to

His lowly dwelling. I bless God to-day for the Christ who healed those lepers of the text and hundreds more of the needy in His day, His miracles of mercy typical of a richer mercy in delivering untold throngs from the foulness of sin. I bless God to-day for the footprints of Christ left centuries ago under Eastern clouds, those footprints showing the path of the grandest Character who ever walked the highways of earth, and those footprints revealing a love that human language cannot measure. So do I bless God to-day for what now beams upon my vision. What is it? Behold it yonder ablaze with the glory of sacrifice and redemption! It is the Cross of the Lamb of God. That Cross is the gateway of life immortal for lost and ruined man. Gather around that Cross, America, Europe, Asia, Africa, the islands of the sea! Then let rise from millions of lips this song of thanksgiving: "Lo, this is our God; we have waited for him, and he will save us: this is the Lord; we have waited for him, we will be glad and rejoice in his salvation!" Ye angels of heaven, hush your notes! Let that song rise to the ears of God unhindered!

The Lifted Christ

As Moses lifted up the serpent in the wilderness, even so must the Son of man be lifted up. John 3: 14.

GEORGE WHITEFIELD preached in his day to thousands of persons at one time, often out under the blue sky, no building being large enough to accommodate the crowds that attended his ministry. In a later day Charles Haddon Spurgeon also preached to vast multitudes in the city of London. So did T. DeWitt Talmage address great throngs in his immense Brooklyn Tabernacle, and, through the press, reaching millions of souls every week whose faces he never saw. But here is a masterly sermon delivered to an audience of one person by the most wonderful preacher that ever lived. Christ frequently cast His marvelous thoughts among a large concourse of people, on one occasion His congregation numbering five thousand souls. It is said that there were five thousand men present, not counting the women and children. If, as is usually the case, the women exceeded the men in point of numbers, what a tremendous auditory that must have been! But Christ also often had only one person to listen to His words. That is what happened in this present instance. But to have missed having that sermon reported would have been to have a blank page in John's Gospel. To

Nicodemus that night Christ opened the very richest vein in the mine of heavenly truth, sinking His shaft deep, and showering upon His hearer double handfuls of sparkling nuggets of gold.

Some of the theological doctors have wrangled about the case of Nicodemus. They have not agreed in their diagnosis. Some have thought his symptoms betokened one thing, and some another. But whatever the motives they attribute to this man in seeking Christ that night, I have long held to the opinion that he was a sincere inquirer. Cowardly he may have been, or politic, or conservative, or anything at all. I do not care. It is my firm belief that he was thoroughly in earnest. Why do I so believe? Do you think that Christ would have talked as He did, if Nicodemus had not really wished to know about the salvation of his soul? Christ told Nicodemus that night some mighty truths that He had not yet revealed to His own disciples. There in that room, right before the eyes of Nicodemus, He pictured the Cross, and Himself hanging on that Cross as the Lamb of God who taketh away the sin of the world.

Nicodemus went out under the throbbing stars that night, and back to his own home, a changed man. The grace of God had melted the ice of Pharisaic formality around his heart and made him a follower of the young Rabbi whose name was Jesus Christ. We afterwards find him, as a member of the Jewish Sanhedrin, protesting against the pre-judg-

ment of Jesus by the chief priests and Pharisees who
had sent officers to arrest Christ. We find him again
at the Cross with Joseph of Arimathea, tenderly caring for the dead body of the Lord, bringing a hundred pounds of a mixture of myrrh and aloes for the
embalming of the mutilated corpse, having a big
purse, and his heart as big as his bank account.

Oh, if men and women would only consent to
talk upon this great subject of the soul's salvation,
instead of listening to sermons, and then immediately going forth again into the world with an increase of hardness in their hearts! This was an inquiry meeting that Nicodemus attended that night,
a kind of meeting that I should like to have after
every evangelistic service. I suppose that there
were many things that sought to hold him back. He
was a prominent man in religious circles; and this
young Teacher, who had but recently graduated into
the ministry from a carpenter's bench, having no
academic degree, was regarded with suspicion, not
being popular in the society in which Nicodemus
moved. I suppose Satan plied the mind of Nicodemus that night with many an objection. Perhaps
the man halted several times on the way to that room
where Christ was, in the darkness of the night de-
bating the propriety of his course. There were grave
issues at stake on both sides of the case. He battled
with himself, Satan furnishing him with weapons
for the conflict, those weapons from the black
armory of hell. But he walks on, coming

in view of an upper chamber of a certain house in the town, the light of a flickering lamp shining through the lattice work of the window, every now and then the wind blowing upon the flame of that lamp, as if to extinguish it, and that same fitful breeze afterwards giving the Christ an illustration of the mysterious movements of the Holy Spirit. Now he has reached the house. His foot is on the stairway outside. Shall he ascend that stairway? What if some of his friends should see him calling at that house? Everybody in the town knows who is lodging there. It is Satan's last desperate chance. If Nicodemus yields, another soul has eluded the grasp of his grimy hand. But Nicodemus will not falter now. His feet are upon the creaking steps. Every argument for his detention is burst from him, as though they are naught but spider-webs. His hand knocks boldly at the door. A gentle voice from within bids him enter. He is face to face with his God and Saviour.

I do not care what you call it, whether God's sovereignty or man's free agency. My belief is that it was both. But that is an entirely different matter from saying that it was fate. There is no such thing as fate. That is one of the exploded superstitions of heathen mythology. But something was drawing Nicodemus to that upper room; something was also trying hard to turn him away; but in the full exercise of his own unhindered will he went to Christ. And that is the history of every real conversion that

ever was or that ever will be. It is God and man
coming together, and because they both want each
other. If God were the only factor in the case, He,
of course, could bring men to Him; but it would be
by reason of superior force. That would fill His
kingdom with unwilling subjects. If man were the
only factor in the case, how many souls would ever
go in quest of God? Silence is the answer. Not
one! Not one! But while the Shepherd is seeking
for His lost sheep, the lost sheep are seeking the
Shepherd; and blessed be God! they find each other.
I do not see why there should be any reluctance to
give God all the glory in the salvation of souls. For
man there is no glory. What would have become
of our world if in it had never been heard the footfalls of a gracious God bent on saving men? To
ask the question is to answer it. The population of
hell would have overflowed like a swollen river.

I say again, if men and women would only consent
to talk upon this important subject, instead of fighting against the truth, resisting the gentle persuasive-
ness of the Holy Spirit, the bells in the crystal towers of the celestial city would never cease pealing
their joy over the return of the prodigals of earth.
I am glad that Nicodemus went up those stairs that
night and engaged Jesus in conversation. I am also
glad that he went of his own accord. Christ was
waiting for him. In like manner, my friend, is He
graciously waiting for you. When will you go to
Him?

Now we are ready for the unfolding of the text. Christ here calls the attention of Nicodemus to a piece of Jewish history with which Nicodemus was perfectly familiar. No occasion to go after a far-fetched illustration. Although Nicodemus was an educated man, Christ did not deem it necessary to tickle the vanity of His hearer. We ministers sometimes sail away in balloons, when we ought to keep close to the ground. Christ was not fishing for compliments that night. His line had been cast into water too deep for that. He was after a soul. He meets that soul on the level. "Moses lifted up the serpent in the wilderness." Yes; Nicodemus knew that. He also knew why that serpent was lifted. It was for the purpose of staying the terrible poison of the fiery serpents that had gone twisting themselves through the camp of God's ancient people on the way to Canaan, those fiery serpents sent among them as a judgment from God for their sins. Repenting of their sins, God commanded Moses to cast a brazen image of a serpent, and set that image on a pole within sight of every tent. Those who looked to that brazen serpent were immediately healed. It was their faith that healed them.

Nicodemus understood all that. But Christ here gives that event an application that had been overlooked by Nicodemus and other doctors of divinity then living. "As Moses lifted up the serpent in the wilderness, even so must the Son of man be lifted up." Why? "That whosoever believeth in him

18

should not perish, but have eternal life." If the
Jews of those days had more closely examined the
symbolism of their Scriptures, they would not have
been expecting a Christ who was to be no more than
a mere descendant of David. Nor would they have
been guilty of rejecting the Christ who came to them.
They were dreaming of a splendid Hebrew mon-
archy, not looking for a spiritual empire. They were
dreaming of a throne, not looking for a cross. They
were dreaming of a king, not looking for a sacrificial
lamb.

What Christ said to Nicodemus that night He said
to the world for all coming time. There was no re-
porter present at that interview. The account of
that wonderful conversation was afterwards given to
the Apostle John, and by him embalmed as an inspired record for multitudinous eyes to read and multitudinous hearts to feel. Those words from the
lips of the Saviour Himself, "As Moses lifted up the
serpent in the wilderness, even so must the Son of
man be lifted up," were meant to teach the world
the necessity of an atonement of blood for the removal of sin. That was what brought Christ to our
insignificant earth. For that, the disrobing of heavenly garments and the putting on of the lowly dress
of humanity. For that the manger of Bethlehem in
exchange for the palace of the skies. For that the
forsaking of angelic praises for the curses of human
foes. For that the wealth of the universe surren-
dered for the poverty of thirty-three years of life in

the flesh. For that the sceptre of omnipotence laid down for the saw and plane and hammer of the Nazareth carpenter shop. Over His Bethlehem birthplace seraphs flashed their wings and seraph choirs poured their songs; but amid all the brightness of that hour there was the shadow of the Cross; and amid all the melody of that hour were the groans of the crucifixion. A Cross beside His immovable cradle in the stable of the inn. A Cross beside His work bench. A Cross on the fishing boat of Galilee. A Cross upon the Mount of Transfiguration. A Cross wherever He journeyed and wherever He tarried. A Cross! A Cross! That Cross was an eternal Cross. It first came to view before human eyes near the gates of ruined Eden. It afterwards showed itself in the dripping blood of sacrificial altars, and was outlined against the sky in the smoke of those sacrifices, that smoke curling upward to kiss the clouds of heaven. It revealed itself in the wilderness in the image of the brazen serpent uplifted by the hand of Moses. Christ came to die, not as other men die, but as the Lamb of God. That was the mission with which He was charged. That was the mission which He fulfilled. His last words, before the spirit left His bruised and mangled body, were, "It is finished!" As He thus spoke, His heart burst, and a place was made within for every sinner of that present age, and for every sinner of all the ages to come, even if this old world should continue traveling through the heavens sixty billion years.

"Must the Son of man be lifted up." In that sentence from the lips of Christ that little word "must" weighs more than the whole world. "Must!" That means that the death of Christ was no mere makeshift, speaking reverently, but an absolutely necessary necessity. There was no other way to remove your sins and mine, or those of anybody else. Had there been, the infinite brain of the Almighty could have conceived it and put it into operation. There was no other way. Ye angels of light, solve the problem! Tell, if ye can, how guilty men can be allowed to go free without violence to the eternal principles of Justice and without shaming the face of Mercy! I see them bending to the task. I see them conferring together in council. They bring to bear upon the question all the accumulated gifts of their superior intelligence. They cannot give the answer. They are speechless. It is a query that only God Himself can undo. Even He can find no other than that of the Cross. No other way! "Even so must the Son of man be lifted up!"

Yet there have been those, and still are, who have made light of the sacrifice of Jesus Christ. But in the very face of all criticism stands that little but tremendously emphatic word "Must!" Against that wall let infidelity batter out its brains, if it will, and lose its soul. But on ladders of repentance and faith many have climbed to the top of that wall, and looked off upon the glories of heaven. O my friend, mount those same ladders to-day, and see for yourself the beauty and richness and grandeur of the Gospel of Christ. God's "must" makes for you the privilege of everlasting salvation. Along with that "must" link your will.

Go back to that scene in the wilderness. Many had been bitten by the fiery serpents. They were writhing in the agony of the poison that had inflamed their veins. Yonder is reared the serpent of brass. The command goes through the plague-smitten camp, "Look, and live!" Those who obey are instantly healed. It mattered not how far the virulence had gone into their system, one look at that image of brass, even though it were the look of a dying man, stayed the poison and brought health. It was confidence or faith in God's promise that broke the malady.

How apt a picture is that of the sin that has fastened itself upon the heart of mankind! A serpent's fangs have been driven into the very life of the race. Wherever you go, you find the people dying because of sin. They have been mortally wounded. There is no place where the sting of sin has not been felt. No spot anywhere on the round earth without the presence of this fearful and soul-destroying plague. "All have sinned, and come short of the glory of God." But there is a remedy—an all-powerful remedy. It never fails. It never has failed. Blessed be God! it never will fail.

Here, again, is another apt picture. For the serpent-bitten Israelites the look at the uplifted ser-

pent of brass, that serpent of brass flashing out in the
sunlight before every eye; for the serpent-bitten
sinner the look at the Cross of Jesus Christ, that
Cross blazing its beneficence in the sheen of nineteen centuries. "As Moses lifted up the serpent in
the wilderness, even so must the Son of man be lifted
up," Himself crucified by human sin and for human
sin, the hatred of men driving Him to Calvary, but
the grace of God making Calvary the scene of an
atonement sufficient for all who will accept it. "Even
so must the Son of man be lifted up; that whosoever
believeth in him should not perish, but have eternal
life." This the Gospel that Christ preached to Nicodemus. This the Gospel that the Apostles preached
as they went forth into the world. This the Gospel
that has come down all the ages, and which, as an
ambassador of Christ, I am privileged to preach in
this pulpit of Buckingham Church to you. Glorious
Gospel! Majestic Gospel! Precious Gospel! "Life
for a look at the crucified One!" Life for you! Life
for whosoever will believe! An angel's tongue cannot proclaim it. God has placed its matchless eloquence upon the stammering lips of those who were
once lost sinners, but are now sinners saved by His
grace. I speak to you as one who well knows what
it means to be a rebel against God. I also speak to
you as one who well knows what it means to be
reconciled to God. This is no coldly intellectual
treatment of this theme. It is the warm experience
of a regenerated heart. Upon that Cross to which I

urge you to look I have fastened all my hopes of heaven. That Cross is the very core of all my theology.

But all through this sermon of mine I have been asking myself a question. What is the secret of this uplifted Cross? One word tells it all. Listen! Love! In this same discourse to Nicodemus there is another emphatic word. The Son of man *must* be lifted up. "For God *so* loved the world, that he gave his only begotten Son, that whosoever believeth in him should not perish, but have everlasting life." That word "so" is charged with the infinite love of an infinite Heart. Behold it yonder, the Cross of Calvary! Human hate is there revealed in the cruel thorns and the sharp-pointed nails; but through the shadows of that hate shines the glory of divine love "God *so* loved the world." "*Must* be lifted up." There was no way for man to be saved; but Love made a way Yet there are hearts so hard they will not be melted by the breath of that love. Is that your heart, my friend? The Holy Spirit awaits your answer. Let it be a negative that shall have in it the tone of a crashing thunderbolt.

Strength for the Day

As thy days, so shall thy strength be. Deut. 33:25.

THIS is a tonic text. A good dose of it will put iron into spiritual blood that is thin. The Bible is full of such tonic texts. Instead of trying the quack remedies of the world, it would be better if God's despondent children should always get their medicine from this divine pharmacy. For a fit of mind depression there is nothing so powerful as the promises of the Bible.

One day Philip Melancthon and Martin Luther were sitting together in utter discouragement. They had been talking about the darkness that was over-shadowing the Church. As they talked, that darkness seemed to be many midnights rolled into one solid mass of gloom. The more they talked, the heavier their hearts became. But suddenly Luther rose up and said, "Come, Philip, let us sing the Forty-sixth Psalm." They sang it—"God is our refuge and strength, a very present help in trouble. Therefore will not we fear, though the earth be removed, and though the mountains be carried into the midst of the sea; though the waters thereof roar and be troubled, though the mountains shake with the swelling thereof. Selah." Having finished the song, the darkness lifted from their souls. The gates of the dawn had opened. Through those gates came the sunrise of hope and faith. There are no shadows that can hang before the light of God's Word. "As thy days, so shall thy strength be."

I. I would apply these words to all forms of anxiety. It was against anxiety that a part of Christ's wonderful Sermon on the Mount was preached. It is useless ever to be in an anxious state of mind. But it is such a mental condition that often troubles the most of people. That was true in all the past centuries. Who will say that it is not true now? It will also be true in the ages to come. The human brain naturally has that sort of a twist in it.

The most prevalent form of anxiety is that of borrowing trouble. Of all borrowing this is the very worst. The old Shylock who gives the loan demands an exorbitant rate of interest. We pay back to that wily usurer, not only a pound or more of flesh, but bitterness of soul, and despair, and shadows through which glide ugly spectres, under the burden of the loan, the face becoming pinched and wrinkled, and the heart beating itself into premature death. At every step we hear the hoarse voice of the usurer crying, "I'll have my bond! I'll have my bond!" Many a man, followed thus by this Shylock of anxiety, has sought to escape him through the clicking of a pistol, or through the stretching of a rope, or through the mixing of a poison, or through a plunge into the waters.

Shakespeare wrote many a tragedy. But it would

take a greater than a Shakespeare to write the tragedies that lie within the human mind. Shakespeare said that all the world is a stage; and that men and women are the actors upon that stage, having their entrances and their exits. But every mortal brain is a stage; and the actors thereon are thoughts—often those actors wrapped in sombre robes, and moving among weird scenery, like the ghostly forms that step along the corridors of a theatre of nightmare. To borrow trouble is to doubt the goodness of God.

I have often thought of the pleasures of the imagination. In the midst of winter, when there is a tempest abroad, and when there is snow on the ground, and when all the streams have been closed by the sheriff of the year, upon their crystal doors a seal of ice, I can sit beside a blazing fire and call up thoughts of summer. I can then see green fields all dotted with daisies and buttercups, and behold running brooks that flash their kisses to the sky, and look upon bright-robed orchard trees adorned like a bride for her husband, and hear the singing of the birds, as they praise God from the gallery of the woods, their notes accompanied by the tones that pour forth from the organ of the wind. I can produce summer in my mind.

Yet this same power that affords pleasure can be turned into an instrument of torture worse than any that was used in the Spanish Inquisition. Under the spell of opium, the imperial imagination of Thomas

De Quincey degenerated into a chamber of horrors. But one can terrify himself without the use of drugs. If you would whip your soul with a knotted lash, or if you would stretch your soul upon a bed of knives, or if you would pinch your soul with heated tongs, just give way to a mental experience of trouble that has no reality.

Yonder sits a mother before the cradle of her child. Giving rein to her fancy, that mother is carried into future days. She beholds that rosy form, now asleep in the cradle, shrouded in the pallor of death, like a lingering flower of the summer covered with the frost of autumn. She beholds the gathered darkness that follows her loss, that darkness hanging in heavy folds all around her home, and hanging in still heavier folds around her heart. The little one is prepared for burial. It is laid in another cradle —the motionless cradle of the grave. The whole scene moves before her vision with all its details vividly painted. But it is all imaginary. That mother is simply hurting herself with what is not true. Borrowing trouble!

But let us suppose that death does come to that child. The mother is almost crazed by grief. But there follows consolation. He who long ago said, "Suffer the little children to come unto me," stands beside her in her real trouble, and comforts her with His grace. Into the surrounding gloom falls the music of a voice that says, "As thy days so shall thy strength be." Under the touch of divine fingers, and beneath the gentleness of divine words, that mother is sustained. "Underneath are the everlasting arms."

So with all fancied sorrows. Men have thought that financial straits, or their removal from good positions, or a hundred other things, for I need not stop to name the whole list, would strike them like a heavy wagon drawn by a pair of runaway horses, and knock them down, and roll out their very life. But when the fancied tribulation assumed reality, they found grace in their time of need. The cloud that their imagination piled up on the horizon, black as the ninth plague of Egypt, came on, and, behold, right beneath its pelting drops, as it spread over the sky, the grass smiled into a richer green, and a thousand flowers burst forth into fulness of bloom! In plain words, God gives His children gains in their losses. Every cloud has an edging of gold. Adversities that come, like the toad of the poet's verse, ugly and venomous, wear a precious jewel in their heads. But often, alas! we fail to see any brightness in the cloud, and fail to see the flashing gem in the head of the adversity.

It is here that my text applies. It says to you and me, and every child of God, "Do not borrow trouble. If there is trouble on the way, wait for it and take its blow." If we have faith enough, that waiting will be like the waiting of a rock-bound coast for the in-rolling waves of the ocean, breaking those waves into splinters of diamond spray. "As thy days, so shall thy strength be."

What is the use in having the spirit of foreboding? What is foreboding? It is an unbroken horse with a timid driver. Faith jumps into the same vehicle, takes the same lines, and the fractious beast moves on as if it had been accustomed to the harness for twenty years. That is just the difference between feverish anxiety and trusting in the promises of God. Our Father tells us over and over again in His letter from heaven to us that He will fit us for every condition of life. "As thy days, so shall thy strength be."

II. I would apply these words to all forms of discouragement. It often happens that good persons are dispirited in their Christian work. After what seemed to be a total failure, Elijah ran away and threw himself down beneath a juniper tree, sobbing there like a disappointed child, and praying for death. Strong natures frequently have such times of mental depression. Elijah's juniper tree still bears leaves. It has sheltered many a discouraged servant of the Lord.

But here is balm for every such wounded soul. Let the very worst come that can come   God provides for every disaster that breaks the heart. "As thy days, so shall thy strength be." There is no use in being crushed by disappointment. When Samson was shut up within the town of Gaza, his enemies thought they had him safe. But with God-given strength, Samson rose up in the night, wrenched the bars of the gates asunder, those gates within the walls of the city, and carried the gates away upon his broad shoulders. So may you and I do likewise with those things that would confine us within the Philistine town of Discouragement. "As thy days, so shall thy strength be."

If there ever was one who had great cause for discouragement, that one was Christ. How few His converts, speaking comparatively! How much scorn He endured! What dishonors were heaped upon Him! But you never find Christ giving way to hopelessness. Christ was the great Optimist of all the centuries. He believed in God. In that case He believed in Himself, for He was Himself the Lord. Even at the very last, in full view of the Cross, He said to His disciples, "Be of good cheer; I have overcome the world." Through the gathering storm of Calvary He beheld the sunburst of victory.

When I was a boy, and was sent out to water the garden, that garden filled with my mother's favorite flowers, I was accustomed to give myself pleasure by making rainbows. How did I make them? Why, I just turned the nozzle of the hose into the sunshine, and the rainbow would appear. I helped to do there on a small scale what the sun often does on a large scale, when behind the retreating shower he springs the iris bow of triumph. My youthful sport gave me a bit of philosophy for future use. We can make our own rainbows. How? By turning our disappointments into the light of God's promises. Look at the gorgeous colors that come into view beneath the brilliance of the text! "As thy days, so shall thy strength be." That is one of the best rainbow-makers of the whole Bible.

III. I would apply these words to all forms of difficulty. There is no difficulty that this text cannot throw. Do you wish illustrations? Look at Abraham! He had been led to hope, for an heir. In the course of time, after long but not very patient waiting, for the saints of the Bible were by no means perfect men and women, the heir came. But when the old father's heart was completely wrapped around his son Isaac, like a sudden crash of a thunderbolt, came the divine command, "Take thy beloved son and sacrifice him." Yonder I see the old man making preparation to carry out that order from heaven. His heart hangs within him like a ball of iron. Yet he believed in God. His faith in God would not allow him to sit down before this difficulty utterly nerveless. He went on with his preparation, feeling that in some way the Lord would open a path of deliverance. God would not rob him. But Abraham was tested up to the very last moment. It was not until the knife flashed in the sun up there on Mt. Moriah, and the father's arm was about to sweep down and drive death into the vitals of Isaac, that the divine order was countermanded. That was a hard road for Abraham to travel; but God furnished His obedient servant with shoes of iron and brass. See those shoes striking fire as they hit the stones up the mountain-side! It was in fulfilment of the promise, "As thy days, so shall thy strength be."

Look at Moses! What? Leave the solitudes of the wilderness, where he was happy, and confront Pharaoh on his throne? It was an appalling commission. But the Lord equipped his servant with the necessary strength for that task. Moses went. Out of that going came a commonwealth.

Look at David! There came an inspiration to him in his youth to go forth and down the boastful Goliath who had been defying the army of Israel. Saul wanted to put his armor on the boy. David tried that armor. It was a misfit, too large and too heavy. Besides that; what did he want of armor? No; he would meet the giant in plain shepherd dress. But beneath that shepherd robe was the armor of God. The whirl of the sling in the deft hand of that stripling, the loosing of a smooth stone picked up from a brook, the swift rush of the missile through the air, an angelic hand guiding it, and yonder Goliath lies stretched upon the ground, a fallen mountain of flesh, a carcass of braggadocio. "As thy days, so shall thy strength be."

Look at Paul! His adoption of the religion of Jesus Christ brought him into many difficulties. But was he afraid? With God's strength upon him, a spiritual Samson, he rocked prisons with earthquakes. With the same God-given strength, he shook gubernatorial chairs and the thrones of kings and emperors.

Look at Martin Luther! God said to that man, "Purge My Church!" The barefoot monk of Wittenberg put on shoes of iron and brass and awoke a sleeping Reformation. What was one man against a corrupt Church that both crowned and uncrowned the monarchs of the world? But Luther walked on, his strength equal to his days, and obeyed God's command. The blows that he struck for the cause of righteousness are yet echoing in the air of earth.

Look at John Knox! He feared the face of no man. Even royalty could not frighten him. A man of iron!

Look at the two Wesleys, one battering the bulwarks of evil with song, the other battering them with prayers and sermons!

Look at Whitefield! His preaching tours bringing him into numerous difficulties; often expounding the Word of God amid a ruffianly shower of rotten eggs and decayed vegetables; yet conquering by his commanding eloquence.

But why go so far back for illustrations? Your own life will furnish them. You have proved again and again the truth of the text, "As thy days, so shall thy strength be." Let those words come home to you at this hour with renewed force. I would write them upon the door of every Christian household, upon the door of every Christian bank and store and shop and factory, upon the door of every Christian school, upon the door of every church auditorium and Sabbath-school room. Behold them, as I trace them there to-day in letters of sunshine! How they glisten! "As thy days, so shall thy strength be."

19

IV. I would apply these words to all forms of sensitiveness about critical opinions. It is from some form of sensitiveness that much of the trouble of life comes. We are all too apt to be mindful of what is said of us. The fear of criticism makes its own trouble. A young man, for example, fails in one of his collegiate examinations. That is nothing at all serious, for some of the world's greatest men have done likewise. At school Adam Clark was a dull youth; so was Walter Scott, who was pronounced to be a perfect dunce. But the failure of the present may become a stepping-stone into future success. That was just what happened in the case of the two boys whom I have mentioned. Adam Clark and Walter Scott both rose into fame, one becoming a learned commentator of the Scriptures, the other developing into a brilliant wizard of speech, his novels taking their place among the classics of the English language.

But the young man who fails is apt to ask himself, "What will my acquaintances say about this? Will they not think that I am of no worth, and that I shall never amount to anything?"

Another young man sets his heart upon a certain position. He does not get it. That, however, is of small moment. Wherever there is a good comfortable niche to be filled, there will be hundreds of applicants. They cannot all gain the prize. But the young man is greatly disappointed. Yet keen as is his disappointment, it is made sharper by the probable comments of those who know him. It may be that the cry will be, "Incompetent! Let him stay where he belongs. It is not well for such as he to have an ambition that is too broad of wing."

I tell you that there is many a man who could walk boldly right up to the mouth of a loaded cannon, the fuse burning, who has not the moral courage to face the opinions of his fellows under circumstances such as these. The people will talk; and talk adversely. Men and women often come together in groups, like students in a medical hall, and dissect other persons' misfortunes. They come together, like a coroner's jury, to investigate dead hopes. They come together like a flock of buzzards, those buzzards flapping their wings, and plunging their filthy beaks and talons into a putrid carcass. Many persons dread criticism far more than they dread the thing itself that sets the cancerous tongue of gossip in motion.

But the promise of the text takes in all such cases. God comes as a loving Father to all such, and soothingly says, "Mind not what men and women think and speak. Rise up, and be a man. Go forward. 'As thy days, so shall thy strength be.'"

"If God be for us, who can be against us?" Blessed the man who believes that! It will always be an inspiration to him, sweetening many a bitter cup, covering many a cross with flowers, throwing a scarf of rainbow over the black shoulders of many a storm. Give me the consciousness that God is with me, and I will go out and lose a battle of Waterloo, and then snap my fingers at a sneering world, as I would snap them at a terrier dog barking at my heels!

Was I not right in calling this a tonic text? Let us take its cheering ingredients. It will nerve us for climbing the hills of the Christian life. By and by we shall stand upon the shining summits of those hills. We shall need no tonic then. The very air that we draw into our lungs will be itself invigorating, for then we shall be far beyond the toils and struggles and pain and heartaches of earth. Up there is heaven.

"Then let our songs abound,
　And every tear be dry;
We're marching thro' Immanuel's ground,
　To fairer worlds on high."

The Angel Upon the Stone

The angel of the Lord descended from heaven, and came and rolled back the stone from the door, and sat upon it. Matthew 28: 2.

I ONCE stood before the sepulchre of George Washington at Mt. Vernon. The dust of that famous man was yet there. That dust was guarded and held imprisoned by Death, the one who unseats all presidents and dethrones all kings and emperors and czars, himself the very mightiest of monarchs. He was crowned by sin six thousand years ago or more; and the same pair of black hands that crowned him then have kept him crowned ever since. I give you inspired proof of my statement. Says Paul, "By one man sin entered into the world, and death by sin."

But there was one illustrious Personage whose tomb Death could not keep closed. Upon that tomb he had placed the seal of the greatest government on earth; and around it were stationed Roman soldiers. Within that tomb the body of Christ had been lying for two whole nights. So far Death was triumphant. He who had raised the dead was Himself dead. Christ lifeless; flat upon his back; locked securely within a wall of rocks. Rocks above Him; rocks beneath Him; rocks behind Him; rocks in front of Him; the doorway of that sepulcher-prison darkened and barricaded by a sculptured rock. But on the morning of the third day, by a key of earthquake, that huge door of stone was unfastened, the rattling of that key in the wards of the lock sending a convulsive jar among those piled up walls of death, and shaking the very foundations of the world. The same hand that held that key, a hand angelic, also rolled back the ponderous stone door of the dungeon and made it a stool, sitting on it. Having unwrapped Himself of His grave clothes, and folded the napkin that bound His head, Christ then leisurely came forth into liberty, His first sight that of a garden all abloom with flowers.

This is the wondrous fact that we celebrate to-day. The lilies, and hyacinths, and crocuses, and geraniums, and jonquils of this Sabbath morning in spring are the lineal descendants of the blossoms that greeted the risen Christ and threw Him kisses, as He stepped forth into the silvery dawn of the Resurrection. The flowers are still greeting Him, and still throwing Him their perfumed kisses. Let no human soul be outdone by the flowers. All hail, Thou living Christ! From the garden of our hearts we gather the flowers of love and loyalty, and twist them into a garland for Thy thorn-scarred brow.

I. I ask you to notice that the women who went to the sepulchre of the Christ, not knowing that it had been opened by an angel from heaven, brought aromatics in token of their love for the Master. Those were dried flowers, the beauty of their blooming gone, but still fragrant. I seem to detect the spirit of those spice-laden shrubs to-day in the odors of the plants that adorn this Easter Sabbath. Right glad I am that those devoted women went to that tomb with their hands full of aromatics. Some of the cowardly male disciples of Christ came stealthily to the sepulchre after the women had gone away; but their hands were empty. With the women love had conquered all fear. They went to embalm the body of their Lord. To woman is given an answering sweetness in the Gospel of Jesus Christ. More women Christians than men. More women in our churches to-day than men. More women than men loyally gathered at the feet of the living Saviour. Woman being the first visitor at the grave of Christ, and carrying there the spices of an affectionate ministry, she has been blessed with pre-eminence in every department of Christian grace and movement. Her love for Christ has grandly flowered through nearly nineteen centuries of time. Accursed be the hands that would pull her down from her Christian exaltation into the dust of bondage! Away with heathenish Mormonism from Christian America! That foul thing would drive woman back into the open tomb of Christianity, and roll again the stone against the door, and bury all her godly refinement and righteousness of character in a charnal-house forever. What we need to-day is an earthquake of moral indignation to rumble over all of this fair land, an earthquake that will pale the brow of political pre-

ferment. Then let an angel from heaven lift the
rock from that sepulchre of feminine degradation
masked as a religion, and sit down on that rock, as
he takes his seat, the force of the vibration shaking
our national Capitol from foundation walls to dome,
and clear up to the cap upon the head of the Goddess
of Liberty! The Lord speed the hour!

Yes; Christianity is aromatic. It sweetens human
life. Let us imitate these old-time women, putting
more of the spicery of the Gospel into our preaching
and teaching, and sending its fragrance everywhere
for the deodorization of the world's noxiousness of
sin. Aromatics! That was what the Magi brought
the infant Christ. He started upon His mission with
perfume. But He did not need it. He was Himself the Rose of Sharon. Aromatics! That was
what the Marys brought for the embalment of His
body. But, again, He was not in need of those dried
shrubs. The open grave, with an angel sitting upon
its rock-door, proclaimed His resurrection into immortal bloom. Yet we can take the hint wrapped up
in those aromatic offerings, and go forth to purify
the world with Christian faith and practice and instruction.

II. I ask you to notice the angelic agent at the resurrection of the Christ. "The angel of the Lord descended from heaven, and came and rolled back the
stone from the door, and sat upon it." Which one
of heaven's distinguished inhabitants it was we do
not know, however much we should like to know.

The Bible was not written to satisfy human curiosity. It does not deal with trivial things. But I am glad to read that it was an angel who performed this great feat. That relieves my mind of the least doubt in regard to the fact of Christ's resurrection. Had it been merely an earthquake that tumbled that rock-door from its fastenings, it might have been that the Roman soldiers would have been frightened away by the phenomenon, the disciples afterwards removing the body and pretending that there had been a resurrection. It was a story somewhat like this that those Roman soldiers were hired by the chief priests to circulate, only that they were to state that the body was stolen while they slept, a most improbable tale, for it was a punishable offense for a Roman soldier to sleep at his post, even as such neglect of duty is with us a punishable offense.

"But," objects some one, "the narrative distinctly says that there was an earthquake." So it does. I had not overlooked that fact. But it says, too, that the angel of the Lord descended from heaven, and came and rolled back the stone from the door, and sat upon it. The earthquake was caused by the descent of the angel. He came so swiftly down and alighted so suddenly upon the world that the impact of his feet shook the very ground beneath him to its far-away depths. Here was a seraphic personality. An earthquake might have jarred the door from the mouth of the tomb, but an earthquake could not have sat upon that door. Besides that, speaking of the

angel, the narrative says that his countenance was
like lightning, and his raiment white as snow; and
that for fear of him the keepers of the sepulchre
trembled, and became as dead men. They swooned
away in fright.   The wonder is that they were not
struck dead.   That same angel was afterwards seen
by the women who were earliest at the grave, having
left his chair of rock and gone inside the tomb.
Luke tells us that he was joined by another celestial.
I can readily imagine that the garden of Joseph of
Arimathea was alive with angels that morning, but
not making themselves visible—angels with folded
wings walking the paths; angels sitting around the
shattered sepulchre; angels standing within the
empty tomb; angels flying through the air; the whole
place rainbowed with angels.   It would not have
staggered my faith had the narrative so stated.

But the presence of the angel of the Lord at the
resurrection of the Christ confirms the belief of the
Christian world in this distinctive doctrine of the
Christian religion.   No angel would have come
down from heaven simply to roll away the stone from
a tomb containing a dead body.   God never sends His
angels forth on senseless missions.   This angel came
to let the living Christ out.   Christ, being Himself
the Lord of Glory, might have spoken but a word,
as when He breathed worlds into existence, and His
grave-prison would have fallen about Him with a
crash.   But He preferred to have a servant do the
work for Him, letting that servant remain behind for

a season in testimony of His rising from the dead. To the women who sought the body of their Lord this angel became a witness, telling them that Jesus was alive, and inviting them into the sepulchre to see the place where He had slept the sleep of death, taking a short nap after His fatigue of cross-bearing. When I find the track of angel feet around the grave of Christ, I cannot help believing in the fact of the resurrection. Into this narrative the Holy Spirit has woven celestial light and celestial pinions and celestial utterance. It is not difficult to give credence to a story that angels have written and punctuated. I dwell on these things because others have not particularly noticed them.

More than that; this angel rolling away the stone from the tomb of the Christ is another proof of heavenly interest in the redemption of mankind. How the gospel blossoms with angels! An angel announcing to the Virgin Mary the miraculous and immaculate conception of Christ. A choir of angels when Christ was born, and chanting His natal song from the starlit gallery of cloud over Bethlehem's hills. An angel strengthening the agonized Christ in Gethsemane, helping to sweeten the bitter cup that was about to be pressed to His lips. Unseen angels closing the shutters of the sky and darkening the death-chamber of open air at the crucifixion of Christ on Calvary. An angel rolling the rock-door from the sepulchre of the risen Christ, and then a pair of angels sitting where He had lain, one at the

head, the other at the feet. Angels after He had
gone up into heaven, those angels suddenly standing
beside the upward-gazing disciples and prophesying
His second advent. Angels! Angels! Angels! The
world celestial in sympathy with the world terrestial.
Not spirits coming to earth on frivolous errands,
coming to rap on tables and ring bells and open
doors, but on their silent wings flying this way and
flying that way on ministries of love. That invisible
world a real world. A definite, localized sphere in
God's universe. The home of our departed kindred
and friends. What was it that Christ said about the
angels? Oh, yes! I remember. It was that the angels rejoice over the return of the prodigals of earth
to their Father's house and heart. Would that they
might be thrilled with that gladness this Easter Sabbath morning! Oh, my friend, what think you of the
resurrected Christ? Answer that question in this
jubilant hour, joining your voice with us in ascribing
to Him all honor and praise and glory and blessing.
Then the waiting angels gathered to this resurrection anniversary would speed back to the throne of
Christ with the news that they like best to bear to the
skies.

III. I ask you to notice that this angel of the resurrection sat upon the stone that he had rolled away
from Christ's tomb. You have often heard sermons
about the angel's pushing back of that rock-door,
but probably you have never heard it remarked that
the angel sat upon that rock-door after he had lifted

it from its place. Why is that sublime fact slighted?
It is suggestive to me of most weighty thoughts.

Well, was the angel tired after that prodigious effort of opening the Saviour's tomb? If that be your
supposition, you do not know much about angels.
They never get tired. You and I will some day excel
them in strength, putting on then our immortal
bodies. That is to be one of the many benefits to us
of Christ's resurrection. But that angel could have
shouldered that stupendous rock more easily than
you or I could pick up a vase of flowers, carrying
his load unbesweated to the very gates of hell. He
sat upon the stone, I think, in token of the complete-
ness of Christ's triumph over death. Men, inspired
of sin, and urged on by devilish foes, had rolled that
stone to its place, sealing it with the impress of the
Roman Government; but now no human hands or no
hands diabolic could roll that stone back where it was
before. The angel sat upon it. Let anyone dare to
imprison the living Christ, and the lightning of the
angel's face would smite the miscreant to death. The
stone that had shut Christ within that tomb had become a throne for a seraph. He sat upon it, thus
symbolizing the fact that man's triumph and Satan's
triumph had been turned into defeat.

I am glad that Matthew did not leave out from his
narrative of the resurrection this angel-topped stone.
I have seen unsightly rocks made beautiful by the art
of God—the same art that throws over the couch of
the dying day robes of cloud colored with sunset,

and, after the day is dead, lays it out in star-embroid-
ered shroud, to wait for the resurrection at dawn.
I have seen such rocks upholstered with moss, making them glorious and resplendent. So here does
God adorn this rock of death with angel limbs and
angel wings and angel face. In the presence of
Christ's signal victory over the grave, death is spoiled
of its terror for the Christian soul. Upon the door
of every Christian tomb an angel is seated. Who
fears death?

In John Bunyan's matchless allegory, as the pil-
grim to the celestial city was entering the gate of the
Christian life, he was quickly drawn in by him who
kept the gate, lest he be wounded by the archers of
Satan shooting their arrows from below. Thus would
Death like to maim and kill those who start heavenward through the gateway of the grave. But an
angel stands there on guard. Bless God for the seraph that sat upon the rolled-away stone of Christ's
sepulchre! "O death, where is thy sting? O grave,
where is thy victory?" Those two questions are two
great diamonds polished by the rhetorical hand of
Paul the Christian lapidary for the crown of the be-
liever's triumph through Christ over the tomb. The
dying school teacher wore that crown when he said,
"Boys, school is dismissed." It was time for him to
close the shutters, lock the door, and go home. The
dying minister wore that jeweled crown when he
said, "I move into the light." Hugh McKail wore
that shining crown when on the scaffold of martyr-

dom he said, "Welcome death! Welcome glory!"
My own aged mother, in her last moments on earth,
wore that crown when she said, using the second
stanza of a hymn I love to sing, the tune Warwick,

"Up to the hills where Christ is gone
   To plead for all His saints,
Presenting at His Father's throne
   Our songs and our complaints."

I was reading that hymn to my congregation in
Chester at the very moment she was reciting its second stanza, I not knowing that she was treading
those radiant hills, a streamer of black crepe con-
fronting me the next morning as I ascended the door-
steps of the old homestead. Paul himself wore that
lustrous crown when from the dungeon of his last
imprisonment he penned the sentence, flinging it as
a challenge into the very face of the destroyer, "I
am now ready to be offered, and the time of my departure is at hand." Millions have worn it, among
them some whose final words you can recall on this
anniversary of Christ's resurrection. An angel sitting on the stone that was lifted from the Saviour's
mausoleum of rock. An angel at every Christian
grave. Aye! The Saviour Himself standing by,
alive for evermore, and saying to those who enter
death, trusting in Him, "I am the Resurrection and
the Life."

Let the women devoted to Christ bring yet more

flowers for the celebration of this mighty victory. Bank every pulpit with flowers. Let every organ roll its thunders. Let every choir voice the sweetest of anthems. Let every bell and all the chimes charge the air with their richest melodies. If nations deem it fitting to commemorate battles on land and water with gorgeous procession along the streets of metropolitan cities, with flags and bunting afloat under the skies, with wide and lofty arches for generals and admirals to pass under, with blaring trumpet in tenor notes and resounding cannon in deeper bass, with oratorical eulogium, then surely is it more appropriate to set forth the result of this more momentous and more glorious conflict of Death and the Captain of our Salvation, Christ conquering.

Heavenly Recognition

And behold, there appeared unto them Moses and Elias talking with him. Matt. 17:3.

WHILE the flowers of Eastertide are yet abloom, I thought that I would go into the garden of the Scriptures and bring you more flowers. Having discussed the doctrine of the Resurrection, it is appropriate now to speak upon a kindred theme, that of Future Recognition.

"Shall we know each other in heaven?" That question is often asked. It is not a query born of idle curiosity. There is a throbbing heart in it. There are tears in it. There is earnestness in it. Those whose lips frame it are anxious to have it solved. As life moves on, as the passing years empty their treasures at our feet, as dear ones begin through sickness to halt along the journey, and as often we are called upon to close the eyes whose light has faded out, we naturally wonder if death is a spoiler of features here familiar. Yet why should we so wonder? We might dismiss the thought as it was once dismissed by John Evans, a minister of Scotland. His wife came one day into his study and asked him if they should know each other in the coming life. He turned to her and said, "My dear, do you suppose that we shall be greater dunces there

20

than here?" He treated all doubt upon the subject as an absurdity.

I. But let us glance at some of the proofs of the subject. There are some shadows upon the theme, but those shadows are silvered. There are stars in the sky.

Walking one summer's day along the graveled paths of a suburban cemetery, I everywhere saw the evidences of Christian faith in the grand, thrilling and comforting doctrine of the Resurrection. All through that city of the dead was carved the ex-pression of such faith. Yonder rose a tall shaft of snowy whiteness towards heaven's blue. Beyond were statues clothed with grace and symmetry. Every mound was marked with stones of beauty. All these were adorned with some sparkling gem from the casket of poetry or with some brilliant from the jewel-case of the Scriptures. I saw these inscriptions: "O death, where is thy sting?" "Asleep in Jesus, blessed sleep." "Thy brother shall rise again." What boldness in such inscriptions! Within the very precincts of the monster who for thousands of years had gorged himself upon human flesh, men, who were themselves waiting to feel that monster's hurtful blow, had dared to lift up a chiseled defiance. Upon the very door of the monster's grim palace they had bravely traced a prophecy of the monster's downfall. To the skeptic this would seem like a felon painting pictures upon the scaffold from which he was about to swing in agony, or like a madman twisting the straw of his couch into an imaginary crown, fancying himself a king. Nothing less than a clear, clean-cut, unmistakable revelation from God could have awakened such faith. Nothing less than a ray of glory from God's throne could have kindled such faith. Nothing less than a quickening of the eye through the power of God could have given such faith to the vision of men.

But what would be the doctrine of the Resurrection without that kindred doctrine, Recognition in Heaven? A father is dying. His family and friends stand weeping around the bedside. All are Christians. What mollifies the pain of that parting? Is it the thought that the clay from which the spirit is about to depart shall survive the destruction of the grave and at the call of the last trump reorganize, coming forth then into immortality? Oh, no! There is another thought. It is that of reunion. The Resurrection and Future Recognition are two doctrines bound together, as were the twins of Siam, by a tie that makes them inseparable.

II. I further remark, that if there is to be no future recognition, then we must believe that death destroys the memory That would make death an annihilation. But we know that the memory is not destroyed. Said Abraham to the rich man who lifted up his eyes in hell, tormented, and begging that Lazarus be sent to him with a drop of water to cool his burning tongue, "Son, remember that thou in thy lifetime didst receive thy good things, and likewise

Lazarus evil things, but now he is comforted and thou art tormented." If the rich man had lost all recollection of the past when he died, it was absurd for Abraham to call his attention to that past; and Christ, Who relates the parable—I say it reverently —practiced a deception. What meaning could there have been to that man suffering the pangs of the damned in the words, "Son, remember," if he had no memory? He did remember, for he recognized the beggar who had sat all covered with sores at his princely gateway and ate the crumbs that had fallen from his luxurious table. If, therefore, the lost remember, the conclusion is irresistible that the saved also remember. Is hell to outdo heaven?

III. I go a step further than this, and positively declare that those in the spirit state of heaven do retain the power of recollection. What is yonder procession sweeping grandly on to the throne of God? How the palms wave! Behold the shining crowns upon the brow! Listen to the song that bursts from the lips of ten thousand times ten thousand and thousands of thousands. What are they singing? It is the wonderful theme of the Redemption—the oratorio of the ages. But how can they sing that song, if they do not remember? When the saved soul enters heaven must it be told over again the story of the manger and the Cross? The question is foolish. There can be no doubt that we shall have the faculty of memory in heaven. That being true, it necessarily follows that we shall be able to recognize those with whom we here parted—our friends and the dear ones who once sat at our firesides with us in loving companionship and made music in our homes.

"But," says an objector, "the body changes, we are told, every seven years. Suppose now that an acquaintance at the age of twenty should go into another part of the world, remaining there until he died, dying at the age of seventy years, you never seeing him again or looking upon his photograph, how would you recognize that acquaintance in heaven? He left you while standing upon the threshold of manhood; he died with wrinkles on brow and cheek and with silvered locks falling towards his shoulders. His features would be so altered that you would not know him."

Well, I reply, taking that question into the spiritual state that immediately succeeds death and into the resurrection state, it is not essential that mere features should be recognized. How do we recognize each other here? Is it only by the color of the hair, or the hue of the eyes, or the shape of the head? By no means. We all have our own individuality, our own characteristics, our own disposition. By these we are known among our fellow men. Just as an author has his own style of writing or an orator his own style of speaking, so that reading their productions we know from whose brain they sprung, so do we recognize our friends and relatives by what is peculiar to them and no one else. The soul is the real man or woman; it has features of its own to make it distinguishable. Even if the body should be left to perish in the grave, there being no resurrection, it is not at all likely that we should go through eternity unknown to each other. What a dreary wilderness of endless monotony eternity would be! As to the resurrection body, while it will be essentially the body we now inhabit, it is to be a spiritual body, an immortal body. Going down into death with the infirmities of age upon it, in the resurrection it will come up renewed, made over again, but with nothing of identity lost. We have a strong hint of this in the resurrection of Christ. His body had undergone a change, but His disciples recognized Him.

These arguments all bring us back to the question of the Scotch minister with which we started, that question denying that the passage from this present life into future life robs us of intelligence. Why, this life is but the preparatory department of the life to come. Here we are in training for higher branches of learning. There we shall go to college. The memory that we now cultivate shall there blossom with quickened power. If we are not dunces here, it is not likely that we shall wear a dunce cap in that university for which we are now making ourselves ready. This world is but the dawn of the world to come. Beyond is sunrise. There shall be no night there.

IV. I remark, again, that there shall be future recognition because the life of heaven is described as one of happiness. How could it be that if we should not know anyone in it? Have you never stood in a crowd of people in which every man and woman and child was a stranger and experienced a feeling of loneliness? Suppose now a soul should enter heaven and be incapable of recognizing any of those who had preceded him? He walks the golden streets, admires the architecture along those streets, looks upon the flashing river of crystal, and listens to the music of angelic orchestras and choirs. But presently the novelty of his new surroundings wears off, and brushing against multitudes of celestial inhabitants, and finding them all strangers, he grows homesick, wishing himself back on earth. He could not be happy in a place like that. Such a heaven would be hell.

"But," says someone, "he might form acquaintances there." Yes, I answer, but meeting those acquaintances again, how would he be able to recognize them? If he could not know those who had gone before him into the heavenly world, father, or mother, or children, what certainty would there be that after taking leave of those to whom he had been introduced in heaven, he should know those new acquaintances at a second meeting? There would be none at all. The idiocy with which he began his heavenly life would continue. He would be a fool forever. You see into what absurd absurdities a denial of this doctrine leads. From such a heaven may you and I be delivered! What a nebulous heaven it would be! Every instinct of the soul is

against such a heaven. Rather let me dream of it
than realize it. A denial of future recognition with-
ers every flower of hope, and reaching up, ex-
tinguishes every star, bringing on a night that piles
shadows into an impenetrable wall of gloom.

V. Again, I remark, that the Scriptures distinctly
tell us there is future recognition. Where? Nowhere in so many words. This is a doctrine that is
taught by implication, it being taken for granted that
the common sense of mankind would lead to an acceptance of it without any questioning. David evi-
dently believed in it. Death had gone into his palace.
No medical skill could keep back the destroyer.
Caring nothing for splendid surroundings, or courtly
attendance, or the royal blood flowing through the
veins of a sick child in that abode, Death placed his
skeleton foot on the stairway leading to the chamber
of illness, and with his bony finger touched the heart
of the princely boy, bidding that heart cease its
strokes. The crimson tide halted in the arteries. The
eyes lost their lustre. The brow became white.
Feeling the wrist, the physician announced the flight
of the soul. Dead! Said the sorrowing father, "I
cannot bring him back again, but I shall go to him."
But what comfort would there have been in that, if
David did not believe that he would be able to recognize his child in the other world?

What is the meaning of the statements made in
reference to the ancient saints when it is said, speaking of their death, that they were gathered to their

people? Is it simply that they went into the grave with their ancestors? I think that it also means re-union with those who had gone before them. Were they unable to recognize those with whom they were reunited?

But in the New Testament we find the fact of future recognition still more vividly implied. Here a stronger light falls upon the subject. Some of the shadows are lifting. What does Christ mean when He speaks of the gathering of the Gentiles into the kingdom of heaven, throngs coming from every quarter of the compass, and in that kingdom sitting down with Abraham and Isaac and Jacob? If those multitudes are to recognize the patriarchs of past days, never having seen them, shall not we be able to recognize those whom we knew on earth? Take again the case of the rich man in the flames of per-dition. Did he not know Abraham whom he had never met? Did death destroy the identity of Laz-arus? What do these things mean, if they do not take for granted an acceptance of future recognition?

In the narrative around the text Christ goes up into a mountain, taking three of His disciples with Him. Suddenly a supernatural radiance bursts upon the vision of those three favored disciples. Christ is transfigured before them, His inward divinity be-coming outwardly visible. With Him are Moses and Elijah, and wrapped about with heavenly splendor. Those disciples recognize both the law-giver and the prophet. What does this teach us? Why, if those men of earth could identify Moses and Elijah, who for centuries had been in the presence of God, and having never seen them before, can it be even thought that yonder, with the dust of this world cleared from the vision, you and I shall not be able to distinguish the features of those who were here with us in circle of friendship and within our homes?

What did Christ mean when He told those weeping sisters of Bethany that their brother should rise again? Death did not change the identity of Lazarus. This was a picture of the future. The reunion of that Bethany home was typical of the reunion of heaven. "Your brother shall rise again." Not a stranger unknown to you, having no memory of the past, out of sympathy with the present, unassociated with all that is to come; but a thorough man, your very brother. So might the words of Christ be paraphrased.

Further, what did Paul mean when he spoke of his Thessalonian converts as his glory and joy in the presence of Christ? How could Paul expect that, if he was not to know those converts in the other world? It is said that there shall be some Christian saints who shall never see death. When the Christ shall come the second time they shall be alive. At the sounding of the final trump, that angelic music-blast to wake the slumbering dead of earth and sea, those living saints are to be caught up in the air to meet the Lord. Standing one moment side by side, and knowing each other, shall they not the next moment, while passing upward and having reached the heights above, continue the acquaintance? To ask such a question is to answer it.

Away with all fog from this subject! While we may not be able to peer through the shadows that invest the future state, we need not be in the least doubt about knowing each other in the life to come. Why should there ever have been any doubt in regard to the matter? I say to those who cavil at the fact what Diogenes said to Alexander as he stopped one day before the tub in which the surly philosopher made his home, "Get out of my sunshine!" If there is no such thing as future recognition, then the Mt. Auburns and Greenwoods and Laurel Hills of earth are naught but masked horrors, their graceful walks, their gleaming statuary, their noble trees, their flashing lakes, their wealth of emerald sward and rainbow-tinted flowers only the sarcastic smile of Death. What is resurrection without recognition?

Said Joseph Cook, speaking of the heresy of a probation beyond the grave, "Give me no guess for my dying pillow." So when we stand or kneel at the bedside of dear ones passing away, or when we come to lie down ourselves in final sickness, what we want in that hour of falling shadow is not the added darkness of a theory, but the unmistakable illumination of certainty. Therefore, when you ask me, as a minister of God, if we shall know each other in heaven, my answer is that the Bible flashes upon your query the light of a glorious affirmative. That Book takes it for granted that the intelligence of earth shall not be blasted by death.

Traveling once down the Delaware River, we started in gloom. That gloom was hung from horizon to horizon, throwing a pall over land and water, But presently there came a break in the clouds, and those broken clouds began to wear the gilding of the sun. Then all the shadows retreated. The heavens were transfigured. The river rolled on like molten silver, its flash irradiating all the miles ahead and all the miles behind. When we reached the bay we were steaming on beneath a sky that would have thrilled a poet and thrown an artist into rapture. It was as if the gates of pearl had opened, letting pass through a whole regiment of fiery splendors with helmets and bayonets and swords of gold.

In like manner, speeding down the river of death, shall the darkness flee and the light of reunion and recognition come as a sunburst to the Christian soul. At that supreme moment we shall have reached the port of the celestial city. The voyage over; the sails furled; the anchor dropped. That will be Jacob and Joseph in each other's arms, clasped in greeting! That will be the prodigal and his father embracing! That will be Home!

Many dying souls have testified to the truth of future recognition. In the fading vision of earth they have seen loved ones long since departed and called them by name. Who doubts that the sight was real? God let those loved ones go forth to accompany those left behind to the great house of many mansions. So shall we behold familiar faces shining over our last pillow and feel the touch of vanished hands. Or if God does not so grant, then in the awakening of heaven we shall certainly behold them and know them. Best of all, we shall see and know Him who redeemed us from the grave. Even will there be no need of an introduction to Him. We shall know Him instantly, as the waking flowers of the morn know the sun, and turn their faces to the glory of the king of day. Christ will be the centre of our attracted gaze, each of us exclaiming, as we meet His radiant glance, "My Lord and my God!"

A Glimpse of Heaven

After this I beheld, and, lo, a great multitude, which no man could number, of all nations, and kindreds, and people, and tongues, stood before the throne, and before the Lamb, clothed with white robes, and palms in their hands; and cried with a loud voice, saying, Salvation to our God which sitteth upon the throne, and unto the Lamb. Rev. 7: 9, 10.

As when a cloud breaks in a stormy sky we catch a glimpse of the infinite blue above, so here through the persecution of the Apostle John we look into the glory of heaven. What wonderful things have issued from the trials of God's saints! Joseph's prison the ante-room of a palace. Job's poverty and bereavement and sickness the prelude to harmonies of faith, those harmonies yet vibrating in the air of earth, and which shall continue to echo until kissed by the music of the final trump. David's exile only the steps leading to a throne. Paul's tribulations the mallet and chisel that carved the grandest character ever produced by Christianity. John's Patmos of loneliness the tramping-ground of supernal splendors and sublimities. Let the shadows of night gather, if they will, over the lives of God's chosen ones; they but unroll to view the hidden stars. Bless the Lord for grief and pain!

But let us gaze at this picture of the text hung up within the gallery of the Apocalypse. Yonder is a throne. Shade your eyes, lest you be blinded by the splendor! It is a throne that no Alexander or Cæsar could have sat upon in all their greatness of earthly power—their thrones but ash-heaps in comparison. This is the throne that governs the universe. Around that throne eternal are three circles. Circle of the redeemed of Christ. Circle of elders and beasts, those elders distinguished personalities, and those beasts symbolical living creatures. Circle of flaming angels. The redeemed of Christ the innermost circle of all. The supremest honors of heaven for those who have washed themselves in the blood of the Lamb. Fellow-Christians, "it doth not yet appear what we shall be." But if you and I could realize only a small part of the "far more exceeding and eternal weight of glory" that shall some glad day be ours, we should never again have an aching heart or a tear-moistened eye.

I. In opening up the text, I ask you to notice the multitudes of the redeemed in heaven. These that John saw composing that inner circle around the throne of God were a great number that could not be calculated. That statement from the inspired pen of the seer of Patmos upsets all mathematical theories in reference to the population of the celestial city. London, Paris, Pekin, St. Petersburg, New York, Chicago and Philadelphia are the great cities of the world; but their inhabitants can be computed. Every few years a census is made, and we know approximately how many people are gathered in those large cities. It is estimated that the surface of the world is now pressed by over a billion pairs of human feet. But if all the throngs of earth were suddenly lifted into the golden streets of heaven, they would be lost in that metropolis of the universe. No mortal brain can figure even the number of the redeemed. John distinctly tells us that in the text. How then is it possible to enumerate heaven's population? The strongest imagination here folds its wings and refuses to fly. Away with human arithmetic! Heaven is a vast place beyond all earthly measurements.

So does John's statement also upset all those narrow notions that some entertain in reference to the number of persons saved by the sovereign grace of God. According to the ideas of some, heaven was built for a very small company. The teaching of the Bible is against all such circumscribed thought. What did Christ mean when He said, "In my Father's house are many mansions?" Why did He not indicate the exact number of those mansions, if heaven is but for a limited number that mortal brain can count? "Many mansions!" That phrase is suggestive of more than a few. What did John mean when he spoke of "ten thousand times ten thousand," afterwards adding to that sublime multiplication an expression that shows the utter hopelessness of going any deeper into the sum, saying, "and thousands of thousands?" In the text he does not even make the attempt of reaching any result, simply stating, "I beheld, and, lo, a great multitude, which no man could number."

A child in the simplicity of his nature thinks that
he can count the stars. He begins. How easy it is
to count them! The glow of the sunset is still in the
sky. The stars twinkle forth one by one. But the
darkness deepens. Then the constellations wheel to
view. So thickly and so fast does the night scatter
her gems abroad, that the child gives up his task.
His puny arithmetic is not sufficient for the enumeration. He cries, "There are too many! I cannot
count the stars!" "No," says an astronomer standing by, "you cannot count the stars my child; but I
can. All these that shine above us I have counted.
Yet listen, child; there are more stars yet that can be
seen only through glass in a tube; and beyond the
reach of that wonderful tube there are millions upon
millions of stars. The stars cannot be counted."

Like the child was the Apostle John in his enumeration of the redeemed in heaven. Then he became
as the astronomer. How useless it was to continue
the count! "A great multitude, which no man could
number!" Even the telescope of inspired vision
fails. Only God knows how many of the saved there
are. But John's statement gives us a heaven that is
as far removed from being a small locality as is a
city like London in comparison with an Indian village.

What a thrilling thought it is that there shall finally
be unnumbered throngs of the redeemed! The grace
of God is not to be frustrated by the machinations of
Satan. In the last census of heaven, after the Cross

of Jesus Christ shall have exerted its magnetic power to the full, I believe that hell in comparison with heaven will occupy but the same relative space as that of a prison in the midst of a large community of law-abiding citizens.   More human souls saved than damned.   That circle of salvation around the throne of God stupendous beyond present thought.   "A great multitude, which no man could number." Praise the Lord!   The all-important question is, Will you and I be among them?

II. I ask you to notice the varied nationalities of the redeemed in heaven.   Listen to the majestic roll of John's language!   "Of all nations, and kindreds, and people and tongues."   That explains what is meant a little farther on in this magnificent Book of Revelation by the statement that the city celestial has twelve gates—a trinity of gates facing each point of the compass.   "On the east three gates; on the north three gates; on the south three gates; and on the west three gates."   Those numerous gates are for the entrance of the representatives of all mankind, whether born in Asia, or Europe, or Africa, or America.   "All nations!"   That there may be no possible mistake as to the world-wide reach of the Gospel of Jesus Christ, John adds, "and kindreds." That not being sufficient, he adds again, "and people."   To still further emphasize his thought, he adds once more, "and tongues."   That leaves no part of the earth out of the blessing of the Cross.

John's language here is not tautological, simply a

repetition of his thought. I am glad that he expressed the matter as he did. Had he only said "all nations," it might have been meant that only those nations that were in existence at the time John was writing would be represented in redemption. But when he piles word on word, saying, "All nations, and kindreds, and people, and tongues," there can be no doubt whatever that he intended to convey the idea of no portion of humanity being missed. No corner of the globe to be left unreaped by the scythe of the Gospel. The redeemed shall come up to the pearl-gates of heaven from every nationality to the end of the world. No race without its representatives—many of the white race, the red race, the yellow race, the bronze race and the black race. No divisions of mankind without its representatives—many of all people in heaven. No language without its representatives—many of all tongues in heaven. Those who object to such a democratic heaven, using that word in its original sense, with no smell of American politics upon it, will have to make a small heaven of their own. The Bible recognizes no difference in mankind except that of character. The only aristocracy that has any weight with God is the aristocracy of kinship with Christ. The Cross of Jesus is a shelter for all who go to it in penitence and faith, whether they be kings or peasants, noblemen or plebeians, rich or poor, wise or ignorant, and whatever be the color of their skin or the speech of their tongues. Heaven is the gathering-place of the redeemed of all humanity in its complex and diverse elements of being as everywhere found on the surface of the globe.

The privileges and blessing of the Gospel being for all mankind, is it not high time, down here in the twentieth century, that the Church should hasten the work of world-wide evangelization? It is often asked why the chariot wheels of the coming Lord tarry. I will tell you why they tarry. They are clogged in the mire of Christian indifference and stinginess. There is no use in praying, "Thy kingdom come," if we are not doing all we can to make it come. When the teamster in the fable prayed Hercules to help him get his wagon out of the mud, the giant god answered, "Put your own shoulder to the wheel!" That was another way of saying that faith without works is dead. The gathering of multitudes of humanity into heaven, as here described by John, can only be when the whole Church of Christ realizes her obligation to take this world for her Lord—a conquest that knows nothing of geographical lines. Those who will not share in this glorious mission must stand aside for those who will. May the day speed on when the vision of the seer of Patmos shall solidify into fact! "All nations, and kindreds, and people, and tongues."

III. I ask you to notice the garments of the redeemed in heaven. "Clothed with white robes." Why not the blue with which God frescoes the sky? Why not the green with which God dresses the fields and valleys and hills? Why not the variegated tints of the woods in springtime and autumn? Why not the lustrousness of the rainbow with which God robes the black shoulders of the storm? Why not in the purple of kings and queens, that hue borrowed from the sunset that enwraps the departing day? I answer that white is all colors blended into one. The redeemed are all one in the union of redemption. No sectarianism in heaven. Methodist and Presbyterian side by side. Episcopalian and Baptist side by side. Congregationalist and Quaker side by side. Lutheran and Roman Catholic side by side. John Calvin and John Wesley together, clasping hands. With them Arminius and Toplady and Whitefield. All metaphysical and theological and ecclesiastic differences gone. All variations of thought and feeling in reference to the unessentials of creeds and philosophies and church governments left as bundles of old rags outside the gates of pearl. All one; all clothed in white robes. Enthusiasts may talk as they please about bringing together the various divisions of the Church on earth, but their dream will never be here realized. It will take heaven to accomplish that glorious result. While the different denominations are closer together now than ever before in fraternal fellowship, they still have their party walls. If I had the power to unite them I would not exercise that power. I might want them all to be Presbyterians! But going into the wardrobes of the King's palace above, we shall all come forth arrayed alike. The air of heaven will clear our vision, and we shall see face to face what we now see through a glass darkly. "Clothed with white robes." That color typical of earthly diversity merged into heavenly sameness. It is only when the colors of the spectrum are separated that they become distinct from each other. United, they form the resplendent light that kisses the world into a blush of beauty. What is grander than sunshine? So shall the blended hue of the garments of the redeemed in heaven reflect the uncreated glory of God. "White robes."

But I like John's inspired thought. He tells us that the garments of the redeemed in heaven have been made white in the blood of the Lamb. It may strike some as being an incongruous thought. How could a garment be made white by washing it in blood. Whatever it comes in contact with blood will stain. Many a murderer has ascertained that fact, and to his everlasting sorrow, science demonstrating before a jury trying him in a court room that blood is itself an unimpeachable witness against such crime, the searching eye of the microscope and the fingers of chemical reagents proving that blood persists in remaining upon the clothes of him upon whom it has been spattered. I once saw the room in which General Mercer died, having been mortally wounded in the battle of Princeton, during the Revolution. The marks of his blood were yet on the floor, over a hundred years having passed away, repeated washing having failed to remove the marks.

Well, I answer, John's expression is figurative, the idea being not that the garments of the redeemed are literally made white by the blood of the Lamb, but that the blood of the Lamb had atoned for their sins, the robes of white they wear symbolical of the cleansing of their nature through the infinite sacrifice of Calvary. Oh, what a wonderful solvent that blood is! It acts even upon scarlet sins, making them whiter than snow. That blood gave David a white robe by taking away the stains of sin from his heart. That blood robed the dying thief in white, that outlaw stepping from a gibbet to a throne in heaven. That blood clothed Paul in white, changing him from a cruel persecutor to an illustrious missionary of the Cross. Oh, the unnumbered throngs that have come under the power of that blood! If, my friend, you expect to reach heaven, your expectation is vain, unless you have been washed by that blood. White robes are only for those whose lives are white.

Yes, John, I like your thought. Men may deride the Cross of Christ or seek to hew it down with the axe of infidelity; but here is a reference to it in the closing book of the Bible that confirms the truth of it in all the preceding books—a final witness corroborating the testimony of numerous witnesses. That Cross eternal. Human philosophy and human scorn cannot destroy it nor mar it. Christ was slain from the foundation of the world. All the white-robed throngs of the celestial city ascribe their redemption to the efficacious blood of the Lamb.

Throughout endless ages you and I shall stand in full view of the Cross of Christ.

IV. I ask you to notice the triumphant gladness of the redeemed in heaven. "Palms in their hands." That was what the children of Israel carried in the Feast of Tabernacles. That was what the people carried at the entry of Christ into Jerusalem, supposing that He was going into the city to be crowned. That is what were given the victors in the athletic contests of the Grecians to carry. That is what were carried in the triumphal processions of Roman generals returned from successful war. The palms of the redeemed in heaven indicating joy and victory. Oh, the blessedness of it! Here we often sit under some weeping willow, our hearts torn of grief, the very soul crushed. How glad we shall be to exchange earthly sorrow for heavenly happiness! Read what John says farther on in the chapter! "They shall hunger no more, neither thirst any more; neither shall the sun light on them, nor any heat. For the Lamb, which is in the midst of the throne, shall feed them, and shall lead them unto living fountains of waters; and God shall wipe away all tears from their eyes." That last clause could never be read by Robert Burns, the poet, without the greatest emotion, it causing him to weep. All trials ended. All heartaches gone. All shadows lifted. "Palms in their hands." The palm-tree, straight as a chiseled column, lofty, royal in bearing, an appropriate emblem of triumphant gladness. It was the long leaf that

shoots out from this tree at the top which was borne
by men in victorious celebrations—the crown of the
tree. Those white-robed throngs holding palms in
their hands look back over the earthly life, and remember the rough roads they traveled, the burdens
that chafed their shoulders, the pangs that trod their
nerves with feet of fire, and the open graves at which
they stood. But now they are exultant in that inner
circle before the throne. Hear the rustling of their
palms! "These are they which came out of great
tribulation." John himself is now with that victorious multitude; and Patmos, bleak, rugged, lonely,
sea-washed, is as though it had been naught but an
angel-punctuated dream.

V. I ask you to notice, as my last thought, the
song of the redeemed in heaven. "And cried with a
loud vice, saying, Salvation to our God which sitteth
upon the throne, and unto the Lamb." What a magnificent song! I have sometimes found myself wondering at the feebleness of earthly song in some
church services. In many churches a paid quartet
does all the singing. I like artistic music, but no
hirelings can lock my lips. I have been in meetings
where the songs rolled from every tongue in a volume of praise that was thrilling. I have been in other
meetings in which the songs were so thin as to be
almost ethereal—starveling songs with no robustness
of Christian experience in their muscles. They
would come forth from the mouth as if frightened,
and die into a mere whisper. I am fond of vigorous

congregational singing, every heart responsive to the sentiment being expressed, whether led by choir or a precentor, and the melody shaking the very walls of the building. I believe that such is the way they sing in heaven. In fact, I know it. John here distinctly says, "Cried with a loud voice." No wonder! What was the theme? The Salvation of God and the Lamb. Under the spell of that mighty theme, they sang with a power that filled all heaven with echoes, some of those echoes, the vibration softened, falling upon John's ears on Patmos.

There are some human larynxes so constructed that harmony is impossible to them. I always feel sorry for persons who cannot sing. But up there we shall all be able to sing. In that oratorio of redemption, you and I, standing with the rest of the saved in the presence of our Father God and Him Who spilled His blood for our sins, shall have a musical part—a full soprano, a tuneful alto, a well-chorded tenor, or a rich, resounding bass—mingling our voices with those of ten thousand times ten thousand, and thousands of thousands, in grand, thrilling, emotional doxologies.

I have read of a legend which says that when persons entered the Temple of Diana they were blinded by the brilliancy of the room, the flashing gold and the sparkling jewels in that room too much for the vision. The janitor of that room always said to strangers visiting it for the first time, "Take heed to your eyes!" But what shall be the effect upon the hearing when the hallelujah of the redeemed in heaven shall break around the throne of God? A stupendous circle of song ringing around that throne. John hearing that song on Patmos, described it "as the voice of many waters." But had it come upon his earthly sense in all its volume of sound, it would have overpowered his auditory nerves, paralyzing them. God grant that we may all some day help to roll that doxology through the air of heaven!

www.ingramcontent.com/pod-product-compliance
Lightning Source LLC
LaVergne TN
LVHW021555230326
834588LV00004B/329